The Last Pub in Fleet Street

A reporter's notebook

Revel Barker

P

Palatino Publishing

First published 2015 by Palatino Publishing
Copyright © 2015 Revel Barker

By the same author:
Non-fiction:
    Round Up the Usual Suspects (Editor)
    Field of Vision
    Crying All The Way to the Bank
        (Liberace v Cassandra and the Daily Mirror –
        Famous Trials)
    Publish and Be Damned! by Hugh Cudlipp (Foreword)

Alternative History:
    The Hitler Scoop

Fiction:
    The Mayor of Montebello
    The Magistrate of Montebello
    The Blood Secret

ISBN: 978-1-907841-15-6

Palatino Publishing 66 Florence Road Brighton BN1 6DJ
United Kingdom
palatinobooks@gmail.com

You cannot hope to bribe or twist,
thank God! The British journalist.
But, seeing what the man will do
unbribed, there's no occasion to.

Humbert Wolfe (1885 –1940)

News is what somebody somewhere wants to suppress; all the rest
is advertising.

Lord Northcliffe (1865-1922)

News is what a chap who doesn't care much about anything wants
to read. And it's only news until he's read it.

Evelyn Waugh (1903-1966)

Journalism is the only form of human activity where the orgasm
comes at the beginning.

Vincent Mulchrone (*Daily Mail*) to the author, 1966

Journalists are always very interested – in what *they* are doing.

Neil Armstrong (astronaut) to the author, 1996

Truth is not only stranger than fiction. It is more interesting.

William Randolph Hearst, publisher (1863-1951)

Nothing is more responsible for the good old days than a bad
memory.

Franklin Pierce Adams, columnist (1881-1960)

Nobody ever said it should be easy.
But it should be fun.
Mike Molloy

1. But I digress...

The announcement of my appointment as a director of the Royal Military College of Science (nowadays the UK Defence Academy) said that in thirty years as a national newspaper reporter I had been deported from a friendly nation, jailed by an unfriendly one and threatened with jail by another that's never been quite sure; I'd been bombed, shelled, shot at, stoned, evacuated from a jungle by helicopter, had jumped out of a burning aircraft, been bitten by a snake and a poisonous spider, and employed by Captain Robert Maxwell MC.

Daily Express photographer Gordon Amory, commemorating my thirty years membership of the Newcastle Pens & Lens Club, had summed up the same career slightly differently: 'A charmed life, including being foreign editor of a newspaper that didn't carry foreign news, editorial adviser to a proprietor who famously never took advice, and publicity director for an organisation that did only top secret work.' Most important of all, Gordon added, 'He taught Bob Maxwell how to swim.'

Thirty years, in not many more words... Not much. Many of the people I had worked with did much more, had more exciting stories to tell. It would be fifty years now, because reporting is an addiction; you can't give it up.

Sadly, the kids who replaced my generation – twenty-year-olds on twenty grand a year (or less) supplanting forty-plus people on forty grand (or more) – often don't believe the stories we occasionally tell them about what have been referred to, mainly by us, as 'the glory days', the great days of newspapers when millions of people relied on them for information over their breakfasts.

Fair enough; we sometimes found them difficult to believe, ourselves.

And they may be right. I can still often fall back on a verbatim recall of quotes (necessary because I was never totally confident of my shorthand notes) and dates, and sometimes of names, but not always. Sometimes – let's be honest – our unprinted stories were improved slightly during the telling and retelling in the pub.

What happens – and among the diminishing number of Fleet Street survivors it still occurs – is that somebody tells a story at a bar. This reminds the person standing next to him of a similar or related incident. And that prompts the memory of another drinker... and so on.

Thus: somebody mentioned the name of photographer Bill Rowntree the other day, which started me reminiscing – from among many experiences with him – about Bill's world scoop photo on the imminent return of yachtsman Robin Knox-Johnston from his single-handed round-the-world voyage, and that got the old grey cells working about a silly story behind the scoop.

See what I mean? I was already mentally interrupting my own memories.

Well, not all of them were originally mine. Roy Spicer told me this one, so I believe it.

Nobody had sailed alone, non-stop, 30,000 miles around the world before 1969. Francis Chichester had tried two years earlier with *Gypsy Moth IV*, and was famously knighted on his return, but he'd been forced to put in to Australia for repairs.

So when Bill, on the *Sunday Mirror*, calculated that Knox-Johnston, on board *Suhaili*, must be getting close to home and to a place in history (in a challenge entirely organised by the *Sunday Times*) the picture desk decided to make contact, and Rowntree prepared to beat the opposition by the simple ploy of finding out where the yacht was and chartering an aircraft to fly over it and take pictures.

['Aerial pictures are easy,' photographer Johnny Robson in Newcastle used to say.' 'You just set the camera on infinity, point it and press the tit.' But back to the story...]

Picture editor Allen Baird had been in the forces. He knew how to do two-way radio on a maritime network. You call the ship's name three times... So he got on to the ship-to-shore operator and asked for a radio link with the yachtsman. After a while he was put through.

'Hello, *Suhaili Suhaili, Suhaili* ... This is the London *Sunday Mirror* calling. Are you receiving? Over.'

Back came the reply: 'Hello *Sunday Mirror*! This is *Suhaili*. Receiving you loud and clear. Over.'

Baird: 'Hello. Could I speak to Mr Knox-Johnston, please…?'

This story was often lost on drinkers in the Stab In The Back who had already forgotten, even during the brief (if uninterrupted) telling, that the entire plot of the tale, and of the voyage, was that it was single-handed. But luckily Roy Spicer was a man of infinite patience, and of good yarns.

He recalled that there was even a fine journalistic postscript, missed at the time by most reporters covering the yacht's arrival. The customs men dutifully went on board at Falmouth and asked: 'Where you from – what was your last port of call?' And they were told: 'Falmouth.'

Mention of Roy always reminds me that before joining us he'd been northern theatre critic of the *News Chronicle*.

He once wrote a review for it that began:

> Slick, sparkling, spectacular, and with some of the most brilliant dancing seen on the English stage, this colourful musical drama has a weakness – its songs. It has no songs to hum or remember.

And the headline, across two columns on the front page, was:

A HUMDINGER – WITHOUT A TUNE TO HUM.

So much for the European premiere of *West Side Story*.

Shortly afterwards he was made motoring editor.

When we shared an office in the *Mirror* Holborn building I'd often walk in singing *Maria*, or *Tonight*, or *When You're a Jet, America*, or even *Gee, Officer Krupke*. And Roy, getting the message but unphased by this intentionally irritating habit, would just shrug and say: 'Sorry, but I still don't think they're good songs.'

But that also reminds me of the time when *Sunday Mirror* editor Bob Edwards offered him the chief reporter's job and Roy said that he didn't want it, but if it meant a pay-rise, he'd take it… on condition that he didn't ever have to speak to the news desk and that his life-style would remain unchanged.

In addition to motoring – which meant he got to drive a brand new car every week – he also organised the Great British Beer Competition which brewers competed for as if their careers depended on it, as perhaps they did, and had Roy constantly driving around in search of The Perfect Pint. We called him our drink-and-drive correspondent.

…Which reminds me that Patrick Mennem, Roy's counterpart on the *Daily Mirror* for 32 years, spent months warning readers about the impending threat of the breathalyser, then was arrested within 48 hours of its introduction, becoming one of the first people to be banned from driving under the new law.

Pat, by the way, was in El Vino one lunchtime when the wine correspondent of the *Telegraph* announced: 'I am going to Bordeaux tomorrow.'

Mennem – a man who always looked as if his face was about to explode in anger – told him: 'One already feels sorry for poor old Doe, whoever he is. But it'll be a blessed relief for the rest of us, in this place.'

*

Anyway, that's how the conversations used to go in the pubs, and there were some of Fleet Street's finest who never strayed further from the office than the nearest bar.

They are all lost to us now, the pubs.

There was the King(s) and Keys, Ye Olde Cock Tavern, The Punch, The Tipperary and the Old Bell; the George, the Devereaux, Coach and Horses, the Cockpit and the Haunch of Venison; the Viaduct, the Harrow, the Witness Box (formerly the Feathers) and the Black Friar; the Hog's Head, Blue Anchor, Printer's Devil and the White Swan; Peel's, the Prince of Wales and Winnie's (or Number Ten); there was the Clachan, Popinjay's, the Red Lion (with a Chinese restaurant upstairs before Soho had a Chinatown) and the Rose and Crown, always referred to as Aunties…

When Fleet Street relocated to docklands The Stab In The Back (known only to the brewers as The White Hart) became a gay bar, then a branch of Pizza Express…

The Cheshire Cheese has been totally overtaken by tourists; it was going that way for years… I fetched up there one lunchtime with northern news editor Ken Bennett, to be told by the friendly head waiter that we should have booked, for the place was full.

'Just a minute,' I said. 'Why is it full?'

'Because it's the most famous pub in Fleet Street.'

'So your punters come in here expecting to see what, or whom, exactly?'

'Oh… point taken.'

He led us to a table in the corner and addressed one of the customers on a bench seat: 'Excuse me, sir, but did you notice there's a plaque on the wall behind you saying that this was Dr Johnson's seat…?'

'Gee, I'm sorry,' said the tourist. 'Has he come in?'

'No, sir. Sadly he is dead but before he died he bequeathed it to Mr Barker and now *he* has come in…'

So everybody shuffled round and made space. And Ken, purely for the entertainment of our fellow diners, opened *sotto voce* with: 'Did I tell you about what Princess Anne said to me the other day, the little minx…'

Up opposite the Law Courts was the Wig & Pen Club – not exactly a pub but part of the same culture. Its fame didn't travel well outside the city and I remember somebody expressing surprise that Wigan had enough journalists to support their own club.

Further still – about as far as anybody could actually walk – was Simpson's In The Strand where another head waiter apologised for the presence of a customer taking lunch without a tie. 'I don't know how he even got in: he's an American. They'll be letting women in next. Or Japanese tourists.'

And now they do both.

And, of course, the famous El Vino, now lost completely to barristers and other merchant bankers, where women were famously banned from standing at the bar and where George Martin, on being told that his guest, a coal-black editor from one of the *Mirror*'s then African outposts, could not be served because he was not wearing a tie, told the manager:

'You tell him it's because he's not wearing a tie.'

What is it, then, this thing about journalists and pubs? Some say simply that it's mainly about unwinding from the stress of a hard day. But not everybody, by any means, had stress or hard days –

certainly not, at least, every day. Nor was it the alcohol, for some drank a little, most drank a lot, but only three or four people in my long acquaintance were definable medically as alcoholics.

George Gale once said that journalists had to 'rub off' each other; that it was their conversation that inspired the best ideas for stories, and there was more than a grain of truth in that. Better still, they actually relished each other's company – fiercely competitive though they might be.

'Journalists need other journalists, to survive,' George explained.

That is how the agendas were set for tomorrow morning's newspapers. We didn't rely on press officers or publicity agents to put stories our way, nor on television programming to decide what was news.

And pubs, truth to tell, were often where stories were to be found. I learnt the value of this at the feet of Sir Linton Andrews, legendary editor of the *Yorkshire Post*, who had signed my indentures as a journalist. While he had been editing the *Leeds Mercury* a young barmaid in the city had gone to a local music hall and been mauled on the stage by a lion. Francis Boyd – already on the *Manchester Guardian* while I was at school and the paper's political correspondent and a director of the paper – had been the *Mercury* late duty man and had missed the story.

Nobody else on the staff would have missed it, but Francis Boyd didn't go on his break for a drink in Whitelock's Turks Head, the office pub where the barmaid worked. He was that odd animal, a non-drinking reporter.

Heigh ho. It was a different age, then. And a different world.

*

So the tales related herein are not (all) necessarily one-hundred-per-cent reliable as actual history. But they are near enough. The names haven't been changed, although maybe some of them should have been. And if any of the escapades are wrongly attributed, my apologies; my intentions throughout are fond and well-meant.

*

For example... We were travelling first class – I don't know what it's like today, but in those days it was an entitlement for all intercontinental travel – on the London to Singapore leg of a flight to Sydney. And like all journalists, anywhere, were swapping yarns about our colleagues. I stretched my limbs (the next row of seats was so far ahead that my feet didn't touch it) and asked Mike Molloy, the editor in chief, whether he remembered the story of John Penrose and Anton Karas.

He said he didn't think he did. But if I'd care to hum the first few bars…

It was the time, I said, when the *Mirror* was trying to persuade its readers to vote in favour of joining Europe, and constantly thinking of story ideas that might suggest to xenophobic Englanders that the Continent could be an interesting place. It produced features on the romance of Paris – lovers walking along the banks of the Seine – on *la dolce vita* that was Rome, on saunas and free love in Scandinavia… but by the time they got to Austria they had run out of ideas. Never mind that Austria wasn't actually a member of the European Community: it was in Europe.

It had been Molloy himself, a dedicated film buff, who had suggested an interview with Karas, the man who wrote *The Third Man* theme – 'the most romantic piece ever written for the zither, which is itself the most romantic of instruments.'

John Penrose (now better known as the sometime Mr Annie Robinson, but then a person in his own right), newly detached from the newsroom to features, was given the job.

[Molloy said that he did not remember the story, but admitted that it all sounded likely enough, so I continued.]

Penrose couldn't find Karas in the phone book, but eventually discovered an address, and set off to Austria, by plane to Vienna, then to Innsbruck, then in a taxi – but sod the expenses, this was *Mirror* features – high up into the Tyrol.

Karas invited Penrose in to his home and asked why he had come all the way from London to see him.

'To interview you. Because you wrote the theme music for *The Third Man*, which is the most romantic piece ever written for the zither, which is itself the most romantic of musical instruments.'

'But why did you come… here?'

'To interview you, of course.'

'But why,' the old zither-plucker persisted – '... why come here?' Penrose asked how else he could have done the interview.

'Well,' explained Herr Karas, 'every Thursday afternoon I play my zither for afternoon tea in the restaurant at Bentall's store in Kingston upon Thames...'

No, said Molloy: he had not heard the story, even though he had been in charge of features at the time. Interestingly, I told him, nor had Penrose heard it – but he had liked it when I'd told it to him, and said that he was perfectly happy for the story to be ascribed to him.

I couldn't remember who had told the tale to me.

But many years later I started an internet blog that became a website and invited old hacks to flood me with daft stories and Plain John Smith obliged with a tale from the days when reporters would be handed 'a wedge of airline tickets as thick as a brick' and be told to 'go off and write something'.

On this occasion the theme of a series was to be Plain John Smith In Search Of Romance for the Sunday *People*. Stuck in a snowstorm in Vienna and trying to work up something about waltzes by Strauss that might amuse his readers, he'd remembered Karas and the Third Man and traced him to a remote mountain village...

> 'Your newspaper is in London, yes?' – I nodded.
>
> 'So why would you come all this way in this terrible weather to see me here in my home?'
>
> 'Well,' I blustered, 'because you are the famous Anton Karas and this is where you live.'
>
> He shook his head. 'Ah yes,' he said. 'But the reason I ask is because every Tuesday and Thursday I play my zither in the tea lounge at Bentall's department store in Kingston upon Thames...'

Well, the saying is 'never let the facts spoil a good story' but then every Tuesday *and* Thursday somehow makes Plain John's story twice as good as my (inaccurate) version.

'So this,' wrote T S Elliot, 'is how the world ends, not with a bang but with a whimper.'

Fleet Street's world ended with both wimps and bankers and with blimps and wankers.

*

It is difficult to put a date on its actual demise – it was a prolonged, lingering death – although some people would time it around July 1984 when Robert Maxwell bought the Mirror Group (on Friday the 13th, as it happened). Some say it was the Murdoch move to Wapping (1986). Others, who managed to survive the Maxwell years, date it to coincide with his death by drowning and the takeover of the group by a consortium led by sometime sub-editor David Montgomery (1991-2), after which the decline was more noticeably rapid.

But at any rate Fleet Street expired when proprietors moved their businesses lock and stock, but no barrels of ink, out of EC4 and (mostly) into Docklands, where land was cheap. The end of an error, some called it.

It was the time when bean-counters replaced experienced newspapermen at the top and a new generation of know-nothings supplanted street-wise people in the vital middle ranks where stories were found and formed.

And that heady epoch leading to the end of The Street – roughly from the fifties to the eighties – is the time-span of this memoir.

We called them the Great Days, The Glory Days.

Were we right?

Well, they were certainly great for us, the journalists – and also for the proprietors, who got rich on our work while shovelling money back in our direction and being generally indulgent in terms of expenses (and sometimes of salaries) for our needs and suggestions and peregrinations.

Glory days? Yes, certainly. The *News of the World* was selling eight million copies every Sunday. The *Daily Mirror* peaked at a figure slightly more than five million. The officially recognised multiplier – readers per copy – meant that the *Mirror* was read every morning by 14.2 million people. The population of England (Scotland had its own 'national' newspapers) was around 42 million... meaning that one person in three was reading the *Mirror* every day. By way of comparison, in 2015 (population 55million) the *Mirror* was selling fewer than 900,000 copies a day – slightly more than the *Sunday Mirror* (six million at its highest). The *Sunday People* (5.6million) now sells 320,000 on a good week. When the *News of the World* was shut down in 2011 its circulation was about 2.8million a week.

How had such massive sales been achieved? The truth is we didn't know. We were fast and we were accurate. We were fair and we were honest. We exposed crooks and wrong-doings, campaigned for justice and refused to flatter fools in high places. We were, I suppose, respected and reliable. In informing and entertaining millions over their breakfasts and on their way to work we were doing something right – we just weren't sure what it was.

Accuracy was paramount. You would be excused for being drunk or idle but could be sacked for getting a fact wrong. Everything was scrutinised. When Hugh Cudlipp, the *Mirror* editorial director, drafted a strap-line for the front claiming THE BIGGEST DAILY SALE IN THE UNIVERSE, chairman Cecil King asked him: 'How do we know?' And it was changed to BIGGEST DAILY SALE ON EARTH.

A banner hanging in the newsroom of the *Daily Express* said: 'Make it fast. Make it accurate.' Some wag had added 'Make it up.' But that was our own joke, against ourselves.

People may have said that 'you can't believe everything you read in the papers', but generally they believed that they could, and they did. They said that 'the camera doesn't lie' – and, before Photoshop, it didn't.

Journalists became national and trustworthy names but those names would now mean nothing to anybody younger than seventy. Not one of them would get through the front door for a job interview today because none had a university degree.

When Bob Edwards edited the *Daily Express* – the World's

Greatest Newspaper ('a bloody awful newspaper', according to Prince Philip) – in the mid-sixties he had the biggest team of foreign correspondents and home based journalists in the history of British newspapers with famous names like René McColl, Chapman Pincher, Peter O'Sullevan, Desmond Hackett and Percy Hoskins among them, in addition to a vast staff working for the William Hickey gossip column. When they published a group shot of the entire photographic staff to illustrate 'the picture power in the *Express*', Lord Beaverbrook counted them over breakfast and was immediately on the phone.

'Sixty-two photographers? You're all quite mad on the *Express*!' But privately, said Edwards, 'the Old Man' was delighted with the presentation.

When Mike Molloy took over the *Daily Mirror* – the World's Largest Daily Sale – in the mid-seventies he inherited an all-star cast including Donald Zec, Keith Waterhouse, Don Wise, John Pilger, Marje Proops and Kent Gavin, but also a motoring correspondent who was disqualified from driving; a gardening correspondent with no garden; a slimming editor who was a stone overweight; a travel editor who was banned from flying on British Airways, and at least one feature writer who hadn't written anything except his expenses in five years.

*

Towards the end of his life, over a dinner in Islington one of the old greats, James Cameron (*Daily Express, News Chronicle, Illustrated London News, Guardian*) summed up the demise of Fleet Street:

'It suffered a massive thrombosis,' he said. 'Which means a healthy circulation, impeded by clots.'

3. Local boy

I saved money as a teenager in Leeds by walking to school. The child's day-return fare by rail (steam train) was only three-halfpence, but I was preparing for O-level maths and calculated I could save four times that amount of pocket money every day by not taking the bus, instead of not taking the train. I would walk – about three miles – or go by bike.

With the money I saved I bought newspapers; morning papers cost two-pence-halfpenny (one new penny) each.

It may be difficult to imagine, after all these years, but TV was still in its infancy; vast areas of England received only one (BBC) channel, and some entire counties could get nothing at all. People relied almost exclusively for their news – and for their news pictures – on the papers. There were two thriving and competing evening papers printed in the centre of Leeds; even two sports papers on Saturday nights on the street within minutes of the final whistle at Elland Road, three evening papers circulating in Bradford (and in York), two rival local dailies in Sheffield.

In the second week of June when I was fourteen the whole country was agog with a court case being fought in the High Court in London in which the colourful and smaltzy pianist Liberace was suing the *Daily Mirror* and its famous columnist Cassandra for libel. And I had the morning papers containing the trial reports.

Memories of that sunny summer (weren't all teenage summers sunny?) would flood back to me fifty years later when I sat down to write a history of the trial. I felt it needed writing: barristers I'd met in court over the intervening years had described it to me as the trial of the century and said the cross-examination of Cassandra (Bill Connor) by Gilbert Beyfus – the top libel man of the day – equalled that by Edward Carson of Oscar Wilde in 1895. It was, and still is, read as an example of brilliant adversarial advocacy. It also contained a lot of lessons about journalism.

In my retirement I had become what's apparently known as a 'macro publisher', reproducing out-of-print histories, biographies, novels and collected columns about newspapers and

16

newspapermen (and women) that I thought ought to be preserved for posterity, and occasionally commissioning new ones. I could therefore publish under my own established imprint and avoid the frustration – known to all authors – of wrangling with the more conventional trade.

I'm still in contact with some of the trial's witnesses but I had to delve into the cuttings of the old newspapers – three pages a day in the *Daily Mirror*, a full broadsheet page in the *Daily Telegraph*, column after column in the *Yorkshire Post*. And an official court transcript the size and weight of a breeze-block.

Cassandra had described Liberace as 'the summit of sex, the pinnacle of Masculine, Feminine and Neuter...'

And he had continued with: 'this deadly, winking, sniggering, snuggling, chromium plated, scent-impregnated, luminous, quivering, giggling, fruit-flavoured, mincing, ice-covered heap of mother-love... this superb piece of calculating candy floss... the biggest sentimental vomit of all time... a preposterous clown...'

There was even a local (Yorkshire) connection. Liberace had complained that shortly after Cassandra's piece had appeared – and allegedly as a result of it – somebody in the audience for his performance at Sheffield City Hall had shouted 'Go home, fairy'. But the president of Sheffield students' union, whose members had made a bit of a rag at the concert, told the court that none of his friends had shouted it. And although the *Daily Mirror* may have been the biggest-selling daily in the known world, nobody at Sheffield University ever read it, he claimed.

*

How much that court case and its insight into the world of newspapers had influenced me I don't know. But my own road to The Street started that year after I had decided against becoming a travel courier or a barrister. Still fourteen, I called on John Algar, editor of the local paper, the *Pudsey and Stanningley News*, with some of my English essays and told him I wanted to be a journalist.

He looked at them, asked whether he could hang on to a couple that would later find their way into the paper, and said: 'Very well – write something for me.'

'Like what?'

'You read the paper. You know what we use in it. Write something like that.'

He told me the going rate for outside contributors was a penny a line. I said that was what Charles Dickens had been paid and that in the middle of the twentieth century it didn't sound like very much. I told him I didn't intend to write a lot, so the income would barely cover my bus fares. (Until 1960 there was a coin in circulation – a farthing – worth a quarter of an old penny, or *one nine-hundred-and-sixtieth* of a pound.)

He looked again at my essays and sighed, then grinned at the cheek of this teenager. 'All right, I'll pay you three-halfpence a line, provided that the others don't get to know about our special arrangement.'

To put this payment in context, apart from being my rail fare, three-halfpence, one and a half old pennies, multiplied by twenty lines meant half-a-crown (twelve and a half new pence) with which, if I'd been old enough to do it, I could have bought two pints of Tetley's bitter.

Miss Beatrice Sharp in the front office handed me a stack of pre-paid 'correspondence forms' that I took home and immediately started writing on. If I wrote on Monday and got them to the pillar box at the top of the street before seven o'clock they would be on the editor's desk first thing on Tuesday. Eight submissions a week: one pound. Some people were starting full-time jobs on less money.

I wrote church notes, Sunday's visiting preachers, bits about the youth fellowship, townswomen's guild and the mothers' union, and gradually extended my domain from the parish church to include the Baptists, Methodists, Congregationalists and Salvationists.

One afternoon our lessons were interrupted when the school secretary came into the form room with a notice to be read to all pupils. Sticks of gelignite had been stolen from a local quarry. If we saw anything on the way home that resembled grey plasticine we should not pick it up to play with but should go straight to a phone box and dial 999.

When the home-time bell rang I went to the office and asked to read the notice – the better, I said, to remember it. I copied it into a notebook.

Back home, I wrote the story. It was too long to fit on a single form so I wrote it on pages neatly torn from an exercise book. It was too important to consign even to the reliable Post Office so I took a bus (three pence) to the *Pudsey News* office and hand-delivered it.

That was Tuesday evening. On Thursday morning my composition was there on Page One across two broad columns:

SCHOOLCHILDREN WARNED OF GELIGNITE DANGER.

'You did right by bringing it in yourself,' said Mr Algar. 'Get an expenses form and claim for your fares. One of the reporters will show you how to do it. I am assuming that you kept the bus tickets.'

There would be no looking back, after that.

At sixteen I left school on a Wednesday and started work as a reporter the following Monday.

*

Pudsey (population 35,000) was a mill town in the Heavy Woollen District of the West Riding of Yorkshire, the buffer state between the two great conurbations of Leeds and Bradford. The postal address was 'Pudsey, Yorkshire' and any letters addressed to the town hall with 'Pudsey, Leeds' on the envelope would be returned unread, and marked No Such Address. Apart from the mills that produced most of the material for Savile Row suits, the borough was proudly famous as the birthplace of several Yorkshire and England cricketers including Len Hutton, Ray Illingworth and Herbert Sutcliffe.

The office of the *Pudsey News*, established 1872, on Lowtown, the main street, was a dusty rickety old building with uneven floors and bulging walls, redolent of newsprint (the paper), hot metal and printers' ink. I would be there for a year, taking private lessons in shorthand on Wednesday afternoons (while the 12,500 copies were being printed in Harrogate), learning to touch-type on an old upright Remington, being introduced to the craft of the reporter, and becoming familiarised with alcohol.

Travelling mostly by bicycle (to save bus fares) I reported local news – similar to the paragraphs I had been writing while at school. Once a week I called on the local jobbing printer to find out about his new orders for work: invitations and tickets, new services, products and premises opening, people needing business cards on promotion.

I also covered amateur dramatics, weddings, funerals, council meetings, the magistrates court, and wrote the children's column (when 'Auntie Pat' was on holiday), reviews of films at the local cinema and births, marriages and deaths (hatches, matches and despatches). On Saturdays I would be at schoolgirls' hockey in the mornings and professional rugby league matches in the afternoons.

Names sold newspapers, they told me; so… lots of them. The committee, the organisers, the helpers, the jumble-sale stall holders… they would all buy a copy of the paper if their name was in it. At a big funeral we would collect, and print, the names of all the mourners.

One of Hugh Cudlipp's first jobs as a reporter on the *Penarth News* (I'd learn, much later) was to cover a performance of Handel's *Messiah* by the local choir. Though he knew nothing about the oratorio he managed to scrape together two thousand learned words by diligent research in *Grove's Dictionary of Music*. But his editor asked for more.

Cudlipp had an inspiration. Opening a new paragraph he wrote: 'The names of the choir were…'

No incident was too trivial to report; no detail too insignificant to mention – although we did hear, all the way from Doncaster, of this dictum being taken to extremes:

> An orange was stolen from a stall at Doncaster market last week.
>
> It was a Jaffa.

Somebody was presumably making a point. As was the case when the *Yorkshire Post* reported on its front page:

> NEW DELHI. – Several people from Yorkshire were drenched yesterday when the monsoon season started in India.

*

Local papers were people papers.

When I quoted a golden wedding celebrant as saying 'Although we've been married fifty years, we still have our ups and downs,' Mr Algar told me to show it to one of the girl reporters and ask her what was wrong with it. 'You need to develop a dirty mind, in order to save your face as a reporter,' he said.

Sue Douglas, a year older than I was, said she had once asked a great-grandmother, on her hundredth birthday, whether she'd ever been bedridden and had been told: 'Yes – and I've been table-ended, but you mustn't go putting that in the paper.'

And there was the Pudsey butcher who, complaining about the rising cost of meat, told a reporter: 'I've had to put my sausage up a few coppers.'

John Algar left to edit the *Leamington Spa Courier* – almost immediately winning it glory as the best designed newspaper in the British Press Awards.

He was replaced by Alan Hepworth, a comparative youngster whose claim to fame was that he'd been a reporter on the *Daily Mail* in Glasgow but whose problem was that he couldn't stand the competition. When the city's national newspapermen had shared a taxi to cover a murder (it must be true what they say about Scotsmen), as the cab turned a sharp corner the *Express* man had opened a door and shoved all the others out.

By comparison, he obviously reckoned, the editorship in Pudsey would be less competitive. He could write – I'll give him that – but as an editor, not even I rated him much.

When Bramley Rugby League Club (near the top of the first division) was beaten 26-0 at York (second from bottom of the second division), I wrote:

> There are only two words to describe Bramley's performance at Clarence Street on Saturday; the first is unprintable and the second is pathetic.

The alliterative headline:

BRAMLEY PUT ON A PATHETIC PERFORMANCE.

Bill Corbridge, club chairman, took offence and said he was withdrawing my 'press facilities' (which was how he generously described a hard wooden seat on a wind-swept terrace) from the Barley Mow ground):

'You should have said we was off colour, but you said we was pathetic, and we wasn't pathetic.'

'But Mr Corbridge, the result shows that you was...'

I reported the 'ban' to the new editor.

'You'd better be right!' he stormed. 'This could get the paper into trouble... into serious legal trouble... and I am not prepared to tolerate that. You'd better watch your step, boy.'

I told him that if a journalist was invited to a match – same as to a theatre – to review and criticise it, a fair and accurate comment was untouchable, in law.

'You'd better be right about that, too,' he told me.

Good grief. At seventeen I was being edited by some callow youth who hadn't even read *Essential Law for Journalists*.

The 'punishment' didn't last a week. As I stood with him at the dressing room door the Bramley team captain told Corbridge: 'No... He shouldn't have said pathetic. He should have said we were crap.' Then club manager Harry Beverley asked whether, as a favour, I would take his place on the bench on the touchline because he wanted to go that afternoon to watch Leeds play.

4. Postscript

I left shortly afterwards to join the *Yorkshire Evening Post* in Leeds as (at seventeen years old) its youngest-ever reporter. By happy accident of birth I had missed conscription – national service – by a couple of years. The teenagers before me had been called up for two years, usually just after their eighteenth birthdays; nobody wanted to employ youngsters who were fairly soon going to be absent, but whose continuing employment had by law to be retained and guaranteed.

Pudsey was emerging as a prime potential circulation area for three rival evening newspapers – the *Yorkshire Evening Post* and *Yorkshire Evening News* in Leeds and the *Telegraph & Argus* in Bradford. The *YEP* wanted somebody who knew the area; I had grown up in it and (briefly) reported it and I was appointed to look after the patch, possibly on the basis of the stories I had sold on to the paper every Thursday after publication in the *Pudsey News*.

This, for me, was the Big Time. My pay soared from three to seven guineas (£3.15p to £7.35p) a week, while my former school chums who had gone into banks, insurance or local government were earning three pounds or less. I still covered Pudsey court and the borough council meetings but otherwise my boundaries and outreach broadened dramatically.

As the youngest reporter (the next youngest was twenty-three, but the majority were in their thirties and forties, which I thought of as being closer to my parents' age) I started writing and editing 'Young Outlook', a weekly page for teenagers, I also got the tickets for pop concerts at the Odeon cinema.

[I should probably also mention – in case anybody wonders why I don't refer to it – that the manager of the Leeds Mecca Ballroom, the venue most popular for teenagers at that time, was one Jimmy Savile, a Radio Luxembourg disk jockey. He was of little interest otherwise, except that he dyed his long hair a different colour every week and once had it done as tartan.]

*

Apart from the specialists (crime, industry and municipal

correspondents), all news reporters did a week in turn covering the magistrates' courts and Leeds Assizes and Quarter sessions that ran non-stop.

There would often be eight or more magistrates' courts sitting every day, with only one reporter from each newspaper to cover the lot.

We overcame this problem (whether with the tacit approval of our employers or not, I never discovered) by scanning the court lists with the competition guy from the *Yorkshire Evening News*, picking out the two most likely cases, covering one each and exchanging notes in the lunch adjournment.

One morning on court duty I spotted the name of the owner of a coffee bar where I sometimes went for a snack before attending an evening assignment. I told Nick Pritchard, covering for the *Evening News*, that I would do that one; the accusation was that he had allowed customers to smoke 'drugs' in his basement.

I bumped into him in the corridor and he immediately started pleading with me not to report his case. When I told him it was my job to do it, he produced a wad of money and started to stuff five-pound notes into the top pocket of my jacket. When I removed them and shoved them back into his pockets there must have been fifty quid, or more.

Reporters had rules about the offer of bribes. First, obviously, they didn't accept them; second, they reported the offer to the news editor; third, they ensured that the story was published.

In the event he received only a conditional discharge and when I told Nick, later, he said: 'Oh, just forget it. The one I have been doing is far more interesting and it's also quite complicated, so we can't be bothered with a trivial case over a few kids smoking pot.'

Next time I went into the coffee bar the owner greeted me like his best friend. 'On the house,' he said. He refused to take my money and insisted so forcibly that I eventually reluctantly capitulated and accepted a cup of coffee and a sandwich, value about a shilling (5p). I never went there again.

By coincidence, my father was on the jury of one of the trials I covered – a doctor accused of performing an illegal abortion.

Because the court list was so full I was only popping in and out at intervals, in order to keep an eye on several running cases. When I got home that night I asked my father how it had gone.

'Oh, we found him guilty,' he said.

'Really? On the brief bits of evidence I heard, I thought he'd have got off.'

'Well yes,' said Dad. '*On the evidence*, he would have done. But in the jury room we discussed it and we thought that, well, the police didn't arrest him for nothing, did they?'

I have been worried about the jury system since that day, even though nowadays a jury of twelve just citizens would be more likely to side against the police, than with them.

One afternoon there was a case of indecent assault (my mother was somewhat concerned about the type of jobs her young son was sometimes covering, so I stopped telling her).

The prosecuting barrister asked the victim to tell the court what the accused man had said to her.

'Oh, no, my lord… I could never repeat it.'

'Perhaps,' said the judge helpfully, 'you could write the words on a piece of paper, so you don't need to say them.' And the court usher handed her a pencil and a piece of paper. It was passed to the barristers, then to the judge, and then to the jury.

In the heat of a summer afternoon one of the female jurors had fallen asleep. The man beside her nudged her to wake her and passed her the note.

It said: 'I am going to shag the arse off you, later.'

The woman folded it and put it in her handbag. The judge asked her to pass it back to him.

'But your honour… it was a private message!'

When a witness was giving evidence about having had sex in a car she was asked by a barrister: 'And did fellatio take place?'

'Oh no, sir,' she told him. 'It never entered my head.'

(Only the *Guardian* reported that exchange – presumably on the assumption that only *Guardian* readers would understand why it was funny.)

A woman giving evidence in a case of indecent exposure, asked what she had actually seen, told the court it was 'a long white thing, with roots'.

The man's lawyer repeated her description questioningly.

'Yes,' she said. 'Like a leek.'

*

Years later I'd do a case at Durham Assizes in which the accused, a petty crook aged 54, had spent every Christmas in borstal or prison since he was nine. He knew no other way of life, and he knew that he would be warm and well fed if he was in jail.

So towards the end of November he had waited in the city centre until a policeman approached and then thrown a half-brick at the window of the Woolworth's store. It bounced back. The policeman told him to move on.

'I'm trying to rob this shop,' he said.

'Don't be silly. Go home.'

So he knocked off the policeman's helmet and was duly arrested.

The judge sentenced him to fourteen days in prison. He'd be out before Christmas.

'But I always get three months for this!'

The judge knew what was going on. 'If you don't behave and be quiet,' he said, 'I shan't send you to prison at all...'

Tom Campbell, when on the *Daily Telegraph*, told me that in his youth covering Edinburgh Assizes there was a judge well known for filling his water carafe with gin. Sometimes he nodded off during a trial, and had to be woken to pronounce sentence without having heard much of the evidence.

Nevertheless the judge was elevated to Lord Chief Justice. The appointment was announced late in the day and made only the Stop Press of the *Edinburgh Evening News*. Too late to check, the headline printed was

SOTTISH JUDGE APPOINTED.

A reader sent the cutting to *Punch* magazine, in the way that, years later, it would have been forwarded to *Private Eye*. And *Punch*, unaware of the judge's reputation, reprinted it, with the comment:

> Now that his Lordship has been elevated, he will hopefully spend less time at the bar.

In the press room the court reporters drew straws and – perhaps because he was the youngest – Tom Campbell drew the short one and went to interview the judge.

Had his honour seen the original and unfortunate misprint? Indeed he had. Had his attention been drawn to the reproduction of it and the scurrilous comment in the humorous magazine called *Punch*? It certainly had.

'We in the press room were wondering... Does your Lordship intend to take any action?'

'No, laddie. I'll just sit tight.'

Judge Geoffrey Baker had a man in the dock at Leeds Assizes accused of impersonating a police officer, but who appeared in court in full jester's gear, complete with bells on his hat.

'Your honour, I thought you might be wondering why I am dressed like this. It's because I am the town clown of Huddersfield.'

'Think nothing of it,' the judge told him. 'Look what they made me wear.'

*

The first mobile phone I saw was 'mobile' only in that it could be moved in a van. We used it for covering urgent and instant news – mill fires and pit accidents, mainly. It had a tall aerial and a telephone handset from which news could be transmitted from the suburbs back to the Albion Street office in the centre of Leeds. The problem was that it required 'line of sight' for its radio waves so transmissions needed to be made from a hilltop. There should be no other hills, chimneys or tall buildings in the way – no easy task in the biggest industrial city in Yorkshire.

Most frequently it was no advantage at all, and the van driver would find the reporter a phone box from which to 'file' (dictate) his copy in the normal way... and even sometimes simply drive him back to the office to type it himself because that would most likely be fastest.

The public telephone system was normally very efficient and hand-operated by women who were still known as 'hello girls'. We had such frequent contact with them that they instantly recognised our individual voices, and we theirs.

But one Saturday for some reason the public phones were out of service all day – a big problem because that was the day we produced the *Green 'un*, the special sports edition with all local and national sporting results. Worse, it would be the day of the Leeds-Sheffield match, a local derby, at the Elland Road ground.

For an important game the writer (in this case it was to be John Bapty, the sports editor) filed five or six separate pieces: pre-match with the players' names, at quarter time, half-time, three-quarter time and on the final whistle. Sometimes he would write a new opening paragraph, when it was all over. He would write as the game progressed and pass the copy to a messenger to dictate by phone to the office.

But with no telephones, what to do?

Then somebody remembered that one of the printers had a 'secret' pigeon loft on the roof of the Albion Street building. Unofficial arrangements were made and the copyboy instructed in the noble art of loading messages onto homing pigeons and launching them. Bapty looked on with interest.

All worked well… until the final whistle. Leeds had scored the winning goal in extra time and the messenger had already checked his watch and gone home. But, as arranged, he had left the last pigeon in the basket for Bapty to take back to the office.

The sports editor knew what to do. He rolled up his copy and stuffed it with his chubby fingers into the cylindrical container on the bird's leg. Then – almost exactly as he'd seen it done on the office roof – he launched the bird… straight into the back of the stand, from where it slithered down… dead.

*

Each reporter had a telephone on his desk but because there was so much noise in the news room – constant shouting, ringing phones, and clattering typewriters – there were also three enclosed wooden kiosks at the back. Every hour on the hour one of the kiosk phones would ring and any reporter doing nothing at the moment would sit inside and do 'the calls' as the switchboard patiently rang all the numbers for him: fire services, police stations, ambulances and hospitals for both the city and the county.

One morning the operator told the reporter taking the calls, first, that there was actually a fire within the building. He kicked open the door and shouted to a colleague: 'Quick! Ring the fire bri-fucking-gade, and get them round to the back door!'

At lunch (a pint of Youngers, a roast beef sandwich and a pickled gherkin) in Whitelock's First City Luncheon Bar I mentioned this interesting example of word-splitting to reporter Malcolm Barker (no relation):

'Fire bri-fucking-gade...?'

'It's called infix, or *tmesis*,' he told me. 'Happens all the time in a newspaper office.'

I was studying A-level Law and English part time at Leeds College of Commerce, but I was learning more grammar, and extending my vocabulary, in the office. And learning more about syllabus law by continuing to cover courts on a regular basis.

I also learnt one of the best lessons about reporting from Malcolm.

The morning after attending a concert by Ella Fitzgerald I had been sitting at my desk, obviously deep in thought; paper in typewriter but no fingers on the keyboard.

'Problem?'

'I'm stuck for what to write. You can't just keep heaping praise on Ella Fitzgerald,' I told him, 'when the whole world knows how brilliant and wonderful she is.'

'Write that,' said Malcolm. So I did, and that was how it appeared.

Malcolm – he would eventually become editor of the *YEP* – had a bright, light touch on news stories that I tried hard to emulate.

One morning Edgar Craven, the chief sub-editor, a big balding man in shirtsleeves and red braces, stormed into the newsroom holding a sheaf of reporter's copy.

'Which one of you fucking Barker bastards wrote this shit?'

Craven was a man of few words, most of them coarse. But since he saw the words as shit I modestly assumed they would be mine, rather than Malcolm's.

I held out my hand to take the copy and identify it.

Craven held on to it.

'It's time you knew that all right is *always* two separate words,' he bellowed.

If we had been told that at grammar school, I had missed it. Nevertheless, it was easy enough to remember.

I nodded.

'Fucking got that, have you? Or do I need to teach you fucking English?'

I couldn't think of anything to say, except 'All right, Mr Craven.'

'All right…? All right…! Are you trying to be fucking funny?'

What this ogre didn't realise was that to me the most important fact in the matter was that he'd been reading copy and couldn't tell whether I or Malcom had written it. It was one of the happiest moments of my young life.

*

The *Yorkshire Evening Post* was selling something around 250,000 copies every night – considerably more than its competition in Leeds or Bradford and about twice as many as its sister morning paper, the *Yorkshire Post*.

Outside the city limits there were also local evening – and sometimes morning – papers in York, Scarborough, Doncaster, Sheffield, and Darlington, as well as in Bradford. Elsewhere some cities, like Leeds, proudly supported two competing evenings. Nowadays some of them would be lucky to support a website.

Rivalry between the two Leeds evenings was fierce and woe betide the reporter who missed a fact that the opposition had discovered.

When a workman was injured on a building site the *YEP* mentioned – but the *YEN* man had failed to learn – that the accident had occurred on his birthday. Next day, when a youngster was knocked down and trapped under a tram, the *EN* reporter crawled underneath to interview him:

'It isn't your birthday today, by any chance…?'

*

During the cricket season and on important racing days the City edition of the *Evening Post* would be on the streets at 10.30 in the morning. The 'First' would be out about noon, the 'Final' at 2pm, the 'One-Star Final' around 3.30 and the 'Late Night Final', for people going home after work, about 4.30. Even then there would be a short single-column space for late news: the Box, or Stop Press, a misnomer because type could be inserted into the paper without literally stopping the presses turning.

(Nowadays there is only one edition of the *YEP*, written and produced the night before, and printed in Sheffield, thirty-six miles away.)

I once ran back into the news room to report having seen a news vendor knocked down by a car.

News editor Ken Lemmon asked: 'One of ours, or one of theirs?'

'One of theirs.'

'So write a par for the Box, then phone for an ambulance.'

When, as frequently happened, groups of people were allowed to tour the office, Edgar Craven would direct their attention to a button on the wall behind his desk. It had originally been on a Leeds bus and engraved within the white ceramic circle surrounding the vital red button were the words PRESS ONCE, so passengers could advise the driver they wanted to alight at the next stop.

This, Craven would pompously explain, was how, when he was finally satisfied with it, he would start the mighty presses and get the next edition rolling. And occasionally he would demonstrate, with the result that just after pushing the button the visitors would feel the tremor from the press room, vibrating the entire building.

One evening, when all the sub-editors had gone home, a couple of us decided to get our revenge on their chief. We took a penknife and carefully unscrewed the bell-push, intending to disconnect it.

In fact there was no wiring whatsoever. All that happened was that Craven knew – to the minute, and sometimes to the very second – when the presses were due to start rolling for each edition, and he pushed the button only for effect.

*

Wandering around the city centre, as we sometimes did (ostensibly in the search for stories) Malcolm introduced me to the West Riding pub and to Ken Yates, the *Sunday Mirror* staffman in Leeds who spent most days inside it, downing Guinness.

'How's that for a job?' Malcolm asked. 'One story a week, and he earns twice as much as I do.'

(I had written nine stories already, that day.)

And then we bumped into Mike Parkin of the *Guardian*, who Malcolm described as 'an angel of a writer'. I asked Mike what was the secret of his beautiful prose – he wrote news stories like literary essays.

'All you need is a beginning, a middle, and an end. But the end needs to be linked to the beginning. Then the subs can't cut it from the bottom.'

*

I started to be given – and also to bring in – some of the lighter stories for the paper. I wrote one about a newly installed lamp post that amused me because it had no obvious purpose and illuminated nothing (LET THERE BE LIGHT). And another about a brick wall that seemed to exist only as a background for constantly refreshed graffiti (READ WALL ABOUT IT).

When a family of geese got lost in the city centre and was relocated to Roundhay Park Lake, I wrote the story as a postcard, as if being written home by the gander.

Pope Paul VI died that day, so I didn't have high hopes for the story making the edition. In fact, bottom centre, with a photograph, and across four columns, it was the only piece on the broadsheet front page that wasn't Pope-related. A couple of readers wrote to the editor to thank him for lightening up the news on such an otherwise depressing day, and congratulating the *Evening Post Goose Reporter*.

Deputy-editor Ewart Clay forwarded the mail to me with a hand-written note: 'I heartily endorse these comments – well done!'

My first of what our trade called 'hero-grams'.

*

There were silly stories that would stay in the memory banks for ever.

Like the time the landlord of The Ostler's in Trinity Street, Leeds, asked reporters Mike Kerrigan and John Beatty for a copy of the *Yorkshire Evening News* Saturday sports edition, long after the street sellers had gone home. They went back to the office and, failing to find a copy, went down to the mighty presses and ran one off for the publican. The problem was that having started the machine they were unable to stop it, and by the time the massive roll of newsprint ran out they were standing waist-deep in green paper.

…Or when the news editor of the *People* wanted to expose the landlord of a pub at Drighlington crossroads for attracting customers by claiming to have a dog that talked – and gave up when Colin Dunne (*Yorkshire Post*) put the animal on the phone to speak to him.

There were also historic stories. In January 1963 when Hugh Gaitskell, leader of the Labour Party (and a Leeds MP), died and an election was being held to find his successor, Raymond Gledhill, who sat at the next desk to me, said: 'I hope Harold gets it.'

'Harold? You mean Harold Wilson?'

The *EP* was owned by Yorkshire Conservative Newspapers Ltd; we didn't refer to socialists by their first names. Raymond nodded.

'Because he's a Yorkshireman, you mean?'

'Not only that… but it would mean there's a chance that he would be the next prime minister. And when we were about twelve years old we were walking together to Scouts and discussing what we wanted to be when we grew up. I said I intended to be a reporter; Harold said he planned to become prime minister.'

'At twelve…? That's fantastic. You should write the story.'

He demurred, so I got him to retell the story to Malcolm, who agreed with me: 'Wonderful! You must write it.'

'I couldn't do that,' said Raymond. 'Harold told me in confidence.'

Malcolm chuckled. 'But twelve-year-old boys don't have confidences.'

'But… he didn't know he was going to be quoted.'

'Yes he did,' I said. 'You had already told him you were going to be a reporter. After that, anything he said to you was fair game.'

(*Essential Law for Journalists*, again.)

Raymond was finally persuaded. He wrote the story and it was reproduced and syndicated all round the world. The Labour Party machine loved it and rather miraculously turned up a photo of an eight-year-old Harold standing at the door of Number Ten. Wilson contacted his old Boy Scout chum, inviting Raymond to join him on election night and the two boyhood pals were travelling back to London in the official car when a police outrider stopped it to inform Wilson that he was the new PM.

*

The problem was that at this tender age I had to review my life.

At school my sole ambition had been to work on the *Evening Post* – and I had already achieved that. Most of my mates who had gone into industry or commerce considered that they were in jobs for life. I thought the world was bigger than that – even (if the thought could be contemplated) larger than Leeds.

I considered my colleagues on the *EP*: without doubt, highly professional to a man. Most of them settled down with families. There were jobs like news editor, diary editor, features editor that might come up for them... eventually. They didn't want or intend to move.

One, Allen Rowley, had gone to London for a couple of weeks to work for the *Sunday People* during his annual holiday and been sent on a story about teenagers who were making an old couple's life 'a living hell' (as he wrote it) by turning the quiet country road where they lived into 'a lovers' lane'. Sounded like good Sunday newspaper stuff.

When he saw the page proof of his story it had been turned upside down, so now it appeared along the lines of 'Leave the kids alone, you miserable old kill-joys!'

While he had been writing his copy the *People* policy had changed. It had been decided to aim at a younger market, in which teenagers could suddenly do no wrong.

'But it is not the story I wrote,' Allen had protested.

'That's not your problem,' the deputy editor told him. 'Your job is to shovel the shit. We will turn it into gold.'

After hearing that story, none of the Leeds pros – all of them used to seeing their copy appear in the paper as they had written it – fancied a move from Albion Street to Fleet Street. Even though it would mean much better money... 'But bloody hell, have you seen the price of houses down there?'

Turning eighteen and still living at home, I could hardly complain.

Often, when I was depositing my pay cheque at the local bank the manager would appear from his office to say hello. He had been at school with my mother.

'Saw your story in the *Evening Post* last night,' he'd say. 'It's good to see that you are doing so well.'

It was big-fish-small-pool syndrome. I was becoming world-famous... in Leeds.

As a reward for something or other I was given my first Foreign Trip – to accompany a group of market gardeners visiting the tulip fields in Holland. Only for a day, but it was also my first experience of flying.

Once a week I'd be at the Leeds Odeon cinema reviewing stage shows by people who were nationally famous and sometimes world famous themselves.

I could understand that the mid-aged reporters weren't especially interested in watching rock-and-roll performers (and as the part-time 'Youth' editor it was in any case my fiefdom), but was surprised that they would rather go home to their families than watch live performances by stars like Ella Fitzgerald, Nat King Cole, and Sammy Davis Junior.

The first time I saw The Beatles, they were the support act for clarinettist Acker Bilk and his jazz band, performing in a converted Leeds tram shed.

Maggie Hall, covering for the *Evening News*, went to interview Bilk. 'Don't waste your time on me,' he told her. 'They're the boys you ought to be writing about.'

But by the time she forced her way through the throng of youngsters to the other dressing room she couldn't get in.

I was there already, interviewing the new phenomenon as autograph books were passed in what seemed like their hundreds through a gap in the door, and photographs slid under it. John Lennon handed me a stack of the books.

'Here you are. Sing for your supper, pal. Help us sign these.'

I looked to see how he, Paul, George and Ringo (they called him Ritchie) wrote their autographs, and I started to copy them.

Fifty years later you could get ten thousand pounds for the four signatures on a plain sheet of paper (much more, for autographs on a photograph of the group). When I read reports of these prices at auction I wonder how many of them might have been written by me.

Before the term acquired a different meaning, those pop and classic concerts – touring the nation with a different venue every night – were known as 'one-night stands'.

Thus, in addition to The Beatles, I reviewed (and usually later, in the dressing room, interviewed) the Rolling Stones, Freddie and the Dreamers, Gene Pitney, Roy Orbison, Herman's Hermits, Manfred Mann, the Hollies, Dusty Springfield, the Dave Clark Five, Susan Maughn, Brenda Lee, Cliff Richard and the Shadows...

Once a concert was announced I'd receive letters from teenage girls: 'I'm their biggest fan. Please-please-please can you arrange for me to meet them in their dressing room? I'll do ANYTHING!' [usually underlined three times.]

It is one small element of history that appears to be overlooked when, maybe forty or fifty years later, some former teenager accuses an ageing performer of having touched her up.

The shows would be introduced by well-known or rapidly rising comperes.

Jimmy Tarbuck told me he had known Cilla Black since they first worked together at Liverpool's Cavern Club.

'Wasn't she the cloakroom attendant?' I asked, having done my research.

'No,' said Tarbuck. 'She just took people's coats.'

I covered a lot of Beatles appearances, arguing with chums on other newspapers about which of us had actually coined expressions like Fab Four and Beatlemania and getting to know their manager Brian Epstein and press agent Tony Barrow.

I took Liz, my teenage girlfriend, to one of the Leeds concerts and during a pre-show chat Tony asked where we were sitting and suggested we come down to watch on-stage, from the wings.

'You'll hear nothing out there, with all the screaming that'll be going on,' he said. 'Often they don't even sing the right words, but nobody knows because nobody in the audience can hear them.'

So that's what we did. John, George, Paul and Ringo stopped for a chat and a breather while running on and off stage for a number of encores – and then slipped out of the theatre before the fans realised, finally, that they were not going to reappear.

Next day at school one of Liz's friends mentioned that The Beatles had been in Leeds the previous night.

'Yes,' said Liz…'Ask me where I was, last night.'

*

There was extra money to be made by covering evening assignments – public meetings, golf club dinners, school speech days – for our morning paper, the *Yorkshire Post* (always referred to as the *Why Pee*). Since I would be attending in any case, for the *EP*, all that was required was a different intro, or a different aspect of the story, for the two papers.

The same deal was available for covering agricultural shows on summer Saturdays – the results would be too late for the evening paper which in any case would be concentrating on sport, so the *YP* could run them on Monday mornings. Even on important regional newspapers – and the *YP* considered itself equal in significance to the *Guardian* – names sold newspapers.

These shows were opportunities for 'light writing' or 'colour' pieces: a description of the scene, which locally prominent people were turning up and sometimes what their ladies were wearing (what's *tulle*?), the number of competition entries, mention of a few of the odder classes and categories (what on earth were pom-pom dahlias?), vivid steam engines, acrobatic dogs, prancing horses and ferocious looking bulls.

The plum job, and I got it, was the Great Yorkshire Show. With hundreds of classes and categories and thousands of competitors, the results, separated by a few photographs, would fill two broadsheet pages in the smallest fount of type all paid for on a linage basis.

There were posters around the show ground: YORKSHIRE POST ON MONDAY FOR THE FULL SHOW RESULTS.

It was no effort, going round the tents or to the judges' enclosure usually by way of the drinks tent and marking 1, 2 and 3 besides the entries in the catalogue. ...Until Monday morning when the results appeared in print and the secretary to the editor of the *YP* asked me to 'pop in' and see her boss, Kenneth Young.

'I've had a friend on the phone this morning, complaining that the results for the Great Yorkshire Show in my newspaper are all wrong. You'd better have a word with him and sort it out, because if they are wrong, we are *not* going to print two pages of corrections.'

I called the chap.

'All wrong,' he confirmed. 'Just look at the results for the Long-Haired Cavies.' (Cavies, I had learnt only at the weekend, were rodents, guinea pigs.)

'... I came second in that competition and you have printed my name – just look at it – as A R Scott.'

I traced my finger down the columns of minuscule type and found it.

'And your name is –?'

'Robert Scott.'

'Not A R, then?'

'No; just R for Robert.'

I realised immediately what had happened. The clue came from him. I had dictated the result: 'second... R for Robert Scott', and the copytaker, mishearing it as 'Arthur Robert' and knowing that because of shortage of space we were printing only initials, no first names, had typed A R...

I wondered how many times that might have happened.

'Okay. Sorry about that. What else is wrong?'

'Er... that's it.'

I reported back to Kenneth Young, who laughed. 'No problem. I'll sort it out with him later, at the club. But it might be better in future if when dictating copy you remember that it should be A for Alpha, R for Romeo. The typists are less likely to make that mistake.'

When I related the story to Geoffrey Hemingway, the *EP* industrial correspondent, he told me: 'Look on the bright side. You have completely fucked your chances of being offered a job on *Fur & Feather*.'

*

My growing reputation for 'light' writing turned out to be a double-edged sword.

Our main competition, the *Yorkshire Evening News*, succumbed to economic pressures and folded, to merge with the *YEP* – for a brief time creating a daily circulation close to half a million copies.

Both evenings printed fairly distinct editions for south Yorkshire (mostly Doncaster, Barnsley and Rotherham; Sheffield had its own evening paper) and the *Evening News* had been stronger in the south. The *EP* needed to capture and retain the market and editor Alan Woodward decided that a bit of 'bright writing' might be the way to do it.

So he sent for me.

'It is a depressing place,' he told me, 'with depressing people. I want you to go down there and cheer them up a bit.'

I didn't want to go.

'It's thirty-five miles away,' he said. 'That's seventy miles, return trip. Every day.'

I was aware of the distance, and could do the maths.

'And we pay three-pence a mile, if you go there by car.'

'I don't have a car.'

'I don't know that you don't have a car…'

Doncaster was best known as a traffic jam on the A1, at that time the main road to the north from London. When there was racing in town motorists could get out of the car and do their shopping, then return to find their vehicle in the traffic where they'd left it.

Predominantly a coal-mining area with a glass works, a tractor factory and a railway yard to cheer it up a bit, it was indeed a grim place, with grim people. There was (and still is) a large village nearby called Grimethorpe. And another, not far away, called Greaseborough. There was even a village (and I occasionally wondered whether my mother had renamed the place) called Heck.

The most frequent cause of death among the local population was pneumoconiosis – the inhalation by pitmen of coal dust – which was measured in percentages to calculate insurance and pensions. One victim had a count of 96 per cent. The coroner's officer, a police sergeant, told me that when the man's lungs were being opened for the autopsy the surgeon's knife had crackled through the coal grit. 'If the poor bugger had spat on t'fireback, it would have burned for a week.'

The exceptions in the gloom (being low lying it was also uncommonly subject to fog) were the reporters who, once they had overcome the bereavement of more than half their number with the loss of a popular newspaper, were as much fun as the people I worked with in Leeds – and generally about half the age.

Through the comradely nature of the trade quite a lot of the *YEN* refugees were offered jobs on the national papers, mostly in the busy Manchester offices where the northern and Irish editions were produced.

Maggie Hall's application had said simply: 'Help, help, help. – Margaret Hall, *YEN*, Doncaster.'

It earned her an interview from which she got a job on the *Daily Mirror*.

What struck me as strange, however, was that it was obviously easier to be offered a job on a national by working for a failed local newspaper, than by working for a more successful one.

In contrast to the reporters, the sub-editors (and the acting editor, who was Welsh so it was possibly not his fault) were older and mostly dour.

I had fun on exercise with the Yorkshire Hussars in Catterick, rode at high speed in a police car on the Doncaster by-pass (one of the first motorways) before it officially opened.

I accompanied the Shah of Persia when he came to look at British power stations.

A chap from the Foreign Office explained the importance of the man: 'The Shah, Mohammad Reza Shah Pahlavi, more correctly referred to as the *Shahanshah* or king of kings, is the latest in a continuous 2,500-year monarchy. He is said to be a direct descendant of Mohammad and is believed by 25million subjects to be the Son of God. But an English duke takes precedence.'

*

I even wrote about the Royal Ballet – well, nobody else wanted to do it.

When their advance team came to town to announce their forthcoming visit, which would last for a week, I naturally wrote about John Field, the director of the touring company, who was a native of Doncaster. I told him I'd never seen ballet and he said I should try it and might even enjoy it. I could review it, he suggested (aware that the Leeds papers had no ballet critics), and he would be happy to guide me in that endeavour.

The *Evening Post* was keen on culture and said that I could spend a week devoted to the ballet if I could find a story a day and write a review every night for the *YP*. I thought that, with John Field's help, I could manage that, and eventually extended my stay, suddenly as the '*YP* ballet correspondent', for their entire northern tour, and even for part of the midlands.

In the intervals of each performance I would meet John Field in the bar and he would tell me: 'The second *pas-de-deux* came in a beat late, and Nadia is dancing as if she has two left feet.' I would go to the phone and dictate it as my review, my 'crit'.

Every morning I attended class, in the hope of finding a story for the evening paper that was paying my basic wages and John – wearing a dark blue suit and hush-puppies – would give them his own assessment of the previous evening's performance and then show them how it should have been done. Not surprisingly, his appraisal was often remarkably similar to mine.

'He's only saying that,' said prima ballerina Doreen Wells one morning, 'because he's read what Revel wrote in today's *Yorkshire Post*.' In fact he hadn't read any of it until he was back at Covent Garden where the press office showed him the cuttings.

'Remarkably accurate,' said John Field, who would later become director of La Scala, Milan. 'That boy originally knew nothing about ballet and now he's writing like an experienced critic.'

Over dinner after a performance in Derby one of the dancers, perusing the wine list, said: 'Oh… Margaux…'

I looked round, expecting to see the world's most famous ballerina entering the restaurant.

Still in his teens, the kid from Pudsey was in a steep learning curve.

*

I wrote about the atmosphere and the crowds attending the racing during Leger Week – carnival time, in Doncaster – and then went to St Germain-en-Laye, just outside Paris, which was Doncaster's twin town, and where I discovered a suburb called St Leger.

There was possibly a connection with the famous horse-race, so I asked whether anybody in the office knew why the race was so called. Nobody had ever thought about it. (It was named after Colonel Anthony St Leger, who had devised the race in 1776.)

'Somebody must know, surely,' I protested. 'It's the only thing the rest of the world knows about Doncaster.'

'Stop showing off… just because you've been abroad,' the racing sub told me.

That was what got to me. There were people sitting round a table editing stories about South Africa and Viet Nam who had never been further south than Bawtry, nine miles away. Not to Leeds, 33 miles north, and certainly not to London, 175 miles south. Nor had the majority of them any wish to make those journeys.

We reporters amused ourselves by cutting snippets out of the morning papers and forwarding them to *Private Eye*.

Customs officers had seized 'a consignment of hemp-ridden pouffes'…

When the *Guardian* misprinted its own name (as *Guradian*) ours was one of a dozen cuttings received at the *Eye*.

There were even occasional errors on the Press Association tapes: SHIT CRASH. 300 FEARED LOST AT SEA…

Followed swiftly by CORRECTION: FOR SHIT CRASH READ SHIP CRAP.

When I wrote:

> Twenty French schoolgirls from Doncaster's twin town were promised an exciting but exhausting time when they met the Mayor of Doncaster today…

… it was one of the women journalists who pointed it out to me. I left it for the first edition, then altered it, and sent the original version to Greek Street.

Every cutting was responded to quickly by an envelope containing a cheque for two guineas each and usually a hand-written note of thanks from the editor, Peter Cook.

Nevertheless, time to move on, I thought.

Escape appeared on the horizon with a call from Tony Hunter, a freelance reporter who with his twin brother Bill covered Leeds courts (all of them) for the nationals. Their friend Bill Freeman, northern news editor of the *Mirror*, was looking for fresh talent and not unnaturally, having worked on the *YP* himself, thought it was the best grounding for reporters. The twins recommended me, and he came to Leeds to meet me over a liquid lunch.

We got along swimmingly, and he said I was what he was looking for. He asked what I imagined it would be like working for the *Mirror* and I said I didn't think it would be easy if I had to cover – picking an idea completely out of the blue – a complicated bankruptcy case in about six paragraphs.

He replied that staff reporters didn't write shorts, only page leads, so no problem there.

On the way out of the Town Hall Tavern he asked my age. I was nineteen. His face fell. He'd give me a job, he said, but not for two years. In those days people 'came of age' at twenty-one. Bill explained that if a story inadvertently got the paper into trouble, he might be asked in court why he had sent a boy on a man's job; if I was twenty-one the question would not even arise.

So temporarily disappointed but imbued with the confidence, I looked around for something to do meanwhile.

There was a men's glossy magazine owned by Michael Heseltine and Clive Labovitch called *Town*, which had started life as *Man About Town* and had later been relaunched as *About Town*. It was posh and stylish and used fine writing and I'd written a piece for it about the Royal Ballet Company owning three pigeons (for use on stage in the French ballet, *Two Pigeons* – they needed an understudy), having discovered that the feathered cast comprised one male, one female, and one homosexual; 'queer as a coot' was my inspired line. So I wrote asking for a job and got a letter by return on beautifully embossed notepaper: 'Dear Mr Barker, When can you come and see me? – Clive Labovitch', and I was on the next train.

Mr Labovitch gave me a couple of folios of copy to read while he did something else, then asked me what I thought of it.

I gave him my considered opinion, based on a lifetime's experience. 'You are not, I hope, thinking of using this,' I grinned, for it was clearly simply a basic test of my journalistic know-how: 'It's crap.'

'You don't like it?'

'Oh come on,' I laughed. 'The man can't even write English. He can't form sentences. He doesn't understand paragraphs. It's all wham-bam-thank-you-mam nonsense. It has no place in a classy magazine like *Town*.'

'Oh dear,' said Labovitch. 'I think we have a problem, then, because I like it.'

He couldn't, I said, be serious. I didn't say it in so many words but I tried to get the message across that he was being advised, here, by somebody who knew how to write, who was getting decent features into the *Yorkshire Evening Post* and who'd been promised a job on the *Daily Mirror*; there was no greater qualification for a writer than that.

'If you don't like it,' said Labovitch, 'I think we might as well call it a day right now, because I am planning to use it in the next issue. I was sharing it with you because I think it is brilliant.'

Well, he was the editor. But I was a reader and I didn't think the piece would sit well in the magazine. It would exasperate readers and he'd have to start planning yet another re-launch. They'd already gone from *Man About Town* to *About Town* to *Town*. Would anybody buy the next incarnation, which would presumably have to be called just *About...*?

'You're entitled to your opinion,' said Mr Labovitch. 'But I think we're going to hear a lot more about this chap, Tom Wolfe.'

All was not lost for at this time they were recruiting reporters for the rejuvenated *Daily Herald*, the paper that was about to become *The Sun* – THE NEWSPAPER BORN OF THE AGE WE LIVE IN. Catchy strapline, or what?

Paul Callan, in the *YEP* London office, trolled along for an interview with the news-editor-designate, John Graham.

According to Callan, Ulster-born John (who I got to know later as one of the nicest guys in journalism) wore a cardigan, cavalry-twill trousers, hush puppies, a wool shirt and a knitted tie, and opened the interview by asking where he was educated.

'Er, public school. Eton, actually.'

Had he realised that this was a trade union newspaper? 'We're not actually looking for public school types.'

And yet, Callan reminded him, Cecil King (the paper's chairman) had been educated at Winchester.

'But he's the guvnor… You're not applying for his job, are you?'

'Not at this interview, no,' said Callan.

He didn't get either job, but kindly sent a message up the line to me and I bunged in an application.

I turned up in my tweed suit – the one I wore for covering the Great Yorkshire Show – and a Viyella checked shirt and wool tie. Instead of Sobranie Virginia I bought a packet of ten Embassy and sat poised ready to be seen placing the two-point coupon in my wallet as the interviewer entered.

It wasn't John Graham.

Barrie Harding, fresh in from New York and, more precisely, from Fifth Avenue, was dressed in a dark blue suit, blue shirt, silk tie and – two fashion items that I identified only later – silk socks and Gucci shoes.

I knew I'd lost it when he said: 'It's not even as if you went to public school.'

So I called Callan and we met for a drink in the Wig & Pen Club.

'It's their loss,' he consoled me. 'You and I are evening paper men and evening men are the salt of the earth in this business. We are the ones who find and write the stories, and all the morning paper crowd ever do is follow us... We, my friend, are what newspapers are all about. I, for example, have just been offered a job I couldn't possibly refuse on the *Evening Standard*. Evening papers... the jewels in Fleet Street's crown.'

I took out my wallet to buy a drink and crumpled the Embassy coupon into an ashtray.

'I suppose,' said Callan, 'you couldn't lend me a fiver.'

Town magazine folded in 1968; the *Sun*, as we knew it, in 1969. Callan still hasn't refunded the fiver.

*

I celebrated my twentieth birthday, still in Doncaster, by covering another Beatles concert. We had prepared a special edition for that night, Page One devoted to a piece I had written based on interviews I had had with them. By total coincidence (because it was the group's second visit to the town) the headline was HAPPY RETURNS, BEATLES. There were four huge head shots of the 'fab four' with facsimiles of their autographs beneath. I didn't know where the subs had sourced them.

At the end of the show, with the cinema besieged by screaming teenage girls who hadn't been able to get tickets, we smuggled them away to their hotel, twenty miles away, in the back of an *Evening Post* delivery van.

Then I applied for, and got, a job with Brenards, the freelance news and picture agency covering London Airport – as Heathrow was then known – for all the nationals and occasionally for the provincial papers. Twenty pounds a week, and a one-room flat with miniscule kitchen in South Kensington, handy for the West London Air Terminal, was six quid a week.

I wrote to Bill Freeman telling him that I was now twenty, so would soon be twenty-one. He replied with a note promising that he hadn't forgotten me.

True to his word, a few months later he wrote again: 'If you are still interested in a job on the *Daily Mirror*, call me.'

I flew to Manchester. 'You'll need to lie about your age for a while,' said Bill. 'But how soon can you start?'

5. Arrivals and departures

So I said to David Niven, 'I'm really worried that I am becoming a bit of a name-dropper. Sometimes I send postcards home to my girlfriend in Leeds and all I write is *Today I interviewed...* followed by a list of famous people's names.'

He told me not to worry. 'When you have just had tea with Sophia Loren' – as he knew I had, that afternoon – 'nobody is interested in hearing about the fucking waiter.'

'I had tea with Lord Mountbatten yesterday. Just the two of us. Real tea, with cucumber sandwiches,' I said.

'Did he have anything interesting to say?'

'Not really. He said he'd been on a fact-finding mission, and had found some facts.'

'An impressive enough name to drop though, even if only on a postcard.'

Niven waved to summon a waiter and order a Scotch for himself and a cold light ale for me, then he started recounting a story about Errol Flynn (or it might have been about Cary Grant, or Audrey Hepburn or Grace Kelly).

Life, covering the airport, was like that. Richard Burton and Liz Taylor in the morning, Marlene Dietrich at lunchtime, Bing Crosby in the afternoon, Sophia Loren around teatime, Niven in the evening.

With one arrival or departure every minute London was the busiest airport in the world. It was also the main hub for Europe, so wherever you flew you passed through it and, while there, would be stuck for an hour or more with nobody to talk to, except maybe a 'resident' reporter. Captive audience.

So, plenty of interviews. At the end of my first week I'd had stories in every Fleet Street newspaper.

The *Express, Mail, Mirror, Sketch* and *Herald* based photographers there; the *Telegraph* had its own staff reporter. The rest was left to the Brenards agency. They wanted VIP interviews and photographs of female film stars and we, the reporters, provided a few lines of copy as an excuse to put them on page one.

Joan Collins on the front page could increase that day's sales of a popular newspaper by five per cent. For the *Mirror*, with a daily circulation of 5.2million, that meant big bucks.

But Sophia Loren – then filming *Lady L* with Niven and Paul Newman – was the picture editors' favourite. And mine. She passed through the airport two or three times a week and after I'd interviewed her a couple of times she'd send her driver to the press room to say: 'Mr Barker, Miss Loren says she is in the lounge, if you wish to join her.'

The film was being shot at Castle Howard in Yorkshire and I'd tell her about some of the parts of the county she wasn't getting time to see. She'd tell me about her always pending marriage to Carlo Ponti (they eventually made it the following year, 1966) and her constant attempts to become pregnant and sometimes she'd give me photographs of herself and a chinagraph pencil and ask me to chalk a cross over any that I didn't like.

She was thirty, I was twenty and like every male of my generation I had seen her undressed – or, at least, wearing only a basque, high heels, stockings and suspenders, and a hat – in the 1960 movie *The Millionairess*.

The most beautiful woman in the world... 'Not true; I have a neck like a *giraffa*!'

Never mind the neck... 'Oh, but everything else is due to spaghetti.'

Liz Taylor, by contrast, appeared significantly overweight.

When I found some way of mentioning the fact, obliquely, she told me it was intentional.

'I'm making *Who's Afraid of Virginia Wolf?* – with Richard, and I need to look like a frumpy middle-aged housewife. So I am on a diet that's almost exclusively avocados because I've been told they're the single most fattening food.'

I told her it looked like it was working.

Poring over a few light ales while waiting to photograph Grace Kelly, *Express* snapper George Stroud asked me: 'What do I call her when I want her to look towards me? Your majesty? Your highness? Royal highness? What?'

I said I thought Princess Grace would suffice.

Came the moment and she stood in front of the photographers' parade. George raised his camera. 'This way please, your grace...'

A few days later George phoned the office to complain about its use of one of his photographs.

'You've used completely the wrong pictures this morning,' he shouted. 'You are a total fucking idiot. You ought to be fired. You are a useless clown.'

The voice at the other end asked sharply: 'Do you know who you're talking to?'

'One of those useless wankers on the picture desk. Doesn't matter which. You're a fucking idiot, whoever you are.'

'This is Bob Edwards, the editor.'

'I don't give a fuck... Do you know who YOU are talking to?'

'I haven't the faintest idea.'

Thank fuck for that,' said George, and hung up.

*

There were politicians, too. More than once I caught George Brown, the deputy prime minister, in my arms when he stumbled and fell, totally drunk, down the aircraft steps and several times helped to pour him into his official car.

He obviously somehow remembered this a couple of years later when, on a visit to Gateshead, he spotted me among the crowd of press men and waved.

'Ah, there you are, dear boy... where can we get a drink?'

I pointed out that it was not quite eleven in the morning, and a Sunday, so still more than an hour before pub opening time. But a kindly copper suggested that the police social club might be willing to serve us, so off we marched, arm in arm, leaving the other reporters standing.

I interviewed Ian Smith before his 'unilateral declaration of independence' for Rhodesia... And prime minister Harold Wilson, on his way to and from Rhodesia... defence secretary Denis Healey... U Thant, secretary-general of the United Nations... More names for the postcards...

*

Muhammad Ali arrived at the airport dressed smartly in blazer and flannels and flanked by his minders in full-length fur coats and chunky jewellery. I asked if I could have a word and he gestured for me to sit beside him then, producing my notebook, I asked: 'I've seen it spelt several different ways, so which spelling of the prophet's name do you prefer?'

He laughed, slapping his knee. 'I like that! Do you know, some English reporter last week asked me, Mr Ali... how do you spell your *Christian* name?'

We seemed to be getting along okay so I asked: 'What's all this Float-like-a-butterfly nonsense? What's it supposed to mean?'

He appeared puzzled. 'Have you seen me fight?'

I said I had, but only on television.

'That's how I move: I float like a butterfly.'

I said I thought he floated more like Fred Astaire.

He rested a big hand on my shoulder and said: 'Don't move.'

(At this point I should perhaps mention a story about the cowboy who was known to have the fastest draw in the West. A youngster asked to see it. The gunman's hands hovered over his holsters and he said: 'Wanna see it again?')

I didn't move, and I didn't see Ali's arm move, but I felt it. Or at least I felt the slipstream from it. He had measured the distance, then drawn back and thrown a punch at my chin, stopping perhaps half a centimetre short. His fist, still clenched, was resting on his knee.

'Wow!' I said. 'That was amazing.'

He grinned boyishly. 'Now,' he said, 'want to go for Sting-like-a-bee...?'

Marlene Dietrich was less gentle. When I tried to interview her over controversy (because she had made anti-German propaganda films in America during the war) about her advertising Lufthansa she hit me in the face with a rolled-up copy of the *Evening Standard*.

When her filming finished Sophia Loren told me: 'We've seen a lot of each other recently and I've enjoyed our chats. But now I'll be away for a short time.'

'I'll miss you.'

'Of course, but I will be back three weeks today on the two-thirty Alitalia flight. So maybe you will put that in your diary.'

'I'll be here.'

'Excellent! Then we have a date...'

Back in the press room, I addressed the gang. 'Okay guys... so who's got a date with Sophia Loren?'

I was pelted by telephone directories, notebooks and half-filled coffee cups.

*

One afternoon I told Niven that Australian actor Rod Taylor was flying to the south of France that evening with Trevor Howard in order to shoot scenes for *The Liquidator*. Taylor had told me that he'd heard Howard was a serious drinker and intended to 'teach him how Aussies drink'. Niven, who knew them both, said he'd like to see that happen and we arranged for him to take a later flight so he could meet them in the departure lounge.

All three of them missed all of their flights that evening.

I had the bright idea of asking these three serious drinkers about their recipes for hangover cures – confident that it would make a feature that I could sell to one of the nationals – and they all chipped in, not only with their own cures, but also with stories about how other famous stars recovered.

I came round in the morning in front of a table with lots of empty glasses and several unopened bottles of light ale. But, never mind, I had a story in my shorthand notebook. The problem was that, beyond names written in longhand – Flynn, Grant, Goldwyn, Olivier, Ustinov, Karloff, Preminger, Sellers, Hitchcock, Burton, O'Toole, Chaplin – I couldn't transcribe a word of it.

*

Six years later when Niven's book, *The Moon's A Balloon*, was published I hurried to buy it and immediately discovered that in all our conversations he had been rehearsing the text, chapter by chapter, on me.

I knew all the stories, and still remembered many of them word for word.

I thought of buying it for my mother; she could tell her friends that she already knew the stories in it, having heard most of them years ago from her son.

But I thought better of it when I realised how frequently he used the F-word in the narrative. She thought the world of her son's friend David Niven and had seen all his films. But she wouldn't have approved of his personal choice of language.

Mum wasn't the only one who rated him so highly. The biggest wreath at his funeral (1983) was from the luggage porters at Heathrow, to 'the greatest gentleman who ever passed through these halls. He made a porter feel like a king.'

*

Brian Hitchen, who would later edit the *Sunday Express* and the *Star*, occasionally covered the airport for the *Mirror* as part of his 'district' patch, the Thames Valley. But he'd usually listen to the BBC World Service in the early hours and then call the office to take advantage of his proximity by suggesting that he ought to be on the next flight out to the latest overseas trouble spot.

In his twenties Brian had an impressive and colourful range of contacts (not to be confused with what the modern generation refers to as 'sources' when they are describing press officers). And on a quiet day he would be allowed time for 'visiting contacts'. Nobody would query the expenses.

Sometimes, if he knew I had the day off, he would take me along. It was an eye-opener.

He introduced me to crooks, thugs, gangsters, members of the Sweeny and to tarts (the type we have heard about, with hearts of gold).

Towards the end of an afternoon he would ask whether I wanted tea, or a G&T, and we would drive off in his Sunbeam Alpine to Mayfair or Knightsbridge to take refreshment with ladies of the night (and maybe also of the day) who would do no more than put the kettle on or open a bottle and tell Hitch what was happening in the big city.

For me, still twenty and about to graduate to Fleet Street and join him on the *Daily Mirror,* the entertainment was no more than watching the pretty ladies in half-open housecoats and little else simply moving about in their tastefully decorated apartments. For Hitch, it was 'seeing contacts'.

Nothing ever happened that couldn't be reported back to his wife Nelli.

In the central glove box of the Alpine he kept a shiny commando dagger. 'Just in case,' he said. He knew how to use it, he said; he had been in the Parachute Regiment.

Good God, I thought, more than once. This is what I joined for... the excitement I craved as a kid reporter.

When he was exposing 'Rachmanism' (concerning the intimidation of tenants by unscrupulous and frightening landlords in West London) the *Mirror* provided him with a minder called (I think) 'Freddie the White Eagle of Poland', who had been banned as a wrestler for biting off the ear of an opponent. One night in the Establishment Club (it may have been the Ad Lib) the singer Alma Cogan took exception to something Freddie had said and, having found a cricket bat in the manager's office (don't ask), hit Freddie so hard over his bald head she broke the spine of the bat. Freddie just stroked his scalp and asked what he could possibly have done to upset her.

Hitch once arrived in the airport press room directly from the India-Pakistan War carrying his Olivetti Lettera 22 and showed me the candle stub still stuck to the casing. A trickle of blood ran through the wax and into the typewriter keys.

He explained that he had used it in the trenches, often at night, to type his accounts from the front line by candlelight. It all sounded dangerous but exciting and even romantic.

And the blood...? He grinned: 'War wound... cut my thumb opening a can of Coke.'

6. Royal flashes

The Great War broke out on the Queen Mum's 14th birthday. That's the sort of information that only those closest to her were aware of, I suppose.

I was in France when she died and learnt about it from the local regional morning paper, which referred to her on the Front as *'la Queen Mum'*.

Not *la reine mère*, nor even *la reine maman*. Such was her personal popularity, even among the Anglophobe Froggies, that she was the Queen Mum, world-wide.

Long – oh, long – before Diana, she was everybody's favourite royal.

We had a chat, once. Well, not much of a *tête-à-tête*, but we conversed. She was about to board a royal flight and the photographers stood respectfully at the foot of the aircraft steps waiting for her to start posing or waving. Her smile radiated, and the shutters clicked. Then her face fell as she looked along the rank of artists-in-light and asked: 'Where is Mr Wallace?'

Tony Wallace, the *Daily Mail* resident photographer at London Airport, was absent from the usual entourage.

In those days photographers knew their place. And it certainly did not include talking to their betters. They shuffled their feet a bit and re-checked the settings on their lenses, and shook their flash-battery packs, but none of them spoke. It fell to me, the token reporter in the company, attending only as the caption writer, to break the embarrassing silence.

'He's off sick, today, Ma'am,' I said.

'Oh dear. I am sorry to hear that. Nothing serious, I hope?'

'No, Ma'am. I believe it's just a cold.'

'Then please,' she asked me, 'give him my best wishes for a speedy recovery.'

'Certainly, Ma'am. I will do that.'

I thought our little banter was getting along well. I was tempted to tell her that I had recently been at Gibside, in County Durham, where she had spent a significant part of her childhood, and maybe to tell her that the railway coal wagons still bore the name of her family, which had owned the Bowes Colliery.

She might be pleased to know that, I thought. Then I thought better of it. Maybe next time; it could keep.

After we had exchanged our waves, I hastened back to the press room in Terminal Two and performed my loyal duty, as I had promised my sovereign's mother – in whose husband's coronation, I could have told her if the conversation had really got going or the subject had come up, my father had been proud to march.

The message had its desired effect. Tony Wallace would make an exceptionally speedy recovery. But first he asked me to phone the *Mail* picture desk and pretend I didn't know his home number, and ask them to pass the message from the Queen Mum on to him.

I was delighted to do that.

'The Queen Mum…? Asking for Tony Wallace?'

'Oh yes,' I said. 'As you probably know, she thinks the world of him. She was really upset to find he wasn't there waiting for her this morning. She told me so, herself.'

'The Queen Mum…' said the picture editor again. 'Asking after Wallace… That is wonderful. Thanks awfully.'

But, as conversations go, it was not awfully significant, you no doubt reckon.

No? Oh really?

Listen. You will learn something.

When Tony Wallace returned to harness, miraculously cured, he bought me a drink and asked: 'Do you know the last time the Queen Mum actually spoke to a reporter?'

Of course I didn't.

'It was in 1923.'

1923… And then, 42 years later, to me.

'She'd made a bit of a faux pas, you see,' said Tony, 'and vowed never to speak to a reporter again, about anything, for the rest of her life. She wasn't even Queen then, of course, just Lady Elizabeth Bowes-Lyon – and a descendant, as you know, of the Thane of Glamis.'

Thane of Glamis… I said yes I knew, but I'd forgotten. Did Tony know that the Duchess of Kent was a descendant of Oliver Cromwell? He ignored me and pressed on.

'...She was talking to a reporter during a photo-session when she got engaged to the – then – Duke of York and she referred to him, just a slip of the tongue, I'm sure, as Bertie. Yes! Our future King George VI (although naturally nobody knew that at the time)... Bertie! He was furious about what he considered to be *lese-majesty* – and she was upset that the reporter had dropped her in it, and not amended her quote more formally before publication.

'So she spoke quite frequently to members of the public, but never to a reporter, after that.

'All we've ever had out of her, since that day, was that smile. Her special smile... But she spoke to you yesterday,' said Tony, joyously. '...About me!'

So everything we had learnt about her, about her feelings, and even her quotes, we had got from third parties.

Hating her brother-in-law, briefly King Edward VIII, for not sticking to the job he was born into and marrying 'that woman', Wallis Simpson, and landing her sensitive, stammering husband with the crown he had never expected to wear, nor been prepared for.

As the last Empress of India (and indeed last empress of anywhere) she apparently believed that Mountbatten gave up India too early and that Britain de-colonised everywhere before the Commonwealth nations were able to cope as independent states.

Ringing below stairs and telling her staff: 'When one of you old queens has a moment, this old queen would like a gin and tonic.'

Of US President Jimmy Carter: 'That man was the only person, following the death of my beloved late husband, to have the effrontery to kiss me on the mouth.'

But none of that came from a reporter.

I know she spoke once to Hugh Cudlipp (but he doesn't count as a reporter), at a Garden Party. She told him she was going to Balmoral that night and – blow security – said that after leaving Kings Cross the royal train always travelled only as far as Doncaster where it stayed overnight in the sidings. Whether this was so she could have a more comfortable night's sleep, or so she could arrive at her destination in daylight for photos, was never satisfactorily established by Cudlipp, to my mind. Anyway, he'd had a brainwave and sent the *Mirror* northern circulation boss, Jimmy Wallace (no relation to Tony of that ilk), to Donny with a set of the first editions. Jimmy found the train and reached up to hammer on the door. It was opened by a (presumably surprised) lady-in-waiting, wearing a dressing gown over a nightie.

He handed up the bundle of papers and told her they were for Her Majesty, with Mr Cudlipp's compliments. She told him to wait.

When she returned she said: 'Her Majesty has asked me to thank you, and to ask you to relay her gratitude to Mr Cudlipp for his thoughtfulness. But she has also asked me to ask you – do you not have a copy of the *Sporting Life*?'

I wouldn't have made a mistake like that.

But then, you see, our relationship was rather different.

*

The royals sold newspapers. During my childhood my grandmother had subscribed to the *Illustrated London News*, solely to see photographs of the royal family. This was before television broadcast their every move, but even when they appeared on TV the pictures were fleeting, and some people liked to study them.

Princess Margaret had been a favourite subject – often found chain-smoking (with cigarette holder) and gin-swigging in night clubs – and Fleet Street took a personal interest in her private life. First up had been her love affair that blossomed in 1953, the year after her sister's coronation, with Group Captain Peter Townsend, former war hero and Hurricane pilot, but a divorcee.

The Church of England refused to countenance marriage of the 23-year-old second in line to the throne to a divorced man and, while she dithered about giving up her royal privileges, Fleet Street involved itself with encouraging headlines like COME ON, MARGARET... MAKE UP YOUR MIND!

It was an excuse to carry more photographs of her. When she eventually turned down Townsend's proposal she was romantically linked with a number of eligible young men until finding and marrying Antony Armstrong-Jones – a royal snapper, no less. No shortage of pictures, then.

In Yorkshire, during my youth, everybody's favourite pin-up was Katherine Worsley – not only beautiful and the archetypal Yorkshire Rose, but a girl with an impeccable county background: her father, Sir William, fourth baronet, had captained the Yorkshire Cricket Club and was chairman of it, he was also President of the MCC and Lord Lieutenant of the North Riding.

So when, in 1961, she married Prince Edward, Duke of Kent, at York Minster, all the Yorkshire newspapers felt it was their own royal wedding.

But somebody in the *YEP* newsroom, with a little help from the subs' table and the print room, produced a spoof front page with the headline

KATHERINE WORSLEY OPENS FOR KENT.

Ewart Clay, deputy editor, was not amused. 'If one single copy of that page leaves this building, or is even referred to outside this office, you will all be fired,' he warned. And it was never mentioned. Until now.

Allen Rowley had picked up a trick of the Fleet Street trade while on his holiday job at the *People*. When we arrived at the Minster for the wedding he passed me a small silver disc.

'The national boys usually remove the diaphragm from the mouthpiece of telephones so nobody else can use the kiosk,' he said. 'So if you find a phone that doesn't appear to work, you'll have this in your pocket. Remember to remove it after speaking to the office.'

I carried the diaphragm in my pocket, and later in the glove box of my car, for years afterwards, but never had cause to use it.

*

The Queen, and her children Charles and Anne, continued to enchant and enthral. And they got to know and I think to respect the royal press pack which, they realised, was only doing the job it was paid for – while also keeping the royal family in the public eye.

When HM noticed the absence of the *Mail*'s Vincent Mulchrone from a royal line-up in Brussels and asked about him, much as her mother had enquired about his colleague Tony Wallace, she was told that he had slipped away to the bar.

'Yes,' she said with a smile. 'He would.'

On her Australian tour *Mirror* photographer Freddie Reed dropped his glass of wine at her feet and she pretended not to notice. But a few hours later, when his flash failed to work, she commented kindly: 'Just not your day, is it, Mr Reed?'

Inevitably however there were occasional complaints of 'press intrusion'. When Bob Edwards was editing the *Daily Express* he received a protest about the activities of one of his photographers allegedly 'harassing' Princess Anne while she was at boarding school in Benenden, Kent. Bob demanded to speak to the snapper but was told that was impossible because the man was in hospital with a broken arm.

'How did that happen?'

'Had a fall.'

'Oh dear, where?'

'Out of a tree. At Benenden.'

Anne's first boyfriend, coincidentally, was Major Andrew Parker Bowles of the Royal Horse Guards (more photo-ops), who would later marry Camilla Shand. Whatever became of *her*?

Complaints from the palace were few. There were two about Princess Margaret being photographed 'dressed for swimming' and also 'dressed for water-ski-ing" (apparently different forms of attire) and one about the Queen being shown 'reclining on the ground'. There was no mention of the fact that in the same set of pictures it was widely decided not to use one of the Queen Mum, also 'reclining on the ground', with a bottle of gin at her side.

But when they thought their image or popularity was slipping, the royals ill-advisedly allowed TV cameras to observe preparations for a family barbecue at Sandringham. The plan, apparently, was to show that they were very much like ordinary people. It backfired by showing that Prince Philip was as inept as most fathers at getting the thing to light. Not the sort of image my grannie had been seeking. The mystique – that the royals were somehow different from the rest of us – had evaporated.

And then along came Di.

Charles had been photographed with a number of gorgeous girls, known to The Street as Charlie's Angels, including Lady Davinia Sheffield, Lady Jane Wellesley (descendant of the Duke of Wellington), Princess Marie-Astrid of Luxembourg and even the actress Susan George. He had actually proposed to Lady Amanda Knatchbull (grand-daughter of Lord Mountbatten and therefore his second cousin), but she turned him down. All wonderful photo-opportunities, however.

Lady Diana Spencer, shy and demur (then) was working as a nursery assistant when she appeared in the frame. Little was known about her... until a story dropped on the *Sunday Mirror* news desk purporting to prove that she had twice made late-night visits to join Charles in – of all unlikely places – the royal train while it was parked in sidings near Swindon.

The train had been there on the nights in question with Charles on board, as was confirmed by the Post Office which had supplied a telephone connection for it.

The particularly damning evidence that appeared to confirm the identity of the Prince's secret visitor was that a car number had been logged by the local signalman. It was not Di's car (her Volkswagen had been damaged in a collision with a photographer's car) but her mother's – a coincidence, it was believed, that nobody could have concocted. Thus:

> The Sunday Mirror today can reveal two late night meetings between Prince Charles and Lady Diana Spencer – the girl many believe will be the next Queen.

The splash headline, in case any readers missed the obvious innuendo, was ROYAL LOVE TRAIN.

Invited to comment just before publication, the Buckingham Palace press office said that there would be no comment.

While the story was on the presses in Holborn Circus my wife Angi and I drove down to Oxfordshire to spend what was left of the weekend with the editor, Bob Edwards, and his wife Brigid.

When preparing for a Sunday lunchtime visit to Bob's local we were surprised by the arrival of a despatch rider from the Palace – bearing a denial on behalf of the Queen. It was to be followed by a hand-delivered letter from Michael Shea, her press secretary, describing the report as 'totally false', a 'total fabrication' and saying that 'grave exception has been taken to the implications'.

I tried to imagine the scene that morning at Buckingham Palace with the Queen reading the papers over her toast and marmalade, getting to the *Sunday Mirror* and summoning her son and heir to explain its front page story:

'Charles, you randy young bugger – what's all this about?'

'But it's not true, Mama.'

'Let's give them a right royal bollocking, then. Send for Shea!'

The editor's response was that 'I cannot publish an apology while I believe we are right.' And perhaps somewhat disingenuously to add 'Certainly we did not intend to imply that anything improper had occurred' (on, ahem, the 'Royal Love Train'). And then to publish the exchange of correspondence in full.

I offered to go down to Wiltshire and try to sort it out, but Bob's view was that the reporters who had written the original story should stick with it. When they returned to the scene they found that the page of the signal box logbook in which the car number was recorded had been ripped out.

Thus encouraged, Bob reminded Shea, in so many words, that his newspaper had been lied to by the Palace before.

It had – over one of my stories.

While working on the *Daily Mirror* and following Princess Anne in what appeared to be a romantic liaison with (then) Lieutenant Mark Phillips, I discovered that the two of them had been caught *in flagrante* in a horse box while fox-hunting together in North Yorkshire.

Even today it would be indiscreet to reveal exactly how I learnt of it, but it was sufficiently sound for me to find a phone box and report:

> Close friends of Princess Anne have revealed that her relationship with fellow Olympic show jumper Mark Phillips has reached a stage where an engagement announcement is believed to be imminent.

And the Page One headline was IT'S LOVE!

Bob Edwards, editing the *Sunday Mirror*, called me and asked for more information about my source, which I partly confided to him. Surely, I said, they have to marry now. He thought the same thing.

Seeking confirmation from the Palace on the Saturday, the paper was told that there was 'no substance' to my story, so it ran the official denial.

But on the following day – presumably after speaking to Princess Anne – the Palace announced the engagement 'with the result,' as Edwards now wrote to Shea, 'that the *Sunday Mirror* was made to look very foolish.'

Of all the repercussions of the Love Train affair perhaps the most severe was that Bob who, having edited *Tribune,* the *Daily Express* (twice), the *Sunday People* and the *Sunday Mirror* and having faithfully supported the Labour Party throughout, could confidently have expected a knighthood on retirement, as happened to the majority of Fleet Street editors.

Instead he received only the runner-up award, a CBE. But what was most stomach-churningly galling was that for the rest of his career the *Daily Mail*, whenever it had cause to mention his name, described him as 'the editor who called the Queen a liar'.

The experience weighed heavily on Bob. Two years later when Norman Lucas (who he billed in the paper as 'the world's greatest crime reporter') produced a story that a petty crook called Michael Fagan had broken into Buckingham Palace, sat on the Queen's bed and asked her for a light for his cigarette, Bob panicked. There's no other word for it.

Unable to seek confirmation from Scotland Yard, fearing that they would leak the story to the opposition and ruin a potential exclusive, he sought advice from Tony Miles, the chairman and editorial director.

'Do we know Norman's source?'

'He says it comes from Sir David McNee, the Commissioner of the Met. I know that they are good friends.'

'Where's Norman now?'

'He's been off sick for some time... suffering from clinical depression.'

'In that case,' said Tony, totally unhelpfully, 'you must use it, if you believe it, but spike it if you are worried about it. Otherwise you're going to have the Queen on your back, again.'

Bob spiked it. Next day the story somehow turned up at the *Daily Express*, where it was given the whole of Page One – and would become Scoop of the Year.

A couple of weeks later I had a visitor in the office, an SAS sergeant major who I had met in Northern Ireland. He told me he was in London 'to check the new improved security on a big house at the end of a wide street.'

How had that gone? 'Oh, I managed to get in and out five times – under, over and through the perimeter, but never through the gates. I was spotted, once, when I was on the roof. The police were called, but I disguised myself as a chimney pot and they didn't find me.'

Shortly before edition time – so that the story would be too late for them to leak – I called Scotland Yard who confirmed that there had indeed been an emergency call from Buckingham Palace about a possible intruder that they had dismissed, after a search of the roof, as 'a false alarm with good intent.'

I wrote it up. Bob Edwards was on holiday but his timidity remained virtually tangible in his absence and my detailed account was reduced to about six paragraphs. Bob didn't even notice it in the paper, but the *Express* did and followed up its scoop big-time and that was where the editor saw it and read it. He called from France: 'Good story in the Excess. Ask Revel to follow it up.'

His deputy, Vic Birkin, told him: 'Well, it could be a bit awkward, Bob, if I asked him to do that...'

*

Generally press-palace relationships remained cordial. Fleet Street photographers would accompany newly-weds Charles and Di to the ski-slopes, take the requisite posed pictures, ski briefly together, and then leave them alone for the rest of the day. But Princess Diana had become the most sought-after face for photographs and the 'paps' – the freelance *paparazzi* – wouldn't stay away or respect their privacy. Every magazine wanted her on the cover and there was big money to be made.

As the royal marriage declined Diana also cashed in on her image as the most photographed person in the world.

Most mornings she'd ring her favourite photographers – at the *Daily Mirror* and the *Sun* – and tell them about her engagements for the day, including personal visits. Critics would say: 'Poor girl – she can't even make a private visit without having the press trailing her around.'

Then they'd buy the morning papers to ogle the latest pictures.

Daily Mirror chief photographer Ken Gavin didn't bother himself with scenery; in fact for several years he didn't bother with much, apart from Diana. So when a colleague suggested a short walk from the Radisson hotel in Agra to look at the Taj Mahal by moonlight, he asked:

"What's the point? Is Diana sitting in front of it?'

She wasn't, so Ken said he'd wait until she was. When the picture was taken next day it seemed to perfectly expose her feeling of loneliness and isolation. The couple divorced a few months later.

She still maintained her contacts while publicly complaining of harassment and frequently asking 'Will they never leave me alone?'

Yet on the last day of her life she teasingly promised hordes of journalists 'sensational announcements to come'.

What did that mean? Was she about to get engaged to Dodi Al-Fayed? Was she perhaps pregnant? Whatever, it wasn't the sort of comment calculated to keep journalists at bay…

*

Before Diana, actress Joan Collins had been the Page One circulation booster. Immediately after Diana's death it would be Posh Spice. What does that tell us about the newspaper-buying public? Fickle… Or What?

*

Many of the royals maintained, and still do, at least nodding acquaintanceships with members of the press. They also have great memories for names and faces.

Twenty-three years after the horsebox incident (and four years after she had divorced Mark Phillips) Princess Anne was introduced to me at a dinner by the chief constable of Bedfordshire:

64

'Your royal highness, I assume you don't know Mr Revel Barker...'

'Oh really? That's an astonishing assumption on your part,' she told him, smiling. 'Mr Barker and I go back' – she paused, ' — many more years than either of us would care to remember.'

When Hannen Swaffer had been sent to enquire after the health of the King, he reported to his editor: 'He is slipping away. He didn't even recognise me.'

That was three kings back and Swaff, who had started his career on the *Daily Mail* in 1902, was still haunting The Street sixty years later.

Haunting was an appropriate word because he was a devoted spiritualist, a firm believer in life after death, to the extent that (possibly in an effort to shut him up) Stuart Campbell, his editor on the *People*, had offered him top dollar for any stories he filed from the Afterlife.

Years later, when the actress Pat Phoenix (who played Elsie Tanner in *Coronation Street*) died, *Sun* editor Kelvin MacKenzie told a reporter to phone Doris Stokes, a popular TV 'medium' and to 'get the first interview with Elsie Tanner from The Other Side'.

Mrs Stokes told him: 'My dear boy... it doesn't work like that. You are not here one moment and there the next. It's a long journey...'

But she promised to leave a message on The Other Side... 'So that Pat can contact me as soon as she has settled down, there.'

When this was reported back to MacKenzie, he was furious: 'What's the matter with the silly old cow! Can't she just make something up?'

But I digress...

It is worth mentioning that when some loony tried to kidnap Princess Anne it was a reporter who affected her rescue and possibly saved her life.

Late one evening in 1974, veteran *Daily Mirror* man Brian McConnell was in a taxi heading down the Mall just in front of a royal limousine carrying the Princess and Mark Phillips, when a car swerved into it and forced it off the road.

Hearing the crash, the cab driver braked and McConnell jumped out to discover a man with a gun threatening the occupants of the limo. He stepped between the royal couple and the gunman and said: 'Don't be silly, old boy. Put the gun down. These people are friends of mine.'

The man reacted by shooting him in the chest and opening fire on several others, wounding two policemen and the chauffeur before being overpowered. Brian went to hospital and later was awarded the Queen's Gallantry Medal, while the gunman, who had a history of mental illness, pleaded guilty to attempted murder and kidnap, and ended up in a psychiatric ward.

A heroic drinker, whose head was most frequently tilted to one side – 'set permanently in italics', as one colleague described it – Brian would modestly explain that he had clearly had too much to drink before setting off for home that evening.

*

Back to the Queen Mum…

She enjoyed the company of newspaper people and once popped in to the London Press Club (they had made her an honorary member) for an hour and stayed for two and a half.

One evening she inadvertently wandered into the wrong suite at the Ritz Hotel and found herself in a retirement party for a *Daily Mirror* feature writer. (We did things in style, in those days.)

She accepted a gin and tonic, spread her smile around the room and eavesdropped on a few unintelligible conversations until being rescued by her lady-in-waiting and redirected to a Jockey Club dinner where she would be guest of honour.

As she was being ushered through the door she looked back and said: 'Oh dear. This one looked as if it would have been so much more fun.'

I was typing up a feature, trying to explain the *Mountbatten Report on Prison Security* in a form that fourteen million readers of the *Daily Mirror* would be able to understand – and wondering whether it was advisable to mention that the author had claimed it would be impossible to prevent anybody with a helicopter dropping a rope ladder into the exercise yard of a top security prison and enabling prisoners to use it to escape – when I was interrupted by the guy at the desk behind me.

Rupert Morters, doyen of the national press corps in the north-east, was also writing. But he stopped and asked: 'What would you do if you suddenly and unexpectedly came in to a lot of money?'

Was he, perchance, drafting his will and intending to include me in it? He was reputedly very well off. He had worked for the *Daily Mirror* before being called up to join the wartime Royal Navy and it was said that the paper had continued to pay him throughout the hostilities. He'd been the first reporter outside London to own a car – and also the first to wear suede shoes. He had a big detached bungalow in about an acre of land at the posh end of Newcastle upon Tyne and an apartment in Majorca.

'How much?'

'Well, let's say enough for you to retire on.'

I was in my early twenties, so not yet contemplating retirement. I replied that I would probably buy a bigger house and a newer car, but would almost certainly continue to work.

That morning I had been drinking gins and tonics with a cabinet minister and learning how the entire communications network for the British Isles was going to be modernised, and I had written this up to inform the *Mirror* readership. I'd spent most of lunchtime swinging on a five-barred gate discussing suspects in a mysterious murder with a detective chief superintendent who swung on the other side of it.

After I'd found a way of getting into my interpretation of *Mountbatten* (I'd been given two days to digest it), I was going to the giant Swan Hunter shipyard to take tea with the Queen. (Not one-to-one, of course; there would be about a hundred other people, but I'd be in the same room, scoffing the same food, drinking the same tea, before she launched the newest Royal Navy destroyer.)

Later, I would be occupying my usual table at *La Dolce Vita* night club, watching Roy Orbison perform and I'd probably go backstage afterwards to renew our old acquaintance.

Next morning I would be in another reserved seat, this time in the Assize Court to hear a judge pronounce sentence on two men found guilty of murder.

At this less-than-great age I had already attended a royal wedding; I'd had tea with Lord Mountbatten, coffee with Sophia Loren and got drunk with David Niven; I'd told Liz Taylor she looked fat, had a punch thrown at me by Muhammad Ali and been swatted by Marlene Dietrich; I had spoken to the Queen Mum, met presidents and prime ministers, and top cops and crooks. I knew The Beatles and the Rolling Stones and had met Ella Fitzgerald, Sammy Davis Junior and Nat King Cole.

You couldn't buy that sort of access and privilege, I thought. Normal people (we called them civilians) couldn't go where I went, and do what I was being paid to do.

Hey! After England's historic soccer World Cup win I had sat next to Jackie Charlton at the Sportsman of the Year dinner…

When Sunderland FC reached the Cup Final I would train with its Wembley squad and later be seen on TV (although I didn't know it at the time) dancing and holding the FA Cup above my head at the Cup Winners' Banquet.

In years to come I would dance – at her insistence – with the Duchess of Kent in the ballroom of the Savoy Hotel.

I would spend two nights at Windsor Castle as a guest of Prince Philip.

I'd go five times round the world and visit every country I wanted to go to (and a few that I didn't).

So… Who wanted to be a millionaire?

*

The job Bill Freeman had picked out for me was to cover England's five northernmost counties – Northumberland, Durham, North Yorkshire, Cumberland and Westmoreland – plus the Scottish borders, for the *Daily Mirror*.

Rupert Morters had been doing it for most of his life but, possibly as a result of it, had suffered a heart attack in his forties. Bill thought he should have a leg-man to race around the area in his stead while he stayed mainly in the office, manning his desk and looking for stories.

He was brilliant at finding them. He could (and once did) find a story in a telephone directory. And when he couldn't find one he'd create one. He didn't actually 'invent' stories, but he would create them. There's a difference.

'Have you heard the rumour…' he would ask, about some well-known figure. 'Ask around. See what you can find out.'

He would ask several people, and tell me to do the same, with the inevitable result that whatever he had enquired about, however unlikely it was, would trickle back in a day or so… as a rumour. It was suddenly a fact – that there was a rumour. Then he would invite the subject of the story to deny it. And since Rupert obviously knew far more about the gist of it than they did, they would usually be happy to do so.

He would also sift the files and re-run timeless stories from a year or more ago. 'They won't remember it,' he would say. And they didn't.

But he mostly occupied his time pursuing a long-running feud with Syd Foxcroft of the *Daily Herald* (later the *Sun*, then the *People*). They had been best friends for years until Rupert decided that Syd had cheated him (he'd beaten him) on a story. Thereafter Rupert referred to Syd only as 'That Little Shit'.

(At Rupert's funeral his wife Hilda asked me: 'What's that little shit doing here?' But Syd told me: 'I never held any grudge, and we had been such close friends for so many years I thought I owed it to him to be here, with my good memories.')

Even without Rupert's inspired input there was never a dearth of stories. But with three morning papers (the *Newcastle Journal*, the *Northern Echo* and the good old *YP*) and countless evenings and weeklies digging up stuff, I generally managed to keep myself busy on the current – and truly genuine – ones.

There was plenty to choose from… massive shipbuilding along the Tyne, heavy engineering on the river banks, coal mining in the counties, constantly busy assize courts and quarter sessions… For entertainment there was the Theatre Royal, where new plays would come for a pre-West-End trial and a number of smaller theatres, and Newcastle was an early hub of the provincial night club scene, with five member-only clubs attracting stars from Tom Jones to Jayne Mansfield, and similar venues a few miles away in Stockton, Darlington, Sunderland, Middlesbrough and South Shields. There was even a burgeoning 'Tyneside sound' starting to rival the 'Mersey beat' including Alan Price and Eric Burdon (and The Animals). Newcastle Big Band with Sting (so-called because he usually wore a black and yellow hooped sweater) on bass guitar was becoming internationally renowned.

*

The Sixties, my first decade in work, was a unique, mould-breaking era. Teenagers were a new phenomenon, expected to be self-confident, and allowed to be stroppy, with their own developing styles of fashion – Teddy Boys and rock-and-roll, mods on motor-scooters and rockers on bikes. The girls riding pillion on Vespa scooters were known as Vespal Virgins – and probably were, for a short time, because the Sixties was also the decade of The Pill (at first available only to married women).

Britain was recovering belatedly from the austerity of the war years and was suddenly considered to be 'booming' in terms of industry, trade and exports. People were being encouraged by an unknown MP representing Buckingham called Robert Maxwell to buy only British goods and promote their sale overseas. The population at large joined in, wearing 'I'm Backing Britain' T-shirts with a Union Jack motif (made in Portugal, because that was the cheapest source).

The *Daily Mirror* played its part by lauding exporters but, being the *Mirror*, it wanted to find the oddities. So I found a firm that was exporting River Spey water to Japan (to freeze into cubes, for Scotch whisky); a Yorkshire mill weaving prayer mats for Arabia, and a firm in Newcastle shipping packets of instant chop suey to Hong Kong.

ICI on Teesside sold millions of tons of chemical fertilizer to China, which sounded like good news until I discovered that the Chinese had no money to buy it – and insisted on paying... with thousands of alarm clocks. An even better, and crazier, story, I thought, until Sir Paul Chambers, the ICI chairman, managed to convince *Mirror* boss Hugh Cudlipp that to print the story 'would be damaging to our export trade'.

Cudlipp decided to invent a series called Boom Cities.

Newcastle, naturally, was to be one of them and this would be celebrated by a massive dinner, four hundred of the great and the good on Tyneside, at a five-star hotel. To illustrate the local boom, I had to persuade first, Swan Hunter shipyard, then the boilermakers union (for a price), to present a tableau in the hotel foyer, with masked welders – sparks flying everywhere – working on part of the supertanker, *Esso Northumbria*, which when launched in 1969 would become the largest vessel ever built in Britain.

So far so good. Former northern editor Bernard Shrimsley told me that Cudlipp was insisting on fresh strawberries for dessert. I checked with the hotel and reported back that, in January, there were no strawberries available, not even for ready money.

'They must be available somewhere in the world,' said Bernard. 'Tell them that you are the *Daily Mirror*. And tell them you insist on fresh strawberries.'

The hotel manager checked and came back to me. 'Okay... I can get you strawberries. But you might like to reconsider. They would come from Florida and the cost would be four pounds a portion – which is half what you had agreed to pay for four courses.'

'I don't think you understand,' I said. 'This is the *Daily Mirror* and we want fresh strawberries. The price is irrelevant.'

Before placing the order the manager sent a messenger to the Newcastle office with a contract for me to sign.

I heard from Frank Corless, my opposite number in Liverpool, the next Boom City, that their dinner was to be on a luxury liner in the docks. When Bernard heard that the guests would come up the gangplank and then have to cross the boat to enter the dining room he said it was unacceptable: the dining room doors had to be on the side the guests would board the ship.

So the liner was towed by tugs down the Mersey and into the Irish Sea where it was turned round and taken back to its berth.

I asked Bernard how much all this was costing.

'It doesn't matter,' he told me. 'It's what Hugh wants. It's only money.'

*

The north-east had been newly designated as a development area with a former Newcastle city councillor, T Dan Smith, as chairman of the Northern Economic Planning Committee.

Dan would become famous, first, as 'Mr Newcastle' and then 'the Mouth of the Tyne' and later infamous for accepting bribes from the corrupt architect John Poulson (and getting six years in prison) for guaranteeing him work on lots of local authority developments.

When he announced that he intended to make Newcastle 'the Venice of the north', I asked whether he didn't think the city was a bit hilly for that prospect.

'No,' Dan said. 'It will be *exactly* like Venice, only instead of canals we'll have roads.'

Durham Jail was being converted into a maximum security prison, chiefly to house the Great Train Robbers, and then for the Richardson 'torture gang', to be followed shortly by the Kray twins and their cohorts. Later with the creation of E-Wing, a prison within a prison, even more evil and notorious inmates – moors murderer Ian Brady and other child killers – would also be confined there.

It probably wasn't a good idea to house so many killers and gangsters in a single space and one of the first things that happened was that some of them broke in to the assistant governor's office and barricaded themselves inside. There was a telephone in it, with an outside line. There was also a copy of the *Daily Mirror* in a drawer, with the Manchester office phone number on the back page.

Dennis Stafford, serving life for the gangland killing of a fruit-machine distributor ('convicted of the murder of a one-armed bandit', was how the *Newcastle Evening Chronicle* once described him) rang the office:

'This is Dennis Stafford and I am calling you from the governor's office in Durham Jail.'

'Yes,' replied Arthur Brooks, nearing the end of his shift on the night news desk. 'And this is Henry the Eighth and I'm speaking to you from the throne room.'

Next was an escape. Walter 'Angel Face' Probyn and John 'Muscleman' McVicar got out of E-Wing and over the wall. A third inmate had been with them but he fell off a roof and landed on a prison officer who raised the alarm.

I had established good contacts among the senior staff, early on, and was producing exclusive stories from the prison on average once a week. They became so frequent and so frustrating for the opposition that other national newspapers complained to the Home Office about what they considered to be 'a high-level leak'.

So no... no shortage of stories.

In fact when the Kray twins had been arrested in a dawn raid in the East End of London, the *Mirror* news desk learnt about it first from me, via my bedside phone in Northumberland. I had been woken by a call from a member of the Richardson family who had heard it from one of the policemen who'd arrested the brothers – including the detail that Ronnie had been in bed with a young boy.

It was because of my familiarity with prisons, and especially with prison security, that I had been given the *Mountbatten Report* to dissect. But after the publication of my account – and following a call to my home from Charlie Richardson's girlfriend asking whether I knew where she could hire a helicopter within flying range of Durham – I was telephoned at the office by one of my prison contacts.

'Don't say anything, but do you recognise my voice?' – 'Yes.'

'You've had an enquiry about hiring a helicopter. I thought you ought to know... that I know. Just be careful what you say over the phone.' And the call was ended.

Although they would all gather in the Post Office Buffet, next to the GPO, on Sunday lunchtimes, on weekdays the national newspapers each had their favourite watering holes in Newcastle city centre. The *Herald* used the Marlborough, near the bus station; the *Mail* had the Forth, near the railway station; the *Express* favoured the Crown Posada on the quayside while the *Mirror* preferred the Magpie, next door to the brewery and opposite the football ground.

It was while I was in there one lunchtime that another unidentified voice telephoned and told me that if I happened to find myself in Durham that evening and fancied calling in on a friend who lived in Old Elvet, I might learn something of interest.

And by coincidence I found myself in that area later in the day and parked a couple of hundred yards away. Lionel Steinhausen, the governor, invited me into his Georgian official residence and told me he had good news and bad news: Bruce Reynolds, one of the Great Train Robbers, had written a letter to me (good), but since prisoners were not allowed to write to newspapers I wouldn't be getting it (bad). The governor actually had the letter in his hand, inside a brown cardboard folder.

It was a pity, said the governor, because he would have liked to help Reynolds, who was serving twenty-five years and was a model prisoner. But anyway, did I like home-brewed beer, because he made his own in the cellar of the house. He would get me a pint of it, if I would wait a few minutes.

When he returned I asked whether the letter was about Reynolds wanting to give back what was left of his share of the £2.6million haul from the 1963 robbery – because, if it was, I already knew about it. However, since the governor appeared to have the original letter in his hands, perhaps I could at least check the facts with him. He said he thought there could be no harm in doing that.

Was I right in my understanding that the money was on deposit in the Banco Nacional di Mexico, in Mexico City, in the name of Keith Miller? Was he intending to send a specimen signature and a thumbprint? Did he say it seemed a damned sight harder to give it back than it was to get it in the first place? Had he spent £20,000 on exchanging his original £150,000 stash into 'clean' money, £12,000 on false passports and £3,000 hiring a private plane to get him out of the country?

The governor was astonished – yes, that was what Reynolds had written to me in the letter that couldn't be sent.

So could I just double-check the name of his solicitor…? Because Reynolds, I said, had given all that information to a prisoner who had been released that morning and told him to phone me, but I hadn't known whether to believe it.

In that case, said Mr Steinhausen, we should have another drink because – although it was his responsibility to ensure that I didn't receive the letter – he could confirm that I had 'a scoop'.

As I typed it up the following morning Rupert was totally dismissive.

'It's not a story, it's a publicity stunt. Reynolds just hopes that if he gives a few thousand pounds back he's got a better chance of parole and an early release.'

'I'm sure he does,' I said. 'But he's not due for review for another seven years. When it comes up he'll be able to show them the cutting from the *Daily Mirror*.'

'If it even makes the paper,' said Rupert.

It made the whole of Page One next day: TRAIN ROBBER WANTS TO GIVE BACK HIS LOOT – MIRROR EXCLUSIVE. Every newspaper and broadcaster had to follow it up, based solely on the facts we printed, but which they were unable to confirm for themselves. There were more complaints about leaks, but the Home Office knew that the letter had been intercepted by the proper authorities and had not been posted to me. They said they understood from their enquiries that a recently released prisoner had passed the information to me.

There was plenty more where that came from: hunger strikes, fights between notorious convicts, a plot by the gangsters to poison the child killers with industrial cyanide smuggled in from a building site, top security prison transfers…

All serious stuff, but meanwhile I was also producing the 'light and bright' features that, happily, the *Mirror* loved.

When an American psychiatrist claimed that youngsters with unusual Christian names were more likely to become juvenile delinquents (one of his unruly patients had been christened Fertilizer Jones, because his dad had made his pile selling that product) I went to Revel, a town in the south of France, and reported that the place was quiet and charming and above all law-abiding.

I wrote about the decline of the Yorkshire woollen industry and blamed the demise on artificial fibres from 'little yellow slant-eyed transistorised sheep, gambolling across man-made moorland.' (The subs cut out the word 'yellow'; racist, perhaps).

I produced a page comprising three short features on lavatories; found a luncheon club where military commanders met to grouse about Whitehall; wrote about the 'lost summer' for the north-east's tourist industry (August 22 had been quite a lovely day).

And even went back to my roots to write about the changing scene in agricultural and horticultural shows that, in an effort to bolster attendances, were now going in for helicopter flights, women's wrestling, vintage cars, parachute jumps... with barely a long-haired cavy or pom-pom dahlia in sight.

They didn't all work out as envisaged. I was driving to the shops on a Saturday morning (the daily newspaperman's usual day off) and listening to the car radio when I heard – or thought I heard – Brian Matthew announce the first playing of a new Beatles record called *When I'm Six-Feet-Four*.

That had been my height when I first met the group (I was still growing) and people kept asking how tall I was. Little Ringo used to say: 'Have you met my friend? – He's six-feet-four, y'know.'

I knew that Barry Norman, then writing show-business for the *Daily Mail*, had once asked Lennon what he thought The Beatles would be doing in, say, five years' time. Lennon said he didn't know, hopefully it would be much the same; he countered by asking what Barry thought he would be doing himself.

'Well,' replied the *Mail* man, 'I'm writing a book about the work of the nonsense poet, Edward Lear. It will be published soon and in five years it will be in paperback.'

Next I heard was a song called *Paperback Writer*... *'It's based on a novel by a man called Lear'*... *'It took me years to write'*... *'His son is working for the Daily Mail, it's a steady job but he wants to be a paperback writer'*... There was no doubt about how that song had been inspired.

And when this latest tune was broadcast – *'I could be handy, changing a fuse...'* it was clearly a reference to somebody's height.

I thought: the buggers! They just sat there in the dressing rooms, talking to us, then they went off to write songs about us.

Sunday's papers all had stories about the new recording so I rang the features editor, Alan Price, and told him they'd misheard the title. They'd all got it wrong. It wasn't *When I'm 64* – it was *When I'm 6 feet 4*. And it was about me!

No, said Alan. He had a copy of it on his desk. It was Sixty-four. Nice idea, though, he said. And I could write it if I liked... about how I'd got it wrong. I thought better of it.

*

There was no shortage of home-based talent on the north-east's newspapers.

Sue Hercombe on the *Evening Chronicle* beat all the prima donnas of Fleet Street to become Woman Journalist of the Year in 1973 – in fact the last ever, because in her acceptance speech she said that, honoured though she was to win it, she thought it was an anachronism to differentiate between journalists on the grounds of gender. And the judges agreed.

Eric Foster wrote brilliant features and could have joined the *Daily Express* if news editor Bob Blake hadn't noticed that the name of Eric's house on his letter of application was 'Beaver Brook' – and thought that he was taking the piss.

Alastair McQueen, recruited from the *Belfast Telegraph* to the *Newcastle Journal*, could often show the national men the way to write a hard news story.

And Colin Dunne, unbeatable with a light story (daft, he'd call it) entertained us nightly in the pages of the *Chronicle* until, like McQueen, he found his natural home on the *Daily Mirror*.

So I was delighted – the word in those days was chuffed – to get a Whitbread Award as Writer of the Year at the annual north-east press dinner.

*

I went to British Honduras in Central America to discover what the Army found to do when, for the first time in its history, it had no wars to fight. Then when 'The Troubles' erupted in northern Ireland flew to Germany to join the soldiers who were training to be sent to the province as 'peace-keepers'.

All the northern reporters would have to take turns to spend two weeks at a time assisting the Belfast office staff in reporting what fairly quickly developed into a bombing and shooting war (but wasn't allowed to be described as one).

During one of my visits I was driving across country with a photographer to watch a planned march where Intelligence had heard of the likelihood of a rooftop sniper, when a petrol bomb, thrown over the high hedges of a narrow lane, landed on the long car bonnet of my hired three-litre Ford Capri.

It appeared to be a vodka bottle, with a burning flame of fabric at the neck and liquid sloshing about inside it. The bottle rolled and rested against the windscreen and I realised that if it stayed there and exploded it would probably kill us both, whereas if I braked it would roll off and explode beneath the car, maybe under the petrol tank.

What to do? I probably said something like 'Oh heck!' Because the snapper said: 'What we normally do is take the next corner very fast, so that the bomb will fly off the bonnet, to the side.'

That's exactly what I did, and the Molotov cocktail shot off and exploded behind us.

We were immediately stopped and surrounded by soldiers who checked our identities (they thought we had caused the explosion) before going in search of the bombers.

Driving on, heart still pounding, I turned to the photographer. 'Just a minute... you said "What we normally do..." So when did that last happen to you?'

'It never has,' he said. 'But I thought that if I just said that I had an idea, or a suggestion to make, you'd have told me to piss off.'

I was also sent from Newcastle to the Republic of Ireland. When the IRA started a campaign of bombing foreign-owned farms I was told to go and find out why.

We had two staffmen in our Dublin office, but they had been unable to answer the question. So I went, but perhaps predictably the bombed farms were unoccupied and the *Gardaí* (the Irish police) said they had no clues.

Sitting in a fairly dispirited state in the dining room of the Gresham Hotel, with nothing to write and no likelihood of finding anything, I noticed a familiar face across the tables. It was Sean Bourke; I recognised him from TV appearances as the man who had sprung British spy George Blake from Wormwood Scrubs in 1966.

I went to join him, introduced myself and told him of my frustration in not getting the story. Bourke wanted to drink and talk and we polished off a bottle of port before leaving the hotel and heading for a block of flats. There was nobody home at the place where we called so we staggered back.

The following morning I woke, fully dressed, on my bed with a scrap of paper in my sweating hand. I called the number on it... it was Cathal Goulding, chief of staff of the IRA. He told me all I wanted to know on condition that I didn't name him as my source. He said he was a painter and decorator so I described him as a self-employed Dublin businessman with strong republican connections.

But the important thing was that I had the story, from the top man in the organisation.

*

Although a lot of stories could be dealt with by phone from the Newcastle office, I was driving thousands of miles every year. My weekly expenses were often higher than my salary. I didn't know about Rupert's salary, but I did know that he visited (or charged for visiting) coastguard stations, fifty miles away, every week, and sometimes for driving to Carlisle, sixty miles each way along Hadrian's Wall, without getting out of his chair.

Every year there would be an official call to cut expenses, usually by ten per cent. It seemed modest enough in itself, but I asked whether, if there should be an incident at Catterick Camp, 44 miles away, I was expected to drive south only 40 miles, and do the story on the phone from the Scotch Corner Hotel.

Years later, on the *Sunday Mirror*, the annual memo suggested that the required cuts could be achieved by reporters and feature writers forgoing the *second* round of vintage port and Havana cigars after lunch with their contacts.

For most of the staff – including desk-bound sub-editors – expenses were a joke.

A photographer in Manchester who walked to the big Kendal Milne department store in the city centre for a fashion show would check the AA book and charge 80 miles each way for having driven to Kendal in Cumbria.

Feature writer Malcolm Keogh, claiming for having his car towed out of a bog by a farmer in Ireland, wrote on his expenses form: 'Money for old rope – £10.' But if anybody spotted the irony in that, nobody mentioned it.

There were probably more stories about expenses in Fleet Street pubs than there were stories about stories.

Rene McColl (*Express*) wrote: To coverage of Suez War – £500.

When told that the accounts department expected more detail, 'taxis, and so on', he amended them:

Taxi from office to Victoria Station – 10s

Coverage of Suez War – £499

Taxi, Victoria Station to office – 10s

One reporter (name unfortunately now lost to history) was asked why he had charged 'more than the going rate' to hire a camel. 'I was the first reporter to reach the front in the battle,' he explained. 'Because mine was a *racing* camel.'

Bill Davis, formerly of the *Guardian* and later editor of *Punch*, says he remembers a reporter sent to Alaska who needed to hire a sled and a team of huskies. His expenses were fully documented, even to the veterinary treatment and later the burial of a sick dog, but they fell fifteen pounds short of the money he had been advanced for the trip. So, handed them back, he added:

Flowers for bereaved bitch – £15.00.

*

Journalists who never left the office traded restaurant receipts – sometimes picking up pads of blank bills from pubs and cafes. One *Express* reporter, whenever he visited a new location, would call on the local printer and, saying he was planning to open a restaurant in the town, ask for sample copies of the types of bills that he produced, then fill them in himself. Editorial executives were generally fairly blasé about signing them but 'management', which often had its own fixed expenses deals, didn't like claims to vary too much because it messed up their budget planning.

It was generally accepted that, in equal measure, they both envied and hated the on-the-road guys who were actually going out – and spending the money – and getting the stories that filled and sold the papers.

On the other hand, the nation was suffering from something called 'pay restraint' which meant that salaries couldn't be increased unless more work was being produced, something that's not so easy to define in newspapers. So instead of pay rises, the expenses levels went up, and additional rewards could be made; when a reporter did a great story he might be told to 'put an extra tenner on your exes' – a lot of money at the time of which I write.

The downside was that 'expenses deals' weren't paid during holidays, didn't go towards the pension and were always subject to management whim. Nevertheless there were some who reputedly never touched their salaries and kept a permanent stash of cash in their back pockets. Got a bill to pay? Ask the news desk for an advance on your exes. And if you happened to be out of town the money would be wired to you at the nearest main post office.

*

Towards the end of the sixties, somebody in *Mirror* advertising had a brainwave. The north-east was effectively an economic microcosm of the whole country and was often used to try out newly-launched products. It also had its own TV station, Tyne-Tees. Four extra pages could be inserted into the paper twice a week, they said, and advertising campaigns run jointly in press and on TV. If it worked, the scheme could be extended to other regional TV areas, and maybe eventually nation-wide.

What made the deal especially attractive to advertisers was that although some of the local evenings were then selling 100,000 a day or more, the *Daily Mirror* alone had a higher circulation in the TTTV region than any three of them, combined.

At least two of the four pages would be advertising, but the rest had to be filled by editorial. Rupert and I were already filing a story a day each, on average, and I was additionally contributing a feature maybe once a week. For more pages we would need more staff. No problem: the increased advertising income would cover it.

Chris Sheridan, recently recruited to Manchester office, was transferred to help us. Tom Buist, who I had known when he was on the *Daily Sketch* in Leeds, came to work with photographer Johnny Robson. Colin Diball, a graduate of the *Mirror* training scheme in Plymouth, came to assist Charlie Summerbell on sport.

We now had an office of three news reporters, two sport reporters and two photographers, plus a series of wiremen leased on a daily basis from the Press Association to transmit pictures. The *Daily Express*, not to be outdone, had three reporters (sometimes four) – one of them concentrating on crime and courts – plus a photographer (sometimes two) and a staff wireman.

Mike Gay, the *Daily Mail* man in Newcastle, worked with a photographer and a wireman. He sent a note to his news editor: 'The *Mirror* has three reporters here, the *Express* has four. Even the *Sun* has two. You have only me. Request advice.'

The response came by telegram: WALK TALL.

Competition was generally friendly and if you had an exclusive you'd usually warn the opposition and tell them where you would be, late that night when the first editions were printed and their news desks wanted the stories. Then you would dictate your copy to them, so that they could quickly rewrite and 'match' it. The night news desks probably wouldn't have wanted to know that happened – on the other hand it worked both ways.

Express reporter Alan Baxter was told by his daughter's primary school teacher that it was a good thing she knew what he did for a living. In her diary the child had written: 'We were all woken up at midnight and Daddy had to go back to Durham Jail.'

Ian Porter, the Home Office chief press officer told me: 'You seem to think prisons are interesting, but they are not. They are boring. You don't even begin to understand what life is like in the place you keep writing about. You don't appreciate the hopelessness of the situation, or even the stench of it. And, trust me, you couldn't begin to imagine the stench.'

Perhaps, I suggested, he should arrange for me to go inside as an inmate for a few days. Then maybe, afterwards, I would be able to understand it.

'Oh we couldn't do that.'

'Well why not ask?'

He came back a couple of days later. No; I could not go inside Durham Jail as a prisoner. But I could go as an acting assistant governor, if I wished, for no longer than five days.

The news desk was happy for me to go 'off diary' for a week. And in I went, listening to complaints, checking the food and the work conditions, hearing applications for parole. I could talk to the prisoners, but not 'interview' or identify them. The only other condition was that the Home Office could see the piece before publication – solely to check there were no breaches of security.

The security wasn't a problem. In fact Porter's only comments on the feature I wrote were: 'Was it really necessary to mention the smell of the place?' And 'Why did you consider it remarkable that there is a wishing well in the prison grounds?'

Following publication of a few more 'leaked stories' another unidentified caller told me I had 'cheesed off' the Home Office to such an extent that they were going to put an end to my interest by reclassifying Durham Jail:

'They intend to convert E-Wing into a top security women's prison. They say you'll quickly lose interest if the child killers and gangsters are moved out and replaced by women.'

'Top security women?'

'Yes, like Myra Hindley and the Price sisters.'

Myra Hindley, moors murderer… and Dolours and Marian Price who had planted four IRA car bombs in central London outside the Old Bailey and Whitehall, injuring 200 people…?

No, I said, the *Daily Mirror* wouldn't be interested in them...

When the call ended I dialled the office and connected with a copy typist.

'For E-Wing,' I dictated, 'read She-Wing...'

Myra Hindley, I suggested, could find herself occupying Ian Brady's former cell.

'Every chance of that happening,' my man on the telephone had said.

*

Life wasn't all about prisons; there were always other on-going national stories, for example a series of miners' strikes – and the north-east of England was built on coal.

Bill Freeman asked whether I could find 'a fourth-generation coal-mining family'. He assumed that there'd be plenty of them, but the only one I could think of were the Londonderry heirs, who had been colliery owners throughout history.

I knew Lord Londonderry (Alexander Charles Robert Vane-Tempest-Stewart, for some reason known familiarly as 'Alistair') because, after his first wife had left him for the singer Georgie Fame, he married Royal Ballet star Doreen Wells in Durham City. It had been a private, virtually secret, wedding, but the only person she knew in the north-east was me, so I was invited.

A few months later I had been a guest at the christening of the couple's first son, Fred. I sat on an oversized rocking horse, holding the baby with a smiling Marchioness looking on. It provided the opportunity for me to mention the title he inherited and to write: 'Marquess of Queensberry rules, okay.'

It wasn't quite the sort of family that Bill had in mind, though.

Our home territory, being in the Frozen North, could also be relied on in winter for stories about extreme weather, storms at sea and snowbound villages in the hills.

When I told the office that the Army was planning to drop feed for cattle from helicopters at farms that couldn't be reached through the snow by road, Arthur ('Henry VIII') Brooks on the news desk said: 'Great story... so we want you and Tom Buist to be at the farms for description and reaction when the food is dropped.'

I explained that the entire point of the story was that the farms were inaccessible. Arthur said: 'Why do you think we pay mileage for your car? Your job, my friend, is to get to parts that the army cannot reach.'

Arthur was considered something of an expert on snow. He once filed a piece about impassibly deep snow in the Pennine village where he lived – THE WHITE HELL THAT WAS SADDLEWORTH. The snow had melted by the time a photographer, despatched to have a look at the scene, arrived there, an hour later. And meanwhile Arthur had turned up in the office, having made the journey on a bus. His six pages of copy were pinned to the newsroom notice board so that everybody could share the fun. And throughout the rest of his career Art assumed they had been posted there as a lesson in descriptive writing for the rest of the staff.

*

Way back in 1933 when it had been bought by Odhams, publishers of the *Sunday People,* in order to occupy the presses that stood idle during the week, the *Daily Herald* had boasted the world's biggest daily sale with a certified circulation of two million.

By 1964 its circulation was in free-fall with the oldest and poorest readership in Britain. IPC (the *Mirror* group, which had bought both papers along with a stack of big-circulation magazines in 1961) decided to revitalise it as the *Sun* – still supporting Labour and the trade union movement, but somehow also targeting the young. To IPC's astonishment the plan didn't work. It had fewer readers than the old *Herald.* So in 1969 it was sold at a give-away price to Rupert Murdoch, publisher of the *News of the World,* who wanted to own a popular daily paper.

There would inevitably be redundancies, because Murdoch considered the paper to be desperately overmanned. The alternative was for IPC to offer jobs to the *Sun* staff. In Newcastle Syd Foxcroft was shifted to the *People* and his younger colleague Clive Crickmer offered a job on the *Mirror* in Manchester.

But – shades of Doncaster and Leeds – Crick was a Geordie, and didn't want to work anywhere else. He wanted to work for a national but if the only job going was in Manchester, 160 miles away, well, thanks, but he'd rather move back to the *Newcastle Journal*. So my erstwhile colleague Chris Sheridan was transferred to Manchester (eventually moving on the BBC and then to ITN) and Crick carried his cuttings books across the city to the *Mirror* office.

He loved writing stories with a 'local flavour'. He had a gift for scouring the weeklies and finding a story hidden halfway down the columns that could be converted to interest the vastly wider *Mirror* readership. As he said: 'If it makes you laugh, or makes you cry, or makes you say Bloody Hell – that's a *Mirror* story.'

I preferred doing the 'national' stories from the region and elsewhere, so effectively we made a good team. Thus, for example, I would go chasing Princess Anne when she came north to hunt, first, a boyfriend, and then foxes. And Crick would write page-leads about girls being sent home from school for wearing ear-rings, or boys suspended because their hair was too long. (This was by now the seventies.)

Incidentally the (unofficial) background to the Princess Anne romance was that she had originally journeyed north in pursuit of Richard Meade, Britain's most successful Olympic horseman, who was training near Richmond in North Yorkshire. She needed accommodation so was housed at Catterick Camp with Colonel Maurice Johnston, commanding officer of the Queen's Dragoon Guards (and who would later be deputy chief of the Defence Staff).

I called to see him, but was told by the guard sergeant that the CO was not in the barracks.

'Then who belongs to that Bentley, parked outside the officers' mess?'

'I wouldn't know, sir. Most of our officers have Bentleys.'

When Meade, the triple gold medallist, expressed no interest in a royal romance, Anne's attention was redirected towards another fellow Olympian, Lieutenant Mark Phillips, who conveniently was a member of the regiment that was hosting her.

But before we could find the couple physically linked, photographer Tom Buist and I had to break away from our country pursuits with the Zetland and Bedale hounds and go hunting for Lord Lambton – another breaking national story.

He had been photographed (obviously without his knowledge) in bed smoking hash with a prostitute and the pictures were sold to the *News of the World*. The paper didn't rate their quality so, next time his lordship made an appointment, they installed their own camera, plus a tape-recorder secreted inside a teddy bear on the bed.

Tony Lambton was Minister for the RAF, but the '*News of the Screws*', as the *NoW* was known in The Street, established that he was not considered a security risk and in an unprecedented fit of propriety decided against running the story. Amazingly they gave the pictures and tapes to the prostitute's husband who tried to sell them to the German magazine *Stern*, then sold them to the *People*... who didn't use them either and handed them to Scotland Yard. And the police, investigating, found cannabis at Lambton's flat.

So the story was anything but secret in Fleet Street, although the reading public knew nothing of it. The Minister was expected to resign and, without the damning evidence, the other newspapers would need to explain why.

Lambton's home was Biddick Hall in County Durham and he was Tory MP for Berwick-upon-Tweed in Northumberland, the northernmost town in England. He wasn't at home and it was unlikely that he'd be in his constituency which he visited more frequently for the shooting than for parliamentary business. But Tom and I decided to call on his political agent and see what we could learn.

The agent lived in one of Northumbria's ancient peel castles and as we crunched up the gravel path we heard the telephone ringing, just inside the front door. Instead of reaching for the knocker we stood outside and waited, politely, we thought, and could hear the conversation – one side of it – perfectly clearly.

'Ah, Tony... at last! Where have you been? No, best not to tell me, because everybody's been looking for you... You want to put out a statement to the Press Association? You want *me* to put it out on your behalf? Okay... What do you want to say?'

It must have been a laborious job taking dictation in longhand, because the agent repeated every phrase and sentence as he was writing it. At the other side of his front door I was writing it more fluently in Pitman's shorthand. The important bit was that, because of the possibility of criminal charges, he had no option other than to resign. When it was finished the agent read it back word for word to Lambton, so I was able to double-check my notes. The statement was not to be issued to PA until three hours later – at ten-thirty that night.

As the call ended, I rapped on the door, and when it was opened said I was looking for Lord Lambton.

'I honestly don't know where he is.' (Fair enough.)

'But have you heard from him at all?'

'No.' (Oops.)

My predicament, I told the agent, was that it was getting late and the *Daily Mirror* needed something – anything – to present Lord Lambton's side of the story in the following morning's paper. So, I said, we were expecting the MP to resign, and if he was going to say anything, could I assume it would be something along these lines...?

And I read my notes back to him.

The agent appeared more than slightly surprised.

'You have spoken to him?'

'No. We haven't been able to find him.'

'Well, I don't know where you heard all that from but what I can say is that if you *had* spoken to him, his response would have been almost exactly like that.' (Almost?)

So we found a phone box and I dictated the statement, telling the news desk that we had at least a three-hour beat on the opposition and would be the only paper to carry Lambton's resignation in the early editions.

Celebrating our success in the eighteenth-century Tankerville Arms at nearby Wooler, we were joined by Brian Cashinella from *The Times* who told us he had also failed to find the MP. I said not to worry because he would almost certainly be making a statement, any time now.

'I suppose so. But what can he say?'

'Oh, he'll resign and most probably say something along the

lines of…' and I told him, from memory because I had heard it several times by now, the gist of Lambton's statement.

'How would you know that?

'Well,' said Tom, 'he obviously knows Lord Lambton pretty well. After all, he's a local MP.'

Shortly after eleven *The Times* news desk called Brian and told him that Lambton intended to resign.

'Bloody hell,' he told me, 'You were spot on. I wish I had taken a risk, and filed it, but, hell! You guys really know your MPs here.'

'Told you,' said Tom.

And Brian generously picked up the bill for all three of us for dinner.

*

The next 'national' story to break and involve the north-east would become known as The Poulson Affair.

It had started quietly enough. An architect called John Garlick Llewellyn Poulson, having become insolvent (meaning that he couldn't pay his debts) filed his own petition in bankruptcy.

At first, only the Bradford *Telegraph & Argus* noticed the case. Nobody followed it up. After all, who was interested in a bankrupt architect from Pontefract? Most reporters couldn't have pointed to the town on a map.

But the mile-high stack of documents – Poulson had never thrown any paperwork away – revealed names of creditors and recipients of the architect's cash, cars, wages, holidays and other benefits. They included a few MPs – some of them household names, such as Conservative deputy prime minister Reginald Maudling and Anthony Crosland (former Labour education minister), and some obscure, including Sir Herbert Butcher, John Cordle and Alf Roberts. There was also a seemingly endless list of officials in both regional and national government. The story was picked up by *Private Eye*, and Fleet Street started to show an interest.

Poulson's firm employed 750 people and was the biggest in Europe. His work was world-wide, from Argentina and Mexico to Malta and the Middle East. But a lot of it, I knew, had been carried out in the north-east. I thought it would be a good idea to make some preliminary local enquiries, being certain that I would be asked about it at some stage.

Leo White, who had succeeded Bill Freeman as northern news editor, said: 'You're looking into Poulson...? Would you like to do it full-time?'

He thought the job could last two years. But he said I would be off the diary for the duration and would have carte blanche to do whatever was necessary and to go wherever the job took me.

It was already being described as 'Britain's Watergate'. Potentially this was going to be The Big Story. It seemed like an offer I couldn't refuse.

So I started to attend the hearings and, as more and more people were gathered into the net and arrested for receiving what looked like obvious bribes, to report the brief court appearances and committal proceedings.

I was doing what I had once worried about having to do – writing short pieces about a complicated bankruptcy case.

8. Tea and sympathy

I was stopped on the steps leading down to the cafeteria beneath Leeds Town Hall (where the Assizes and Sessions – newly renamed the Crown Court – were housed) by Detective Chief Superintendent Dennis Hoban and we stood exchanging old memories. He was now head of the city CID and we had been neighbours and good friends when I worked in Pudsey and on the *Evening Post*. He had even taken me along with him when making arrests.

In the basement were more familiar faces: solicitors and barristers who earned their living at the petty and judicial courts on the ground floor; a few small-time crooks; and the Chapeltown ladies who appeared at fairly frequent intervals to pay their nominal fines for streetwalking: a sort of tarts' licence. They looked considerably more than ten years older, and were blissfully unaware that an animal called the Yorkshire Ripper would soon curtail their trade – and in some cases their lives.

As I reached the cash desk to pay for my coffee I was joined by another familiar face. I gestured towards his cup of tea: 'I'll pay for that, too.'

John Poulson and I had been staring at each other across courtrooms for the best part of a year by now. Each time he would enter the dock, gaze about him in apparent bewilderment, and nod automatically in my direction when he recognised a face.

Now he said: 'No… you can't do that.'

I smiled, because I knew what was coming next.

'I make it a strict rule, not to accept gifts.'

This was a man who – the Number One Crown Court upstairs was about to hear – had handed out more than two million pounds in bribes. The prosecution described them as 'corrupt gifts, rewards and favours'. Bribing on a lavish scale to ensure work for his architectural practice, he had eventually gone bankrupt with debts totalling nearly £250,000.

'For goodness sake,' I said, slapping the money on the counter. 'It's only threepence… I can get it back on my expenses.'

I let him go ahead and followed him to his table.

'May I...?'

He shrugged. 'I can't talk about the case.'

I told him I understood that. He had never talked to a reporter. So we chatted about Leeds United, a subject on which I knew nothing, except that he used to have a season ticket. A staunch Methodist, he didn't care for it so much these days because of the bad language on the terraces.

I raised an eyebrow when he took a silver foil packet from his jacket pocket and produced a single sandwich.

'Marmite,' he said. 'I used to eat fillet steak, but these days...'

Barristers would describe him as 'ruthless, ambitious and very probably friendless'. What I saw across the table was a tired old man (he was 63) in a tired Savile Row suit, shambling, shuffling and confused. He was mystified by the law's decision that he couldn't do what he'd seen every other developer and architect do: pay bribes to win contracts.

It was (or had been) commonplace for builders who wanted to land contracts to fly councillors and officials away on all-expenses-paid trips to Europe with their wives (or secretaries) on the pretext of examining a similar development – a housing estate, town hall, swimming pool, office block or hospital – usually at some pleasant destination, and almost always with sunshine.

Between these visits they would ply them with cases of Scotch, chickens and turkeys for Christmas, accommodation in lavish London apartments (sometimes with paid companions), family holidays, and even with jobs and sometimes mortgages.

Determined to be the best at that game, and to secure the most and the biggest contracts, John Poulson had gone a few steps further. For George Pottinger – Scotland's most senior civil servant who now stood beside him in the dock – he had bought Savile Row suits, paid expenses, provided a car, arranged family holidays and even built a house, in order to ensure that his tender would be accepted to design the Aviemore ski village.

But it wasn't until he heard the prosecution list the amounts of his largesse and when Pottinger described him as being 'like a rich uncle', that he started to talk to me about the case.

'I never realised I had given him so much,' he said. 'Now it turns out that he's had more of my money than I spent on my own family.'

It had taken more than a month over the tea and marmite, but Poulson realised that his time was running out (both men would be sentenced to five years) and now this 'very probably friendless' man wanted somebody to talk to.

He had plenty of tales to tell, even though they couldn't possibly be told until his trial had ended.

The gravy train on which he had bought a first-class single ticket to ruin had departed from Leeds Central Station. It was there that he had 'bribed' his first 'official' – tipping the booking clerk for telling him when important people were travelling to London, then reserving him an adjoining seat so he could spend the journey extolling the virtues of his architectural practice.

By the time he was convicted I could have written the book. In fact I was commissioned to produce one, but it was eventually abandoned for fear of litigation from people who had not yet been caught up in the net, and nobody knew for sure when it would end.

The *Daily Mail, Sunday Times* and *Daily Express* each had as many as six reporters working on the Poulson case and the trial. Most of the others had two or three. I referred to myself as the *Mirror* Poulson Team. Why did none of the competition simply come and sit at our table as we talked, most lunchtimes?

The answer is that they did. But every time we were joined by a stranger Poulson would clamp his hand across his mouth and not remove it, not even to nibble at his sandwich, until they left. He would stare at me with eyes like a spanked puppy.

I would usually say something like: 'So, Mr Poulson, did you get to Elland Road for the game at the weekend?'

He wouldn't even shake his head.

So my colleagues would give up, and ask whether I might be able to get some statement out of him, that we could all share, after he was sent down. I'd say I hoped to do that – as eventually I did – and they would leave us to the apparent silence and adjourn to the pub.

The best story he told me was THE DAY I SHOCKED THE QUEEN.

He had secured – at the time the event took place he thought he had secured – the contract to build a new general hospital for the Maltese island of Gozo. He was entitled to feel confident. The building was to be funded by the Crown, mainly due to pressure put on the British government by Reginald Maudling who at the time was shadow Commonwealth Secretary and a mover of considerable influence.

Poulson was paying Maudling £5,000 a year as chairman of one of his subsidiary – job-finding – companies. He had also given a job to Maudling's son Martin, who had left Oxford without a degree, and had made an annual covenant of £22,000 to the Adeline Genee Theatre Trust of which Mrs Maudling was a patron and fund-raiser.

When the Queen flew to Malta to lay the hospital foundation stone, Poulson was there in the line-up. Prince Philip, who had met him at previous prestigious inaugurations, shook his hand.

'Ah, Mr Poulson! – You are obviously the architect for this hospital project. Good…'

'Well, sir, I hope I am the architect. But in fact no tenders have been accepted for it yet.'

'No tenders?'

'No, sir. But I expect to be the architect, just as this man expects to be the stonemason, that one the glazier, that one the plumber, that one the aluminium supplier…'

'No tenders? – Then what are we doing here?'

'I don't rightly know, sir. It all seems to be a little bit premature, with respect…'

According to Poulson the Prince called the Queen back and told him: 'Tell her what you've just told me.'

She was as amazed as her husband: 'You mean I am about to lay a foundation stone, but the design for the place hasn't even been agreed yet?'

Poulson, using a good old Yorkshire expression, told me 'she was right vexed' by the news.

'She went ahead and laid the stone – it was in the wrong place anyway, smack in the middle of an operating theatre, and it was taken away on a lorry immediately afterwards – and when she got home she sent back the silver trowel she had used for the ceremony, and that they had presented to her as a memento, as a sign of her disapproval. The entire procedure had been a farce. The Queen had been brought there under false pretences.'

I couldn't use the story while Poulson was still in the dock, but I made enquiries in Malta and established that the ceremonial trowel had in fact been returned.

When he went to jail I called Buckingham Palace and asked them to confirm that the Queen had sent it back. They said they couldn't confirm it, although they couldn't actually deny it, or even find it, either.

I asked what other gifts the Queen might have returned in recent months or years.

'Oh… come on… let's be realistic,' said the bored Buck House spokesman. 'What would Her Majesty want, with a trowel?'

A fair point. How long did they need to check the facts?

The rest of the day, at least.

I told them to call me with the answer that night. Otherwise they could ring me next day – by which time, I said, I would be in Malta.

*

In contrast to the cold spring Yorkshire weather, Malta glowed hot in the sunshine, the light reflecting golden rays off the ancient sandstone buildings. I had two points of contact on the island: a local stringer called Godfrey Grima, formerly on the *Financial Times*, and a Maltese developer whose name Poulson had provided.

Grima had found a brief reference in parliament to the return of the trowel that he translated for me from Maltese; it confirmed the facts that the Palace had been unable to substantiate.

Poulson had shown me a letter he had written to the businessman; it congratulated him on the way he 'handled' local politicians – adding that it was much the same way as he handled the same sort of people back home.

His letter had enclosed a cheque for £5,000 – a lot of money in those days – for a totally unnecessary 'equipment contract' for the building.

At least, it was unnecessary except for greasing what Poulson called 'the always outstretched palms of the Maltese government'.

Since the letter was written there'd been a regime change on the island. The bribes had been paid under the Nationalist Borg Olivier government; now Socialist Dom Mintoff was in power. It made little difference. The developer who had been bribing contacts declined to speak to me, as was of course his right. I later learnt (there were few real secrets on the island) that he had immediately telephoned Borg Olivier who had in turn called Mintoff.

The result was effectively a 'dawn raid' (6am) at my hotel with detectives ordering me to leave Malta on the first available flight: 'You can make your own way to the airport. Or we take you in handcuffs and they don't come off until the aircraft lands.'

Leo White, on the news desk, told me to file my copy from Malta and then to leave the island without making a fuss.

'But they're putting me on the first flight out – and it's to Rome!'

'Have you been to Rome? No? Oh, you'll hate it. And you'll want to punish somebody, so you'll arrive there and find there's no seat on a direct flight to London until maybe Sunday' (this happened on a Thursday). 'So you'll book yourself into a posh hotel and spend lots of money and charge the firm…. Okay, I'll get you fixed up, somewhere.'

I heard him speak to Maxine Kay, his secretary: 'Book Revel into the Ambasciatori Palace on via Veneto and tell them to send the bill here, and get some cash sent to him at the main post office in Rome.'

By some cock-up in cashiers I was sent £500 spending money which, converted into lira, made me an Italian millionaire.

Yes… things were different, in those days.

*

The first Poulson trial had lasted fifty-two days and cost an estimated £1.25million although given the number of high-living reporters and photographers, Fraud Squad detectives, barristers, solicitors and witnesses – all of them on expenses in luxury hotels – the city of Leeds must have been experiencing an unprecedented economic surge.

There were at least six more to come so the judge offered a deal: if he would plead guilty to the outstanding cases, he would add only two years to Poulson's sentence (making seven years, in all) but avoid the 'cat-and-mouse game' of bringing him back and forward to court.

We reporters had no such reprieve. Reporting the trials was fairly intensive work; we had to record almost everything because mostly we didn't know for sure where the evidence was leading and who it might involve.

There were a few light moments. One reporter – a TV man – returned from a heavy lunch and fell asleep in the press benches. When he snored, his neighbours nudged him and he half woke but, with eyes still closed and forgetting where he was, he lighted a cigarette.

As the smoke billowed around the newsman's head Poulson's barrister, Donald Herrod QC, told the judge: 'M'lud, I appear to have some competition for the jury's attention.'

The smoker's neighbours prodded him again and somebody behind him slapped him on the head, He awoke fully with a start, realised what had happened and threw the cigarette down, stamping on it. But each footfall only increased the oxygen around it and created more clouds of smoke.

The judge, George Waller, looked on, intrigued.

'We'll wait a few moments,' he told the court.

When the smoke subsided he said simply: 'Please continue, Mr Herrod.'

A good judge.

At one stage he had warned the reporters against frequent comings and goings as they left the benches to phone their copy. He said that, apart from being a distraction for the jury, he might want to warn the press about not reporting evidence that could prejudice a future trial – so they should stay in their seats until the lunch adjournment.

This ruling would obviously most affect the evening paper men who were updating their reports almost hourly to meet edition times so one of them, Jack Miller from the London *Evening Standard*, rose noisily to his feet, coughed loudly and having got the judge's attention told him:

'With respect, my lord, you can't do that.'

We all knew that Jack, who normally covered the Old Bailey, had more court experience than the rest of us. We also knew that nobody talked to a judge like that.

'Excuse me?'

'You simply can't decide when we enter and leave this courtroom. Some of us have deadlines to meet.'

'Stay where you are, for now,' the judge told him, firmly. 'Then come to my chambers when we adjourn.'

It was chokey for Jack, we all reckoned. He would be banged up in the next cell to Poulson.

In fact all that happened was that the two court experts reached a deal. When potentially prejudicial evidence was looming, the judge would announce a 'red light' to the press. If they then went to phone copy they wouldn't report any part of the proceedings that occurred until he announced his 'green light', possibly including a warning about the reporting of it.

Another sensible judgment.

When Poulson, giving evidence in his own defence, appeared to be confused about why he had been brought to court, Judge Waller asked him what he had thought the Fraud Squad would find when they started their investigation into his business affairs.

'I thought they would discover all the good works I had done.'

'But Mr Poulson,' the judge said kindly, 'the Fraud Squad doesn't investigate good works.'

*

We were still waiting for further arrests. The one Poulson wanted to see in the dock – and more importantly in jail – was Alderman Andrew Cunningham. To describe him as a leading figure in trade unions and politics didn't do the man justice.

He was a member of the national executive of the Labour party, leader of Durham County Council, northern president of the General & Municipal Workers Union (biggest union in the north-east), chairman of the police authority…

When being introduced to Poulson his first words had been 'What's in it for me?'

Poulson hated him. 'But I was told how he reacted if people disagreed with him. He would be very vitriolic with anybody who failed to fall into line. He frightened me.'

So he paid for family holidays and gave Mrs Cunningham a job – advising on what colours to paint school corridors and classrooms – because that was what the alderman asked for.

In the north-east, councillors and journalists alike referred to him, quietly, as 'Back-handy Andy'.

Unstoppable, just before his arrest (he was sentenced to five years, reduced to three on appeal) he asked the deputy chief constable of County Durham: 'Suppose somebody is sent to jail, how do they guarantee a job in the prison library?'

I was sitting in my car outside Dan Smith's house when members of the Fraud Squad arrived to arrest him. There were no photographers present but a picture of the detectives coming out of the door with him would make the front page.

By lucky coincidence I saw Leo Dillon, the *Mail* photographer, driving past the end of the street and when I flashed my headlights he came to see me and waited to take the desired picture.

I gave the *Mail* some words and Leo gave us a copy of the photograph. It appeared on the front of the next morning's *Mirror* as 'By Tom Buist'.

The picture desk wouldn't have wanted to know.

I remembered that Leo had once missed a photograph that *Express* man Gordon Amory had got, and Gordon helped him out with a picture. Next day Leo phoned Gordon to thank him. It had been so good, he said, that he'd had a herogram from the picture desk that morning.

'I hope they don't study it too closely,' Gordon told him. 'Because you are in it.'

Dan Smith got six years after the judge heard that he had received a total of £156,000 from Poulson for 'public relations work' and had channelled more than a million pounds worth of business Poulson's way.

*

Not one of the MPs who had taken the architect's money would appear in court through a remarkable and suddenly discovered 'loophole' which ruled that MPs could not be considered to be in charge of public funds.

I continued to pursue Maudling. He admitted to me that he'd received more than his MP's wages as salary from Poulson, that the architect had contributed to his wife's theatre trust, employed his son and built him a swimming pool, and even that there had been a £70,000 intra-company debt that had never been repaid.

But he had at least resigned and the consensus appeared to be that, finally, enough was enough.

The Poulson Affair started to peter out as the Fraud Squad, the law officers and the newspapers lost interest, after a total of nineteen successful prosecutions and with no more prominent names in the frame.

*

It was all quiet on the north-eastern front so I took a holiday and came home to be reminded that my patch also included the north-western front.

Northern news editor Leo White had heard from a fisherman about a Japanese ship being seen coming in to Barrow-in-Furness with a 'nuclear cargo'. Since nuclear energy was being produced at and sold from Britain's reactor at Windscale, surely this was the wrong order of things? Perhaps I should take a look.

My old boss at the *Yorkshire Evening Post* who had thought of Doncaster as a depressing place should have seen Barrow, the biggest iron and steel centre in the world, at the windswept end of a twenty-mile cul-de-sack. Towns, even seaports, just do not come any more miserable. Because of its shape the peninsular (the Furness) had been named after an Old Norse word describing a female sexual organ. And Barrow was right up it.

It took some time but eventually British Nuclear Fuels Ltd came clean (so to speak).

The UK sold nuclear energy to Japan in the form of giant doughnuts. But Japan's constitution interestingly forbade the storage of nuclear waste, once the energy was extracted, so they returned it – still radio-active (a half-life of 250,000 years, according to BNFL) to the UK.

It was part of the deal, said BNFL. It was all about trade and exports. We couldn't sell the stuff unless we agreed to accept the waste products back, and store them for eternity. Not only Japan…

It made the front: BRITAIN BEING USED AS WORLD'S NUCLEAR DUSTBIN.

I wasn't inclined to hang about there, so it was back to Newcastle office, and the comfort of the Magpie pub, until Dan Ferrari, the news editor in London, called.

The Poulson Affair apparently hadn't quite finished yet.

*

There was a story flying round that Ted Short, deputy leader of the Labour Party (and MP for Newcastle Central) had a secret Swiss bank account, with funds received from Dan Smith, presumably originating from Poulson. Was there yet another MP on the take?

'What do you think?' asked Ferrari.

I didn't believe it. I liked Ted Short. He was quiet and seemed straight and had a sense of humour.

When he was Postmaster General I'd been planning a story about the unreliable phone service in the regions.

I rang him and told him he owed my pal Clive Crickmer a pound. I said I'd had a tip for a horse but had been unable to pass it on to Crick because the bloody phones were not working – again – between Newcastle and South Shields, about five miles away.

If I had been able to contact him, Crick would have invested half-a-crown in a bet on the horse, I said. And it had come in at eight to one, so…

'Well,' said Ted. 'I am responsible for the telephone service, so I will give Mr Crickmer the money – on condition that you give me your word of honour that, if the horse had lost, he would now be sending me the half-crown he would have spent.'

I liked that.

'You'd better come down here, my dear, and sort it out,' said Ferrari.

Ferrari was on the phone, talking to a reader, when I arrived.

'You've invented a time machine and can use it to go backwards and forwards in time, as you wish...? In that case, can you tell me the winner of the 2.30 at Kempton Park today...? Oh... only full days backwards and forwards... I see. In that case, yes of course we are still interested. I'd like you to come in and see me, and bring the machine with you. Let's say at ten-thirty... yesterday.'

There may have been a rumour about a Swiss bank account, but there was nothing to back it up.

Dan told me that the story about Ted Short was all over The Street, and was being widely whispered about in Parliament. People had seen a bank statement, he said. But the *Mirror* hadn't been able to get its hands on a copy.

My first job – that everybody else had seemingly failed to do – was to find the statement.

I didn't believe that such a thing existed. But if anybody was going to invent evidence, and start a smear campaign...

I telephoned *Private Eye* and reminded Peter Cook that he remembered me.

He had also heard the rumour, but hadn't seen any paperwork. If I found some, he'd be grateful...

I called *Time Out*, then very much an 'alternative' magazine, and Tony Elliot, the editor, said that, yes, he had a copy of 'the Ted Short Swiss Bank Account' on his desk.

It was a few minutes' walk up Grays Inn Road.

Dan and I pored over the document. 'That's his full name, Edward Watson Short,' I said. 'And that is the address of his place in the Lake District. Somebody has done their homework, but I still don't believe it.'

'Well, my dear – either stand the story up, or knock it down.'

The London boss of the Swiss Bank Corporation didn't appear very helpful at the start. He could not and would not tell me whether anybody had an account with his bank.

Could he tell me if somebody *didn't* have one? –'Of course not, because... well, what if I couldn't deny it?'

But what he could tell me was that the type face on the copy I had was quite different from the one the bank used: they had a unique fount, for security reasons, and to identify forgeries such as this one.

It was the bank's stationery all right – or it had been, until a few pints of Tippex had been applied to remove the original typed information. So somebody had an account with the bank, somewhere. But possibly not, in this instance, Edward Short MP.

Suppose somebody knew he had a bank account, and forged a copy of what they thought it would look like, in order to give it credibility?

'You don't believe there is such an account, do you?' asked the banker. I shook my head.

'Nor do I,' he said.

So we were left with a rumour we didn't believe, in fact that we believed to be a lie. But no peg to hang a story on.

I told Dan Ferrari: 'I know what Rupert would do.'

It was a bank holiday weekend and Ted Short had been travelling north while I had been heading south. So I drove to his house in the Lakes. The narrow roads were clogged with cars and caravans. It took hours, but Short invited me in to the holiday home that he had bought for his retirement. He'd been 'telephonically besieged' by reporters, he said, but had refused to speak to any of them.

And yet: 'Well, the *Daily Mirror* and its man from Newcastle...'

We would be denying a story that the general public wasn't even aware of. On the other hand, there had been an attempt to smear the name of a leading politician.

He provided the headline himself: DIRTY TRICKS DEPARTMENT.

As I headed towards the car, he called: 'By the way... did we ever settle that bet?'

9. Miss World exclusive

I was sprawled diagonally across a double bed in London's Tower Hotel, when Helen Morgan, who had been crowned Miss World only six days earlier, announced that she was taking her knickers off. I pretended not to hear.

I screwed up my eyes so she could see I wasn't peeping.

'What about you, Revel?' She had a beautiful soft Welsh accent. 'Are you going to keep your pants on all night?' It's the sort of quote that, when uttered in the illicit atmosphere of a hotel bedroom by a recently-crowned Miss World, stays with you for the rest of your life.

At this stage in our relationship we'd been together for two days, almost to the hour. I knew everything about her. I'd already written her life story twice. She was only twenty-two.

The most interesting part of the tale, apart from her 'coronation' as Miss World, was that she was an unmarried mother, who might be named as 'the other woman' in a divorce. Julia Morley, who organised the beauty competitions, had always known about the baby, but discovered the other fact after the crowning ceremony and decided to sack her.

She confided in Kent Gavin, the *Daily Mirror* photographer, and he convinced her to delay the actual dismissal, but to summon Helen from Carlisle (where she'd been opening a supermarket for the Co-Op) and discuss the matter face to face.

That was where I'd come in. I met Helen at Newcastle central station – I'd had to buy a morning paper to find out what she looked like – introduced myself, and got on the train with her to London.

And now here we were, 48 hours later, in a hotel I'd booked under an assumed name, with her inviting me to take my pants off.

'Come on,' she said, 'I'll run them under the tap with my things.'

That was the height of our intimacy. Like a good tabloid reporter, I made an excuse and left for the bar.

Helen had arrived In Newcastle with a security guard, hired to act as her chaperone, which obviously meant keeping her safe from unwanted attention such as perverts and pressmen. But he had a Geordie accent. 'You must live round here,' I guessed.

'Aye: Wallsend.'

'Well don't bother about going off to London, I'll look after her,' I offered generously. 'I'll see she gets safely to Mrs Morley.'

'Will you really do that for us?'

'Course I will. Look, that's why I'm here. I've got to go to London, anyway. There's no point in our both going. Don't worry, I'll not let any reporters talk to her.'

It was a promise that was remarkably easy to keep. The security man told me I was a gent.

Clive Crickmer walked with us to the 11.15 night train and Tom Buist took some photographs of Helen signing autographs and walking under a sign that said Way Out. Then Clive went to file the copy – 'she really was magnificent', he quoted the security guard as saying. 'I don't think anyone suspected anything was wrong' – and Tom to wire the photos while Helen and I settled into an empty first class compartment. I pulled the blinds on the windows.

'Lend me a lipstick.'

'What for?'

'I thought I'd write *Just Married* on the windows. Nobody will come in then.'

'I'd rather you didn't,' said Helen. 'In case somebody does come in… In case we're found out.'

It was wise advice, as it turned out. When the train pulled in at York half a dozen reporters boarded it. I'm still not sure how they knew which train she was on, but to my horror they stationed themselves in the corridor outside (presumably) the only first class compartment with its blinds drawn. I could hear them outside the door, discussing tactics. I even recognised some of their voices. Astonishingly, they tapped at the door.

'You're asleep,' I hissed at Helen.

I slid the door open a couple of inches. 'Yes?'

The elected spokesman was not a face I recognised. 'Could we speak to Miss Morgan, please?'

'I'm sorry, Miss Who?'

'Look, we know she's in there. Helen Morgan. Miss World. We just want a few words.'

'I see. I'm sorry, but she's asleep just now.'

'Can't you wake her up?'

'I would, but you must realise that she's had a very tiring day. Pestered enough already by the newspapers. I think she's entitled to a bit of peace, don't you?'

The lads conferred. 'Look, if she wakes up before the next stop, will you give us a shout? We'll be in the compartment just down there.'

Of course I said that I would, and slid the door shut.

It's difficult, when one hears stories of press harassment or intrusion, to reconcile that: one of my rare experiences at the receiving end, as it were, of the national press. They were incredibly polite, decent, and gentlemanly... not to mention incompetent, negligent and idle. I'll never know why they didn't simply open the door and sit down beside us while they fired their questions at Helen. Nothing I would have done could have stopped them.

And then I had a pressing problem. I'd been summoned onto the story from the pub with no time to discharge the early evening's intake of lager.

'I need to go to the toilet,' I confided to Helen.

'What about all those men outside?'

'They're not actually in the corridor. Look, as I see it, there's two options. I can stand on the arms of the seats and pee out of the window...' I indicated the small sliding ventilator above the main pane of glass, '...or I can go to the loo. Frankly I don't want to leave you.'

'It's better than the alternative,' said Helen. 'Just try and make it quick. I'll stay asleep.'

'If anybody comes in and so much as touches you to wake you, scream rape,' I said. And ran off down the corridor, in the direction I thought was safe.

Only they'd changed compartment.

I didn't realise until I'd passed them. And they didn't seem to notice me. I dashed to the toilet and dashed back.

Again they didn't notice. It was some sort of relief.

Shortly before Doncaster there was another tap at the door.

'Is she awake yet?'

'Sorry. She's just clapped out.'

'Could you wake her and just ask her for a quote about how she feels about getting the sack?'

'She hasn't been sacked.'

'Can we quote you on that?'

'I'd rather you didn't.'

'Are you from Mecca? Or from the Miss World Organisation?'

'No. Look, I'm nobody.'

'Just a friend…? Hey – you're not the boyfriend, are you? The father of the, er…?'

'Not at all. Look, if you want a quote, you can say that she says she's tired out and very upset. Today's events have been very distressing. But she's under contract as Miss World and she can't say anything until she's spoken to Mrs Morley.'

'That's great. A direct quote, you say? Smashing. But if she wakes up before Doncaster, will you let us know?'

'Of course.'

They came back when the train stopped at Doncaster.

'Has she woken up yet?'

'No. I went to look for you, I knew you'd be pushed for time, but you weren't in the compartment you'd told me you were going to.'

'Hey thanks, mate. That was good of you. The problem is, the lads don't know whether to stay on the train and wait for a quote, in case she wakes up.'

'You've got a quote. A direct quote. What more can she say, even if she does wake up? But look at her.' I generously opened the door another inch. 'She's totally shagged out. If I was you I'd get off here and file what you've got.'

I said *file*. I realised as soon as the word crossed my lips. Only a newspaperman would refer to copy being 'filed'. They didn't notice. They left the train at Doncaster. And filed their quotes.

We had a peaceful journey to Peterborough, chatting about Helen's life in Barry, Glamorgan, as a freelance model, her 18-

month-old baby, Richard, and her boyfriend, Chris Clodes – 'He's just one of my boyfriends. I have no plans to marry him.'

I wrote it all in my notebook, and as I read back each page of shorthand she signed it as a true record.

'Will I get paid for this?'

It was the question I feared. 'I don't know; I've never had to pay anybody for a story in my life.'

'But I've heard of people getting lots of money from newspapers. I mean hundreds of pounds.'

'Well, I can't guarantee it, but suppose you spent the day with us tomorrow, posed for some pictures, a bit more interview, before going to see Mrs Morley. Or suppose we get Mrs Morley to come and meet you at the *Mirror*. I can't promise – you must understand that I have no authority to offer you any money at all – but I'd try and get you, I don't know, maybe a couple of hundred pounds.'

'Two hundred pounds!' I could see her walking out on me.

'Well, I only said...'

'No, you did say it! Two hundred pounds! For only one day's work!'

It was the start of a beautiful friendship.

The trouble was that I could not guarantee it. Newspapers are so fickle, their interest-span so fleeting, that I wasn't sure they'd think the story would be worth two hundred pence when we arrived in London in the morning. Suppose the Miss World Organisation snatched her away from me at the station. Suppose Mrs Morley refused to travel to Holborn to collect her Miss World from the *Mirror* building. If there were six reporters at York, how many would there be at Kings Cross? How could I, unaided, deal with the Fleet Street heavies?

At Peterborough, there were photographers as well as reporters waiting for the train. By this time the message would have been relayed from Doncaster to confirm, for those who didn't know it, which train we were on.

I picked up Helen's bag and told her to be ready. It sounded melodramatic, but when the train moved out of the station we were going to jump off.

There was an outer door almost directly opposite our compartment door.

When I heard all the doors being slammed shut I wandered, humming, into the corridor and dropped the window and leaned out as if taking the evening air. The corridor was full of strangers, all looking interestedly in my direction. Some had cameras slung around their necks. At the first judder I reached back for Helen's hand, opened the door and pulled her onto the platform. We pelted towards the barrier with me hoping that Peterborough would run to a taxi at that time of night, or morning, that the taxi driver would be willing to drive to London, and that the news desk would be sufficiently interested in the story to pay the fare when we arrived.

There were no taxis. But there was a photographer who flashed one snap as we ran into the darkness. Then a voice shouted 'Revel – the blue Volvo!' And I dragged Helen towards it, wrenched at the back door, which was locked, opened the front, opened the back, shoved Helen in, climbed into the front passenger seat – and found myself staring at a total stranger.

'For God's sake, let's move!' I yelled.

It is perhaps worth pausing at this point to look at how the *Daily Mail* reported that little moment of history:

> At 3.37am on Platform Two of Peterborough's general station, Helen climbed down from the London-bound express and, shielding her face, walked to a waiting car.
>
> In front of her was a young man in a check jacket and black slacks. Behind were two other men.
>
> Two photographers were pushed aside as the group headed off down a side exit from the station, missing the ticket barrier. They jumped into a dark blue Volvo and accelerated away.

In the early hours Peterborough was quiet enough for us to establish that we were not being followed as we 'accelerated away'. But I had no idea whose car we were in. I feared that Helen and I had acted out a silly scene worthy of a spy B-movie – only in order to walk into another newspaper's hands. There was only one thing for it.

'Let's ring in,' I said.

We stopped at a phone box. The driver left the keys in the ignition, but he dialled 100 and asked the operator for a Freephone number I'd never heard before.

'It's me,' he said, when the phone was answered. 'I've got Revel; he's standing here beside me, and Helen's in the car. They got off at Peterborough and there were no problems. Nobody saw us, except one photographer, and he hasn't followed us. We'll go straight to my place.'

At this stage I decided that I'd been duped by the *Daily Mail*. It was a stunt that their assistant editor Jack Crossley or reporter Harry Longmuir would have pulled, calling out my name, and then being weirdly non-committal on the phone. Still, two could play at that game. The chap was smaller than I, and slightly built, and the keys were in the car. I could leave him in the telephone kiosk and drive away with Helen. Surely stealing a car could be justified if Miss World and a *Daily Mirror* reporter had been kidnapped. Unless... I reached towards the telephone.

'Do you want to speak to Revel? Oh. Ok.'

He depressed the receiver rest with his fingers.

'They say well done. You've done a great job.'

There'd be another chance. I followed him meekly to the Volvo.

We sped south. Helen was asleep in the back seat, either confident of her safety or simply past caring. I had no idea where we were, nor where we were going. The driver didn't talk much.

It was still pre-dawn dark when we pulled in at his home. There were no lights on. We stayed in the car while he unlocked the door and illuminated the place. I demanded to see where Helen was going to sleep, and told the driver to make a hot water bottle for her bed. She huddled beside an electric fire and I, with our host occupied, went to work on his bureau. After a few minutes I had found a pay slip and established his identity: he was Ian Sellars, deputy night news editor of the *Daily Mirror* – a man I'd spoken to often, but never met.

'Thank God you turned up when you did, Ian, you old bastard,' I said when he reappeared with cups of steaming soup. 'What an operation, eh!'

'I just had this thought,' he said modestly. 'I said, old Revel's on the train and he's bound to think of getting off somewhere en route. I mean, any professional would, wouldn't he? So I sent a man to every station. My car was the fastest, so I took Peterborough.'

We woke in the Sellars home in Hitchin, and listened to the news. We – Helen and I – were the main item, with the BBC soberly explaining that by leaping off the train we had thwarted more than two hundred journalists who had been waiting for the train's arrival at Kings Cross. The Beeb has an almost pompous method of reporting newspaper activities, ignoring the fact that it's a newsgathering organisation itself... and that with BBC TV news, *Nationwide*, BBC radio news, local radio, and probably *World Service*, all travelling mob-handed with sound and lighting technicians plus cameramen, Auntie BBC probably accounted for the largest single proportion of that journalistic horde.

Julia Morley, known as Mrs World, was impatiently anticipating Helen's arrival at the Shaftsbury Avenue headquarters of Mecca, the contest organisers.

'Gavin's on his way,' said Sellars, pouring the first of many cups of coffee. 'And they're sending Merrin up as a minder.'

The deadly duo arrived early, as even Fleet Street's finest can when they smell a big story. They had picked up father-of-the-child Chris Clodes on the way. He wore stacked shoes and his hair was parted in the middle.

'Hello, darlin',' said Kenneth George Gavin as he emerged from his primrose-yellow Daimler. He spoke in the cheeky cockney way that photographers affect when addressing models and Miss Worlds. 'Wotcha, sweetheart,' called Merrin, another cockney who looked like a cross between a Kray twin and Henry Cooper, only bigger and more threatening.

'Kent!' Helen screamed with delight and ran over to kiss Gavin. She had to run past Chris Clodes to reach him. Gavin told her: 'You're all right now, darlin'. Just stick with us and we'll see everything works out fine.'

I was, therefore, delighted and flattered when these two Big Time Operators abandoned Helen, explaining:

'We've just got to sort things out with your man, here.'

They walked down the garden with me.

'Look, Revs,' said Gavin, 'This is serious. Have you had her?'

I was speechless.

'Did you give her one, or what?'

'You do realise, Mr Barker, that Mr Gavin here does need to know the score on this point,' said Merrin, smiling, menacingly. 'In fact, at this stage in the game there's absolutely nothing that you could think of that's more important.'

'I think it's ridiculous,' I blustered, 'even to suggest that I'd do such a thing.'

'A simple Yes or No would suffice,' said Merrin. 'Where did you sleep last night?'

'Downstairs. And she slept upstairs. Do you really think I'd do that – to a story?'

'Nah,' said Gavin. 'Where they slept, where they actually slept with old Torchy creeping around the house is not the question. Did you have your evil way with her on the train?'

'It's very important,' Merrin reminded me. '– Because, you see, he's had three Miss United Kingdoms, but never while they were reigning, and never a Miss World, yet. So if you've beaten him to it,' explained Merrin, 'young Mr Gavin here is going to throw himself off Tower Bridge and the office will hold you responsible.'

I was able to assure them that the life of the chief photographer was safe in my hands, so we moved on to other vital matters.

'How much have you promised her?' Merrin wanted to know.

'Well. I haven't exactly *promised* anything.'

'How much is she asking?'

'I don't know. I mean, in my world we don't normally have to pay to get people to talk to us. How much should I have offered?'

'Anything she asked for. Come on, you must have talked money at some time during the night on that train, at least, when you weren't touching her up.'

'Well, I told her that we would probably want her to stay with us for the rest of today, and she's agreed to that.'

'Great! How much for that?'

'…And I said that we'd probably want Mrs Morley to meet her on our premises, so there'd be no other papers present, and she agreed to that.'

'How much? *How much*?' Gavin and Merrin were ecstatic.

'Well, nothing definite, but… well, there's nothing in writing, but I thought about two hundred quid.'

'Two hundred quid!' The Big Time Operators stared at each other open mouthed. 'Are you serious, or what? Two hundred bleedin' quid! Mr Gavin, tell me I'm dreaming.'

'Oh shit,' I said. 'Have I screwed up?'

*

And so we said farewell to Ian Sellars, who had served his purpose and enjoyed his moment of unreported glory, and set off towards London. Before we did anything, we needed an up-to-date set of photographs, so we turned our back on misty Hertfordshire for the more familiar setting of the capital.

They talked about locations for the shoot with the insight that Londoners obviously have. Lacking such nous, I suggested Trafalgar Square, the Mall ('after all, she's been crowned'), and Downing Street ('she's a world leader'), but my knowledge of London landmarks fortunately expired before they told me to shut up.

Somewhere near Mill Hill we pulled up alongside a phone box so that Merrin could check in.

'That Morley cow's gone ape-shit,' he explained when he returned. 'She's gonna sue us for abduction. She's called a brief in and Miles is waiting for the injunction to drop. Miles is named on it as editor, and Jacobsen, as well as every other piddling director, and there's a blank space for Mr Barker's name when they discover it. Then she says she knows Helen's not well and if her health is damaged she'll sue for that as well – bodily harm, I expect. Plus, all those hacks and monkeys who were trained on Kings Cross have rebased in Holborn Circus. Four hundred, now. They've had to lower the bombproof barriers to keep them out, and now the bleedin' staff can't get in.'

'Did they say what we should do?' I ventured.

'Just stay out of the way. Keep driving round the north circular 'til we think of something, I suppose. But the hunt is on for yellow Daimlers, so we'd better keep our heads down.'

'I know,' said Gavin. 'Victoria Park!'

'Like fuck! Every snapper in London knows you go there for all your outside shots.'

'But I wouldn't go there when I'm in hiding, eh?'

Double bluff. So we went to Hackney.

Gavin, not surprisingly, had first met Helen when, as Miss Wales, she won the Miss United Kingdom contest. When she ran for Miss World, she became newsworthy as the first unmarried mother in the competition. On the eve of the contest the bookies made Miss Belgium 8-1 favourite, with Helen at 9-1. *Mirror* woman's editor Joyce Hopkirk had tipped Helen to win, but Gavin, confident that the judges would never pick an unmarried mother, had plumped for Miss South Africa, a leggy blonde called Anneline Kriel. Gavin's judgment had been swayed by Eric Morley's confiding that Mecca was nervous about the possibility of Helen winning – not, he said, on moral grounds, and the publicity would be tremendous, but because the tough regime which faced all Miss Worlds might be too much for a young girl with an eighteen-month-old son.

After she'd been crowned Eric Morley told Gavin that she'd proved her point and been the most beautiful girl in the contest. 'But I still think it might be better if she handed over the title. As an unmarried mother it's going to be very difficult for her to do the work demanded of a Miss World.'

Gavin had danced with Helen at the 'Coronation Ball' and repeated the conversation to her, as Eric Morley had asked him to. But she'd heard it already: the Morleys had urged her to resign and suggested some financial arrangement with the successor so that Helen wouldn't lose out totally on all the money she could expect to earn from personal appearances.

Clearly, the Mecca Organisation had realised that two Miss Worlds were even better for publicity than one unmarried mum.

The following morning Ken had photographed her – 'looking as if she hadn't a care in the world' – sitting on a bench... in Victoria Park.

A dispatch rider was sent to meet us at a secret rendezvous in order to pick up Gavin's film. Dan Ferrari was coordinating the operation; he'd sent a message with the motorcyclist: 'Mr Ferrari says on no account tell anybody where you are, just keep driving round. On no account go to the office; it is bedlam. On no account go anywhere near Mecca; it is worse. You can't drive down Shaftsbury Avenue; it's blocked by newspapermen.

On the one-o'clock news Mrs Morley accused us of abduction. She feared for Helen's safety, and her health. She was already in breach of her contract, but that didn't matter – if only she could hear Helen's voice, telling her that she was all right...

About this point, I made an executive decision: 'Ring in,' I told Helen. 'Don't say where you are; tell her that you're with the *Daily Mirror* voluntarily – not against your will; tell her that you're well; and tell her that you can't go to the Mecca office because it's surrounded and you're frightened to go back there. Tell her you'll think of a place to meet her when it's quietened down.'

Helen did all this, while Mrs Morley tried to cajole and then to threaten her. Standing beside Helen in the telephone kiosk I could see the effect it was having on her. 'Say you've got to go now,' I whispered. 'Just say you'll ring back.'

Back in the Daimler Helen squeezed her hands between her knees and said plaintively that she just didn't know what to do.

'Take my advice, gel, and get out of it,' said Gavin. 'You don't think this aggravation is going to stop, just by going to see Julia, do you?'

'The question,' said Merrin, 'is whether you think the title is worth all the unpleasantness. Me, I don't.'

Helen looked across the leather seat at me. 'You've been voted Miss World,' I reminded her. 'You *are* Miss World. What's Mecca going to do when you roll up at the door? I'd resign, while I was winning.'

It was as if a weight had been lifted from her shoulders. Helen sat up, and smiled. 'That's what I'll do.'

'Got your notebook handy, Mr Barker?' asked Merrin. 'I think I can feel an abdication statement coming on.'

Together we composed – well, Merrin mostly dictated to me – an official communiqué from Helen Morgan to announce her resignation as Miss World. We actually wrote it in a pub. Merrin had gone in first to make sure there were no Fleet Street faces and given us the all clear. Helen, her face only partly covered by her coat collar, smiled sweetly as she ate a sandwich. Other drinkers actually noticed, and remarked on, her beauty. But nobody recognised Miss World, in spite of the fact that her face must have been the most photographed and most published face for the best part of a week. And currently the most sought-after face in London.

Once finished, the statement was telephoned to the *Mirror*'s copytakers, rushed to Dan Ferrari, shown to the lawyers and then delivered by hand to the Mecca office, and simultaneously released to the Press Association.

Incensed, Mecca issued a statement: Julia Morley was en route to the South African embassy where she intended to offer the newly vacated Miss World title to Anneline Kriel, who had come second in the contest.

Around four o'clock we checked in with Ferrari.

'There's nowhere safe,' he told us. 'You'd better go down to my place. At least, even if they trace you there, they can't get at you.'

Off we went to deepest Kent and to an ancient, wood-built mill-house with a stream running through it. There were five acres surrounding the building, and a set of former stables where we secreted the primrose yellow Daimler. We introduced ourselves to Mrs Ferrari – Joyce – who took one look at Helen and sent her to bed. She allocated an attic bedroom to her husband's three colleagues and Merrin and I sat down to write the story:

MY LOVER, MY BABY, AND ME.

In fact, once again Merrin did it. I had the notes and had read them through to him. He picked up the phone, asked for copy and dictated:

> Beautiful Helen Morgan told yesterday of the torment and the tears behind her decision to quit as Miss World after only four days – point, par – Helen, a 22-year-old

unmarried mother, said she was giving up the coveted
title to protect her baby boy – point, par, quote – I put
motherhood before the Miss World title comma quote she
said – point par still quoting.

He handed the telephone to me.

My baby Richard is more important to me than all the
beauty titles in the world.

'Shall I mention the boyfriend, here?' Merrin nodded.

As she spoke, Helen hugged 26-year-old Chris Clodes, her
boyfriend from schooldays – point, par, quote – Chris is
Richard's father, she said proudly – comma quote – I have
never made any secret of this – point par.

We had actually lost Chris, somewhere along the way, but we
went on, the handset passed back and forth between us every time
Merrin thought up a new bit of narrative, or felt the need for a
quote from my notes.

We finished the Page One splash and Merrin immediately
started dictating the centre spread feature:

I DON'T SLEEP AROUND - MISS WORLD'S OWN STORY.

I watched the lights of a car being driven up the long, straight,
approach to the house and wondered whether it was Dan coming
home in triumph. But it was a stranger who knocked at the door.

'Could one of you deal with this,' asked Joyce. 'It's the *Daily
Express*. I've asked them to go away, but they won't take it from
me.'

I went, on the basis that for anyone who knew them, the
appearance of Gavin or Merrin at their news editor's home would
confirm any suspicion. It was a girl reporter.

'Can I speak to Miss Morgan, please?'

'Sorry, you've got the wrong house,' I lied.

'No I haven't.'

'You have. This is a private residence. It's Mr and Mrs Ferrari.
Nobody called Morgan lives here.'

'Well, we'll just sit here in the car 'til she appears.'

'No, you can't do that; this is private property, and I must ask
you to take the car away.'

'Well I won't.'

'Tom,' I called, 'would you speak to the driver of this car?'

Tom ambled down the steps, the two Ferrari Alsatians at his heels, and addressed the driver, a photographer: 'Would you like to move this car, please? Or would you like me to move it, with you and your lady friend in it?'

'I'll move it,' said the photographer, clearly upset by Merrin's smiling face. And he drove off, leaving the reporter to run after him down the drive.

Dictating copy had kept the telephone engaged for a long time. But as soon as it was free it rang. Brian Hitchen, now news editor of the *Daily Express*, wanted to speak to Joyce. 'How are you, darling? I was just checking that Helen was comfortable.'

Joyce knew Hitchen fairly well – he'd been Dan's deputy on the *Mirror* news desk and had been to their home...

'Helen?' she said. 'Helen who?'

And then Leno, their eldest son, arrived home from his job as a reporter on BBC TV *Nationwide*. I was introduced to him as 'a friend of Daddy's, down here from the Newcastle office.'

'Don't talk to me about Daddy!' said Leno. 'You can't believe how he's ruined my day. He's got Miss World hidden somewhere – did you know? – And I've spent every single minute of the day telephoning hotels and guesthouses all over England trying to find them. I'm absolutely shattered! I'll just have to go and freshen up, and change my clothes.'

'Of course you must, darling. But not in your own room, use Simon's room...'

'What on earth are you taking about – not in my own room?'

'Well,' said Joyce, 'I've let somebody borrow it. It was the tidiest, you see...'

'Not... not...' He looked at his mother, and then at me, the truth finally registering. 'Oh, Mummy!'

About this time, the phone went dead. Hitchen's team had been ringing and re-ringing in the hope of scotching our operation, preventing our filing, or maybe even on the off-chance that Helen herself would answer the phone. Eventually, they simply left their receiver off the hook so that it was unusable. Still at his desk in

Holborn, Dan managed to get the GPO to clear it and then the *Mirror* news desk kept the line open with the arrangement that each end would listen in every half-hour in case either side had any message for the other.

When Dan came home he found his property surrounded by *Express* reporters and photographers.

'We've nothing to lose, now,' he said. 'Let's go for a drink.'

There was a pub almost at the end of the drive and we went in to order supper. Gavin opted for lamb chops on the basis that the curry wouldn't be hot enough to satisfy him. I was to learn that he only ever ordered lamb chops or vindictive curries. Merrin and I had a moderately hot curry.

Halfway through the meal Hitchen waddled in.

'You might as well produce her now, Dan,' he said. 'We'll get her anyway. I've got twenty-two journalists here with me: there's no way she can get out.'

'Twenty-two?'

'The full team. Thanks, I'll admit, to your cryptic clue. They've been on the story all day and nobody leaves 'til we've got the story.'

'Cryptic clue?'

'It wasn't easy, at first, but I worked it out soon enough.'

'What was the clue?' asked Merrin.

Hitchen beamed at his former colleague. 'I rang Dan and congratulated him on a scoop well-handled. And I said since he'd had her all day he could share her with us. I just asked him where she was hidden. Dan said I'd be sick if I knew. So I sent reporters round all the places he knew where I'd chucked up – and then I remembered his own house.'

'But you'd sent reporters and photographers out, twenty-two in all, to the other places,' I queried. 'Eleven places.'

Hitchen turned on me. 'That reminds me,' he snarled. 'I'm not amused by this stunt at Peterborough station. You beat up one of my photographers!'

'Who did?'

'You did!'

'What did your photographer say?'

'He was there when you got off the train. Helen Morgan and you and another *Mirror* heavy. You smashed his camera and blacked his eye.'

'And you believe it.'

'Naturally. It's what he told me.'

'I think calling me a *Mirror* heavy is the nicest thing you've ever said to me, Hitch. But I'm not heavy. I'm not a heavy, and there's only one of me. The only other person getting off the train was Helen Morgan – though admittedly she was wearing trousers and the photographer might have made a mistake... and there was Ian Sellars waiting in the car.'

'And he's not a heavy,' everyone said at once.

'I'll have that bastard in the office in the morning,' said Hitchen. 'If he doesn't have a black eye when he comes in, he'll sure as hell have one when he walks out!'

'What really distresses me, Brian,' said Ferrari, 'is that in all the time we worked together you didn't learn my first rule of news editing.'

'Which is? –'

'Never associate yourself personally with a failure,' said Dan.

The *Mirror* team walked triumphantly out, leaving Hitchen with the bill for dinner.

But the night wasn't finished. A guy came down from the *Mirror* publicity department wanting to record Helen reading her *Mirror* story so it could be used as an advertisement for the paper on commercial radio. I explained that, since Mecca's lawyers were holding me responsible for her health, she had to get her sleep, and I sent him back to London.

Then the *Mirror* office doctor, Janet Bentley, arrived to check Helen's state of health.

'She'll obviously be run-down, exhausted,' Janet told me.

'That's why I won't let you wake her up to examine her,' I said.

The following morning, true to its news editor's word, the *Express* team was still there. And it was augmented by other Fleet Street newspapers who were eventually getting wise to the *Mirror's* scoop. It was still a big story, mainly because no other paper had obtained a single word other than our hastily-written abdication statement – from the 1974 Miss World, an unmarried mother who had resigned to look after her baby and incidentally been named as 'the other woman' in a divorce case.

The lads and Helen had breakfast while Dan telephoned his neighbour. Then he took me into the corridor for a confidential chat.

'How much have you offered her?'

I didn't really know...

'Less than ten?'

Ten...?

'What? Oh yes, definitely less than ten.'

'Then offer her nine. It's been great. They showed the front page on *News At Ten* last night and ran the whole thing for nearly ten minutes. Nine's fair.'

'Nine what?'

'Nine big ones, of course!'

Shortly afterwards a slim-looking young chap in a donkey jacket, Wellington boots and a waterproof hat left the side door of the house with the Alsatians and walked across the grounds towards a stream that bordered the grounds of the Ferrari house. The reporters and photographers, some of them perched in trees, paid no attention. A few minutes later I followed, wearing a pair of Dan's waders. Beside the stream, and hidden briefly from view by shrubs, we posed for a photograph, then I balanced the 'slim young man', who the previous day had been Miss World, on my shoulders and entered the swollen stream. It was wader-deep, and in flood. All I could think of, as I picked my way across the rocky bottom, was how much the writ would increase if I dropped Miss World, even the ex Miss World, in the water.

Eventually, we made it, and slithered on our stomachs across next door's lawn until we reached the side door of the garage. We crept in and into the back of a Jaguar. 'If you lie down behind the seats, with the young lady on top of you, I can cover you with this travel rug,' advised the neighbour.

Me, I thought it better not to argue.

My task was to deliver Helen to the office in Holborn while Gavin and Merrin created a diversion. When I heard that the *Express* had managed to get reporters (admittedly former *Mirror* staffmen, who had defected with Hitchen) through our security and onto the *Mirror* editorial floor I'd denounced all arrangements as 'crap' and Dan had said then he'd leave the planning to me.

The scheme I devised involved the neighbour driving us to a lay-by nominated by Gavin where we transferred to a discreet office car. On Blackfriars Bridge we were to meet a *Mirror* dispatch rider who would drive a hundred yards ahead of us and signal the opening of the shutters on the ground floor of the Holborn building. The shutters would close behind us and we'd go straight to the inner entrance of the front door (closed because of IRA bomb threats and *Express* trespassing) and into the executive lift to the third floor where, I insisted, I was to be met by a face I recognised, or Helen and I would continue up through the building.

It worked like a dream, security even joined in the fun by placing two delivery vans between which our car sped, and the vans crashed into each other to ensure that nobody could follow.

John Penrose met us and took us straight to the editor's office where Tony Miles greeted us with a bottle of Champagne.

Back at the house Dan had dug out an old parrot costume, created as part of a joke for Hugh Cudlipp's farewell from the *Mirror*. Either Dan or Merrin wore it, sitting in the back of the yellow Daimler beside the other, who had a blanket over his head. Dan had called the police to clear his gateway and the photographers all snapped away as the trio drove out, and started a merry goose-chase around the back roads of south-east England.

There was more Champagne for us at lunch in the directors' dining room where we celebrated a classic scoop.

Ferrari joined us bringing the latest on the saga. 'Her boyfriend says there are no skeletons in Miss South Africa's cupboard,' he read. 'She is Snow White.'

'That's asking for it', said Mike Molloy, the deputy editor.

'Tomorrow we name the seven dwarfs,' I said.

'Can we do that?' asked Miles, apparently suspecting that I

knew some personal secrets of Miss Kriel's.

'Dopey, Sneezy, Grumpy, Doc...'

'We can't do that,' he said. 'You'd better take Helen round and make peace with the Morleys.'

It was weird. Julia Morley and Helen hugged and kissed each other, then Mrs Morley turned on me. She shouted at me, and said I was personally responsible for wrecking the Miss World contest and that Mecca would be suing me for every penny I had.

Mrs Morley was leaning against the edge of her desk as she harangued me. She was wearing a colourful midi-length skirt and thigh-length peach-coloured suede boots. I interrupted her.

'Mrs Morley, do you think I could ask you a personal question?'

'What is it?' she barked.

'I have this problem, you see…'

'Believe me, you don't know half the problems you've got!'

'I have this other problem. It's that, well, I'm a boot fetishist...'

'A what!'

'I'm sorry, but... well, it's those boots you're wearing. I was wondering how far they went up the leg.'

Astonished, she executed a part-twirl, spinning the pleated skirt to reveal the top of her boots and her fine legs.

'Mrs Morley,' I said. 'Those really are the most beautiful boots I have seen in my entire life!'

'I think,' she said, 'that you can call me Julia.'

That was the night we stayed at the Tower Hotel, booked under assumed names.

The following morning, checking out and attempting to pay by credit card, Gavin, Merrin and I suddenly found ourselves surrounded by the hotel's security. Our cards, of course, were in different names from the rooms. I asked for the manager and told him confidentially about Miss World. He'd been following the story on TV. I told him that Gavin had taken lots of pictures of Helen in her room overlooking the bridge and we would send him a set.

'You should have told me,' he said. 'I'd have laid it all on for you. We're used to that sort of thing, do it all the time. Especially for the *Daily Mail*. I mean, if Mr Crossley or Mr Longmuir ever have anybody they want to keep under wraps, they always bring them here to hide them. Discretion is our watchword.'

I thanked him and said that I would, of course, keep what he had said in mind, and would make a point of telling my news editor.

The following day Gavin had organised a fashion shoot for Helen, to model next season's swim suits. As soon as we arrived they disappeared to the studio and when he showed me the prints I started to write.

> She's still the most beautiful girl in the world because she's been voted more beautiful than the girl who's officially Miss World.

Woman's editor Joyce Hopkirk liked it. It was Friday and the piece was schemed as the centre page spread for Monday morning's paper.

'You can get rid of her now,' Miles told me. Give her some money and get her a taxi to Paddington. Get her on her way home to Wales.'

'What shall I give her?'

'How much have you promised?'

'Well, I never actually promised anything. At the start we talked about the possibility of two –'

'Two thousand? That's fair enough. Write a chit out and I'll sign it so you can give her the cash and get rid of her.'

'How do I get rid of her?'

'Christ knows, cock. Take her to the Stab and ring for a taxi, I suppose.'

'But everybody's still looking for her. They'll be in the Stab.'

'Then take her there and sell her if you like. But get rid!'

I told Helen that although I'd promised her only two hundred pounds she'd been so cooperative that, although it had meant putting my job on the line, I'd said it had to be two thousand or nothing; I couldn't allow her to be misused. She appeared grateful, so I took her to the pub to await the money and the taxi.

There were two old friends of mine, Sunday newspapermen, drinking just inside the door. They offered me a drink and congratulated me on the Miss World scoop. They'd been working on it themselves all week, but were generous enough, by Friday night, to admit defeat.

'By the way,' I said, 'I don't think you've met Helen.'

They offered her a drink, too.

'It must have been a funny old week for you, love, wasn't it?' Trevor Aspinall suggested.

'What do you mean?'

'Well, old Revel here has been holed up all week in hiding with Miss World, hasn't he? You must have been a bit worried about what he was up to with her, eh?'

'Not at all,' said Helen. 'I knew that he would always behave like a total gentleman.'

Then the money, and the taxi arrived. And I never saw her again.

Molloy joined us in the Stab and said well done. I said it wasn't finished yet, and reminded him we had Monday's spread all finished and ready to go.

'We're not using it,' he said.

'Don't be daft.'

'We're not using it because she has hairy arms.'

Gavin joined us. 'What does that mean?'

'Revel's described her as the most beautiful girl in the world and the most beautiful girl in the world does not have hairy arms.'

'Just a minute,' I said. 'Her arms aren't that hairy, and by the time the pictures are reproduced in the paper nobody will know whether her arms are hairy or not...

'Not the point', said Molloy: 'Helen Morgan has hairy arms and therefore she cannot be the most beautiful girl in the world, therefore I have spiked it.'

'Does Hopkirk know about this?' said Gavin. 'She'll go bananas.'

'Yes she does. I admit she's not happy, but she accepts it.'

'Hang on a minute,' I said. 'There's no problem, I'll go back and re-write it. I'll do a different intro.'

'No you won't, said Molloy. 'I've told you, it's out, spiked, finished. End of argument. Now give me some money and I'll buy you a drink.'

'He's pulling your leg,' Gavin told me. 'He always gets like this at the end of the week.' But he wasn't sure.

'Ere,' he said when Miles joined us. 'Mollers says he's spiked the swimsuit spread.'

'That's right.'

'But he can't do that!'

'He's editing the paper on Sunday night. He can do what he likes.'

'Well you tell him!'

'No, I agree with Mike.'

'You know your trouble,' said Gavin. 'You know fuck-all about news, fuck-all about pictures, fuck-all about sport, fuck-all about features, in fact, fuck-all about fuck-all.'

Miles grinned at me, the visitor. 'I don't know why I let him talk to me like this.'

'It's 'cos you know I'm right,' said Gavin.

'I believe you're right when I sign your expenses.'

*

The rest of Fleet Street was as generous in its praise as the two pals in the pub.

The *Sunday Times* compared the handling of the story with *Front Page*, the Hecht and Macarthur play about Chicago newspapers in the thirties, which was enjoying a London revival. Other newspapers, unable to cover the Miss World story, covered the Miss World scoop, instead.

Ever the gent, Hitchen sent a congratulatory telegram to Dan.

And the threatened divorce-case-citing never materialised.

Years later, at a party, I reminded Molloy of the hairy-arm story.

'I had to find a quick excuse to stop it,' he explained. 'There was a chance of selling the *Mirror* to Tiny Rowland and the board told Miles and me to drop the Miss World saga. It had been running for three days and the board classed it as a "sex scandal" and thought it was bad for the paper's image.'

Back down to earth, I had lunch with Leo White, my immediate boss, and pointed out to him that I hadn't had a bad run with major national stories... Princess Anne, Lord Lambton, the nuclear dustbin, Poulson, Maudling, Ted Short, Dan Smith, Andy Cunningham... and most recently Miss World.

I said I wanted to do more of the same.

The other papers called it 'Investigative Journalism'; on the *Mirror* we called it 'Reporting'.

In the way of things, these stories threw up dozens more allegations of corruption and dastardly doings by people of influence – politicians, trade union leaders, public officials and big businessmen – many of which proved impossible (or, at least, too complicated) to substantiate.

But there had been sufficient for me to propose a *Daily Mirror* shock issue entitled BENT BRITAIN.

I even helpfully suggested artwork to illustrate the point: a map of the British Isles twisted into the shape of a pound sign.

But the *Mirror*, perhaps mindful of the motes in its own eye – including the unchecked travel and entertainment expenses paid to journalists who never left the office, shift payments to printers who didn't exist, the accepted theft of thousands of copies of the papers from the print-room every night – decided against it.

In the event, the government took up part of the task itself, establishing a royal commission into *The Standards of Conduct in Public Life* in December 1974. My ultimate boss, editorial director Hugh Cudlipp, who had killed my shock-issue proposal and had recently been knighted, was appointed a member of it and, in between filing stories for the newspaper, I found myself being constantly asked to feed him memos with information and examples about where public standards had clearly fallen short.

Leo said fine – I should continue to do it.

'But you are aware that, historically, the *Mirror* is a Labour-supporting – or anyway at least an anti-Conservative – paper. It might be appreciated by the powers-that-be if you could turn up a bent Tory.' He said he'd give me three weeks to find one. 'Visit your former colleagues at Yorkshire Conservative Newspapers,' he suggested. 'Talk to your pals in the Labour Party and the unions. Go see your old friends John Graham and Chris Buckland in the Commons. I am not saying "bring me the head of a Tory", but I wouldn't object, if you did.'

It was an excuse for a number of good lunches and, not surprisingly, nearly everybody I spoke to could name 'a bent Tory'.

Nobody, however, could produce a single jot of usable evidence. Everything was unsubstantiated rumour and innuendo.

Over lunch in the House of Commons John Graham, by now political editor of the *Sunday Mirror,* called over Chris Buckland, the *Daily Mirror* political correspondent who had been chef-de-bureau in Belfast when I had gone to help cover The Troubles.

'Old Revel here has got a doddle of an assignment,' said John. 'They want him to find a bent Tory.'

'Pick a name,' Chris told me. 'There's about three hundred of them in this building.'

'Okay,' said John. 'So let's help him find one.'

But you can't just wander through Annie's Bar, the Terrace or the Members' Lobby and say – as I had said more or less in confidence to John – 'I'm looking for a bent Tory MP'.

We got busy (there were seventeen bars and restaurants in Parliament), talking to other journalists and MPs, and enjoying the occasional drink while fairly obliquely directing the conversation into the direction we hoped it would go.

'Something will come of this,' said John, with absolute confidence.

Nothing did... at least, not until I was back home in Northumberland and wondering how to break the news to Leo of my miserable failure.

The phone rang. 'Are you the guy I met in Annie's bar who writes about what MPs get up to, outside the Commons? The one who did Poulson and Maudling and Ted Short? I might have a story for you...'

Jeffrey Archer opened the door of his home with a warm and welcoming smile. 'Revel!' he said. 'Good to see you again. Come in.... what would you like to drink?'

I had telephoned him the previous night, a Saturday, and said I wanted to see him. He'd suggested I should come round in the morning, 'after church', which I thought was a nice touch. I opted for coffee and when he reappeared with a tray he repeated: 'It's good to see you again. How long is it now, since...?'

The Tory MP for Louth, Lincolnshire, seemed so delighted to see me that I felt almost ungracious in accepting his hospitality while informing him that, in fact, we had never met.

'Come on,' he said, as if jogging my memory or even playing along with a silly joke while I tried to find room to place a saucer among his coffee-table books ...'We were at Oxford together!'

No, I said firmly; we were certainly not at Oxford together, and Archer immediately corrected himself: 'I mean we were *in* Oxford, *at the same time.'*

It appeared to be a touchy matter. 'At Oxford' implied that you were there doing a degree. Archer was slightly sensitive about the fact that, although he had studied at an Oxford College (Brasenose) and had represented the university in athletics as 'an Oxford student', unlike the rest of them he had never been there as an undergraduate. He didn't have the O-level in Latin that was a *sine qua non* for admission to an Oxford college; he hadn't even passed O-level English. He had been taking a diploma in education – a DipEd – rather than a degree and, as far as I was aware, he hadn't completed it, even though he spent three years on what was normally a one-year course. I never discovered where (if anywhere) he had gained the BSc or the BA that was sometimes tacked after his name.

But I wasn't there to discuss semantics, nor did I wish to embarrass the MP about his dubious history; I was interested only in his current predicament.

Archer, however, wasn't ready to give up. 'Are you sure you

weren't up at Oxford when I was there?' he asked, as if it might somehow have slipped my mind. 'Because when you telephoned and said who you were, I knew your name immediately.'

I told him that might be because he would see it, most days, in the pages of the *Daily Mirror*.

'I see lots of names in the *Daily Mirror*, every day,' he said. 'Why would I have remembered yours?'

'Probably,' I told him, 'because I write mainly about bent politicians.'

'So,' he asked with an air of apparent mystification, 'why have you come to see me, then?'

*

Our extensive cuttings library hadn't had much on file about the life, to date, of the 34-year-old MP. There was no mention of his jobs, teaching physical education at a couple of public schools, of his officer cadetship in the Duke of Wellington's Regiment of Yorkshire, nor even that he had briefly been a constable with the Metropolitan Police. He had made little impact as an elected member of the Greater London Council or as an appointee to the Inner London Education Authority. There was, however, no shortage of rumour and innuendo about his past.

While at – or, rather, in – Oxford he had discovered that he'd a natural flair for fund-raising and had enlisted the support (albeit it fairly remotely) of The Beatles in a campaign on behalf of Oxfam. He had arranged a meeting with the group and with Prime Minister Harold Macmillan, which went awry when The Beatles failed to turn up for it.

He did get them there later. In the gents toilet Ringo asked the critic Sheridan Morley, then a student at Merton, if he knew 'this Jeffrey Archer bloke'. Morley said everyone in Oxford was trying to work out who he was. Ringo told him: 'He strikes me as a nice enough fella, but he's the kind of bloke who would bottle your piss and sell it.'

Thereafter there would be stories floating about of discrepancies between the amounts projected or reportedly raised by Archer's efforts and the cash actually received, by Oxfam, the National

Birthday Trust, the United Nations Association and the European Movement

He was known as 'Mr Ten-per-cent' on two counts – it was said that he had offered to write the expenses for fellow GLC councillors in return for a tenth of the amounts they claimed, and that he had asked for a similar deal with money he raised for charity.

Harold Wilson had reportedly withdrawn his personal support for the European Movement saying that if he persuaded a rich businessman to donate, say, £10,000, he would consider it objectionable to see £1,000 of it going automatically to a private fund-raiser. Meanwhile, Humphry Berkeley, who was chairing the United Nations Association, let it be known that he was unhappy about Archer's own claims for expenses – including charges for taxis where a car had been sent for him, and for restaurant meals that other people had paid for.

Apart from fairly broad and meaningless hints, very little of this ever stood up well enough to make it into public print. The word commonly used to describe him was 'controversial'.

He certainly had no shortage of enemies who would tell you, *inter alia*, that he had represented Oxford as an athlete (he ran 100 yards in 9.6 seconds 'with the wind behind him') and even become president of the OUAC while not actually on the books of any college. He gained a Blue competing against Cambridge – which still rankles among the 'official' Blues at Oxford even more than it does with Cambridge who his team thrashed at the White City stadium in 1966.

They said he claimed to have been at Wellington College, rather than at the less prestigious Wellington School; but, if it was true that he ever did that, I found no evidence of it. Oh well, countered his detractors, if anybody else said that it was Wellington College Archer never bothered to deny it...

From the age of 29 he had enjoyed the benefit of the safe Tory seat in Louth. Provided only that he kept his nose clean, he had a job there for life. But after almost five years he was going nowhere politically. Youth and energy were on his side but he was overlooked for even minor government roles.

Although he projected himself as a popular figure, the truth was that he was anything but that. What most people seemed to object to was that he was a pushy self-promoting young – and apparently rich – MP who claimed to be the youngest member in the House, whereas in truth there were several who were younger, starting with the 22-year-old Bernadette McAliskey (better known as Bernadette Devlin).

Worse, he let it be known that he was a millionaire.

This, he certainly was not; the story I had uncovered was that he was actually well out of his depth in debt.

It was straightforward enough. In the autumn of 1972 Archer had been given a tip to buy shares in a Canadian company called Aquablast developing a component to reduce exhaust emission in cars that was likely to be adopted by all car manufacturers.

His problem was that he didn't have any money to buy them. Looking round his wealthy contacts he targeted Anthony Bamford, son of J C Bamford, the boss of JCB earth-moving vehicles. Bamford junior had been hailed as Young Exporter of the Year (in those days Britain still took manufacturing and exporting seriously) and Archer talked him into a loan of £172,000 to buy 50,000 shares at £3.40 each.

In 1972-74 £172,000 was serious money. An MP's salary was £4,500. Archer's main home, a Georgian-style house in The Boltons, South Kensington, was worth an estimated £100,000 – it could be closer to £100million at today's (2015) prices.

Bamford told me: 'He said the shares would be the next Poseidon and it was too good an opportunity to miss, so I loaned him the money. He said there was no way I could lose on the arrangement.' The deal was that since Bamford was putting up all the capital but taking none of the risk, he would receive one-third of any profit, while Archer would keep two-thirds.

Both men must have been aware that shares in Poseidon, a nickel-mining company in Australia, rocketed in 1969 from 80 cents to well over $300, and then in 1970 crashed just as quickly. And when Aquablast shares plummeted to a few pennies each, the Canadian stock exchange suspended dealing and ordered an
132

investigation into fraudulent trading. At this stage Bamford asked for his money back and Archer obviously didn't have the wherewithal to pay him, nor anything like that amount of money.

Therefore Archer was insolvent and Bamford told me he was prepared to make the MP bankrupt in a bid to recover his own outlay.

And that, I was now telling the MP for Louth, was why I was visiting his second home – a converted farmhouse in Brigsley, near Grimsby, worth about £23,000 – and suggesting that he resign as a Member of Parliament. I said I didn't need to remind him that bankrupts were not allowed to be MPs.

Archer's face went from cheerful to black. 'Get out of my house!'

I told him I hadn't finished my coffee and his natural sense of hospitality briefly took over.

'Finish it,' he said. 'And leave.'

While I sipped slowly from the cup I told him that I could be helpful to him. The story would come out anyway. He could explain his side of it to me and I would report it faithfully and fairly. The alternative would be that all the newspapers would go at it, reporting bits and pieces, probably getting parts of it wrong and keeping it going for weeks – whereas if he gave the details to me it would be no more than an overnight wonder, and would then almost certainly be dropped and soon forgotten. But I needed him to tell me that he would resign as an MP.

'Finish your coffee,' he said again, 'and leave. What you are saying is completely libellous. You will be hearing from my solicitor.' So I gave him my business card and left, mildly protesting that I thought this was a regrettable way for him to treat an old Varsity chum.

His solicitor telephoned me that same Sunday afternoon and told me I clearly did not understand the laws relating to reporting bankruptcy.

Victor Mishcon was, I knew, a lawyer of fearsome reputation (years later, as Lord Mishcon, he would be adviser to Diana, Princess of Wales) – and also a Labour politician. I said that after two years shadowing John Poulson there was probably little that I didn't know about bankruptcy law, but I would be obliged to hear his point of view.

The lawyer's interpretation was the same as mine: that you could not report any pending or likely bankruptcy as such, you had to wait until it happened, or at least until the debtor admitted it – which was what I had been hoping to get Archer to do.

And that might have been the end of my involvement or interest in the story except that both Archer and Mishcon complained about me to *Mirror* chairman Hugh Cudlipp who, reasonably, thought that I had done nothing wrong. He said that, while the *Mirror* would never countenance harassing anybody to get a story, there was no reason why I shouldn't maintain contact with the MP, and check from time to time whether he had changed his mind about telling all to our newspaper.

Archer, to be fair, was always polite. He said on one occasion that his friend Bamford didn't have a case because everybody knew that the stock market was a gamble and that shares could go down as well as up. But I obviously needed to remind the MP that Bamford had not actually bought any shares – the clear documentary evidence was that he had loaned Archer money, and now he simply wanted the loan repaid. On Cudlipp's advice I logged each conversation with the head of the *Mirror* in-house legal department and on August 22 the lawyer phoned me.

'Your friend Archer is a fool,' our barrister said. 'He has just announced that he will not be seeking re-election because of what he says are severe financial problems. It is now open to you to say what those difficulties are. Just... well, you know... skate around the use of the actual word bankruptcy.'

The following day's rival newspapers carried the bald statement, as Archer had issued it to the Press Association, saying that he would not be standing in the next general election. The *Daily Mirror* carried the front-page exclusive story that I had been sitting on for about four months, detailing the reasons behind his financial embarrassment.

In contrast with his earlier days his life thereafter has been well documented. With no proper job to occupy him he immediately took to writing books. His advances were soon reported (at least by him) to be millions of dollars and it must be said that he apparently repaid every penny of his considerable indebtedness.

Chris Buckland met him one day in the departure lounge at Heathrow and, perhaps rather sarcastically, enquired about what he was doing.

'I'm writing books,' Archer told him.

'Oh, good. Have you had anything published yet?'

'All of these…' said Archer. And he stepped aside to reveal the W H Smith display stand of hardback and paperback copies of *Not a Penny More, Not a Penny Less* (1975), *Shall We Tell the President?* (1977), and *Kane and Abel* (1979).

Chris rang me from the airport. 'If Archer wasn't a millionaire when you first met him, he surely is one now,' he said. 'Thanks to you.'

That wasn't quite the end of my distant relationship with Archer. In 1980 I walked into the office of Nick (now Sir Nick) Lloyd when he was deputy editor of the *Sunday Mirror* and found him talking to Jeffrey Archer. Nick had edited *Cherwell*, the Oxford student newspaper, while studying at St Edmund Hall and had run stories in it about Archer's fund raising activities with The Beatles for Oxfam.

I apologised for the intrusion and as I withdrew Archer said: 'I know him!'

'Of course you do,' said Nick. 'That was Revel Barker.'

'Oh yes,' said Archer. 'Wasn't he at Oxford with us?'

Later still – in fact while the first of his several trials was taking place in the Royal Courts of Justice at the other side of The Strand – while keeping an appointment for lunch at the Savoy Grill I realised that I needed to walk past the table where Archer was sitting with his wife Mary (an Oxford graduate).

He caught my eye and stood up to greet me as an old friend. As we shook hands he said he didn't think I knew his wife, and introduced us. We also shook hands and as I moved away I heard him answer her quizzical expression: '…He was at Oxford with us.'

*

Sorting unsubstantiated rumour and innuendo from the truth, fact from fiction, wheat from chaff, was what reporters were supposed to do.

Harold Wilson was supposedly 'an agent of influence' for the KGB. MI5 believed it, for a time, and bugged his office and the Cabinet Room. They also bugged between sixteen and twenty MPs, most but not all of them members of the Labour Party.

'I am not going to tell you their names,' my source said. 'But you can probably work them out for yourself.'

John Stonehouse, former Labour postmaster general, former minister for aviation, was believed (rightly as we later established) to be in the pay of the Czech secret service. He obviously wasn't being paid sufficiently well because, while Jeffrey Archer was agonising about his own financial status, Stonehouse, at the other side of the House, was going bankrupt. It was no secret that his ambitions were to become a millionaire and then prime minister, but he didn't have either the luck or the nous for the first, nor the party popularity for the second.

In an effort to make some money to support a wife, three children, and a mistress, he started a parliamentary consultancy company. When that failed he started another, knowing as an economist that with a little creative accounting he could transfer debts between them. After the second company failed he opened another... until he had twenty-four in all, by which time he had attracted the attention of the Department of Trade and Industry.

Rather than face the music he decided his best course of action would be to disappear completely and started making plans. He was inspired by a book and a movie, The Day of the Jackal, in which a man took a dead person's identity and adopted it as his own.

In late November 1974 a pile of his clothes was found on a Miami beach. There was no sign of him and it was assumed he had gone swimming and either drowned or been eaten by a shark. When his business dealings became known it was considered as a possible suicide. (A remarkably similar story, a TV comedy called The Fall and Rise of Reggie Perrin, in which the lead character faked his death by drowning, was actually broadcast only after the event.)

'Another MP for you, my dear,' called Dan Ferrari from London. 'And looks like another fraud. Get yourself down here to work on it, will you?'

One minute's silence was held in Parliament to mark his presumed passing. But Dan's gut reaction had been to doubt the suicide story, and even the death, from the start. But if Stonehouse was no longer in America (which he thought likely) where would he be? Most probably back somewhere in Europe, thought Dan.

When I arrived in the London office reporters John Penrose and Richard Stott were patiently working through the RAC *Continental Touring Guide,* phoning top hotels to ask after anybody called Stonehouse booking in as a guest.

My scouring of his company documents suggested that the MP was anything but broke: he could possibly have taken tens of thousands of pounds with him – except that it wasn't his own money. He had also taken out six separate life insurance policies with his wife as the beneficiary.

Then a break: police in Melbourne Australia had spotted an Englishman behaving oddly. He was transferring money between bank accounts in different names; he was also avidly reading the British newspapers.

They wondered whether he might be Lord Lucan – who had disappeared two weeks before Stonehouse after killing his children's nanny in Belgravia – or maybe even John Stonehouse. They asked Scotland Yard to send photographs of both men. Dan's hunch had been right; it was Stonehouse.

Another wayward and bent MP was exactly what Fleet Street wanted for Christmas.

The *Daily Express* put twenty reporters on it, including its cricket correspondent who was already there; the *News of the World* sent nine journalists with £15,000 in cash to attempt to buy the MP's story while *The Times* told its Sydney-based opera critic to cover it.

The *Mirror* waited until Scotland Yard headed for Heathrow, then sent one reporter. Richard Stott (later *Mirror* editor) was our Stonehouse Team. He got the interview and the best story.

So how had the MP got there? Syd Young in the New York office had also started calling hotels. One of them told him that a guy who looked like the picture in the papers had stayed there, only he hadn't been called Stonehouse. He was – 'Just a minute, while I check the files' – calling himself Joseph Markham.

Had he made any long-distance telephone calls while staying as a guest at the hotel? – 'Oh, we couldn't possibly tell you that.'

So Syd asked to speak to the manager.

'Here's an astonishing coincidence,' said the hotel boss. 'I'm British, from Burnley, and when I was at school I sat next to a kid called Syd Young, who always wanted to be a reporter…'

Friends reunited and Syd called the office with a London phone number that had been used by Markham, aka John Stonehouse MP. And we quickly established that Joseph Markham was the name of one of his (dead) constituents in Walsall North who had been born in the same year as the MP.

The number belonged to a small hotel in Belsize Park, Hampstead. A quick call to it produced nothing, so the information was passed to Scotland Yard who, as was their wont, leaked the information to everybody. Dan sent a reporter who found the hotel besieged, and the front doors locked against hordes of pressmen.

Assuming that none of them would know me by sight, I rang the hotel, said I was in London for the Smithfield Show, and booked a room.

Allowed in, I dropped my membership card to Newcastle Farmers' Club on the stairs as I was being led to my room. The owner's wife found it and brought it up to me.

'Thank god you found it,' I told her. 'You know, you can get great discounts at the Show if you have this card.'

She wasn't to know that the 'Farmers' Club' in Newcastle was actually an after-hours drinking dive near the station, mostly favoured by railwaymen and reporters.

I asked her what all the fuss outside was about and she told me that journalists were trying to find out about a woman called Sheila Buckley, who had stayed at the hotel a couple of times recently – and coincidentally had been given my room. 'She worked for that MP who has gone missing, John Stonehouse.'

Sheila Buckley did more than that, I knew. She was both his secretary and his mistress.

But I told her I didn't think there had been anything about that story in the *Northumberland Gazette*.

My room was an opportunity for a photograph, so I went down to the front door, unlocked it, and waved *Mirror* photographer Harry Prosser inside. He took pictures of my room but was spotted with his camera as he was leaving.

The manager, built like a rugby forward, picked Harry up bodily and ran with him, using the little snapper as a battering ram, opening the double glass doors with Harry's head (and cracking the glazing, in the process). Then, because I had been with him, he turned on me and punched me in the stomach.

As I collapsed into a chair his wife told him: 'You shouldn't have done that – he's a guest, not a reporter! He's just come down today from Newcastle.'

The hotelier apologised. 'I'm at the end of my tether,' he explained. 'I am sick of it. That MP, John Stonehouse, rang here from Hawaii a couple of times to speak to his secretary and now all hell has broken loose, as you can see.'

'When did all that happen?'

He produced the hotel register and read the dates.

'It's a pity you're not licensed,' I said, because my stomach really hurts where you hit me. I need a drink. Do you have a back door I could use?'

No worries, he said. He had called the police. When they arrived he asked them to see me safely to my car. 'Don't let those people get to him, he's a guest.'

I drove to a call box and rang Dan, who was staying back late to supervise the developing story.

'Excellent,' he said. 'Now get back to the office sharpish. They are opening champagne in the newsroom.'

But by the time I arrived it had all been drunk.

When Dan eventually left for home the entire newsroom – reporters, photographers and sub-editors – stood and applauded him.

I suspect that was a first. It may also have been a last. Journalists simply didn't behave like that.

*

Nor did they behave in the way that, we were to learn to our horror, the succeeding generation of reporters acted. There were no cell phones to 'hack'. Even the security services required (at least in theory) Home Office permission if they wanted to bug a phone. No self-respecting reporter would dream of employing a 'private detective' to make his enquiries for him. Technology was in its infancy, but even if it had been available, we didn't need it.

I was once loaned a gadget that purported to tell whether a phone was bugged. It seemed to work, but was of no practical use.

A friend gave me a device that would bug a room and transmit to an FM radio about fifty feet away, but I had no occasion to use it.

An executive on the paper asked whether he could borrow it 'to play with over the weekend, for a bit of fun'. He plugged the transmitter, which looked like an innocent three-way adaptor, into a socket in his dining room and, while entertaining guests to dinner and clearing the plates with his wife, went into his kitchen to listen to the conversation.

What he heard was:

'Why did you tell her that was delicious? It was absolutely fucking terrible.'

'I know. I was just trying to be polite…'

The *Daily Mail* investigations team persuaded a Labour councillor to take a small portable tape-recorder into a meeting where they would be choosing what was likely to be a 'loony left' candidate for Parliament.

He sat with the reporters in their car while they showed him how to use it, and practised with it.

When the selection process started the councillor reached into his pocket and pressed the button… The wrong button. The committee room was suddenly filled with the echoing sound of *Testing, testing, one-two-three-four… Mary had a little lamb…*

The most sophisticated equipment any of us ever had was probably a telephone recorder – and even that was illegal unless
140

you warned the person at the other end of the line, at the start of the conversation, that it was being recorded.

*

Dan Ferrari said he didn't know, off the top of his head, how many reporters and writers he had at his disposal, north and south and world-wide. I thought it would probably be about a hundred.

'Say that on at least two days every week, a hundred days a year, the front page is decided for us with breaking news,' he said.

'Now what if each member of the staff brought in or found and developed an exclusive angle to a story, only twice a year... Wouldn't we have the best newspaper in the world?'

'We already have the best paper in the world,' I said.

'Yes,' said Dan. 'I suppose we have.'

13. Sunday best

When Bob Edwards was appointed editor of the *Sunday Mirror* in 1972 it got him into the *Guinness Book of Records* as 'the Fleet Street editor who has worked on the most titles'. Not an earth-shattering achievement, perhaps, but a record of sorts. He would remain in the job for nearly thirteen years, itself a record on that newspaper.

He had identified his future career – his ultimate ambition being to edit the *Daily Express* – when he won a prize for writing in the school magazine. After national service and the *Reading Mercury* he joined the Labour Party and met Michael Foot, editor of *Tribune*.

He was offered a job and by 26 was the editor. He came to the notice of Lord Beaverbrook and was offered a pay rise and a leader writer's job on the *Evening Standard*; Foot had already been recruited. Edwards stood for parliament as a Labour candidate and refused to write leaders supporting the Suez War in 1956. He nevertheless moved quickly up through the system, becoming deputy editor of the *Sunday Express*, then managing editor and eventually editor of the *Daily Express*.

An accomplishment, unnoticed by *Guinness*, was that Bob, uniquely, held the editorship twice. He could – and would – stop conversation at dinner with the words, 'I remember when I was fired as *Express* editor, for the *second* time...'

It was a good story. His son, Josh, told him the report of his dismissal had been on the BBC TV six o'clock news. Bob said he shouldn't worry – they would keep the house, the car and the yacht, that there was a mysterious freemasonry called 'the editors' club' and he would be found another job, somewhere. He had misread the youngster's concern: Josh feared his school chums might rib him, hearing that his father had been fired. Bob told him: 'If that happens, just ask them, if their daddy had been sacked, would it have been on the six o'clock news?'

Shortly after the first firing, Beaverbrook had relented. He sent him to Glasgow to edit the *Evening Citizen* and after a year in exile brought him back as editor of the group's flagship daily, where he remained until 1965, the year after the proprietor's death. Those were heady days: the *Express* had the biggest team of journalists in the history of British newspapers. In 1963 Edwards introduced the paper to cheque-book journalism by buying up Christine Keeler's memoirs for £2,000. Inspired by the lay-out genius of associate editor Harold Keeble, he also created Photonews – allotting the top half of page three to the best photograph of the day.

With sales of 4,382,500 during his first term as editor the paper was the largest selling daily on earth. It targeted the aspirational wannabes of the Swinging Sixties. Hugh Cudlipp sneered that 'it pretends to have a readership of two-car families with 2.4 children in semi-detached mock-Tudor homes – but they're not like that, they are merely people who want to be like that.'

The point was not lost on the editor. When his assistant, George Millar, pointed out one night that the paper had four stories about public schools, whereas their readers couldn't afford private education, Edwards, who had been a prep-school boarder, told him: 'I know they can't. But they like to think that the editor thinks they can.'

The *Express* would be toppled as best-seller in 1965 by the *Mirror*, which achieved five million a day – but only after Edwards had left. The editorship of the *People* (1966-72) was more comfortable politically for him, if only because he no longer needed to follow the 'ludicrous political persuasions' of his megalomaniac former boss.

Edwards – effectively a champagne socialist with Savile Row suits, hand-rolled cigars and a castle in Oxfordshire – always claimed to be working class, sometimes describing his father, who had never troubled Bob's mother with the formality of marriage, as 'a milkman', although in fact he had been a director of United Dairies. Now he had a totally Labour-supporting – and non-aspirational – mass readership drawn almost wholly from the downtrodden classes.

From Sam Campbell he took over a fiercely campaigning newspaper that under legendary crime reporter Duncan Webb largely cleaned up the protection rackets and brothels of London's Soho. Edwards continued in much the same spirit, exposing bent detectives on the take from pornographers and 'vice kings'. It required a certain amount of bravery: Webb's life had (allegedly) been threatened so often he worked behind a screen of 'bullet-proof' glass. This was during an era in which Sir Robert Mark, the Met police commissioner, said he aspired to arrest more criminals than he employed. And when Scotland Yard got nowhere tackling internal corruption, Edwards, *Express*-style, put teams of hard-nosed reporters on the job.

The *People* circulation, already more than five million, increased while he was at the helm; but it dropped 250,000 in 1970 when he fearlessly exposed a 21-year-old cold-blooded British army massacre of Malaysian civilians suspected of harbouring terrorists, a scoop that many readers (and politicians) considered to be disloyal to 'Our Boys'...

His final editorship, of the *Sunday Mirror*, suited him best. Now the readership was what would become known as the 'sane left', and what Bob would describe as 'nice people'. In fact he saw them as being very much like *Express* readers (more than 40 per cent of whom, according to a contemporary readership survey, also voted Labour).

But despite his record-breaking achievements he was seen as cautious; under him the tabloid was never reported to the Press Council (almost certainly another record). The *Sunday Mirror* was the first newspaper to learn the sordid details of the 'Jeremy Thorpe affair' from a dossier brought in by builders who discovered it while clearing a house. It was a story for which his contemporaries would have given their eye-teeth, but Edwards handed it to the politician, keeping a copy in his safe until it was exposed by rival papers.

After – and sometimes during – the reporting of Poulson, Maudling, Ted Short, Lord Lambton, Archer, Stonehouse and the rest most newspapers were establishing what they described as investigation departments. The *Sunday Times* had already set up 'Insight', which exposed the evil effects of thalidomide and the

144

manufacture of nuclear weapons by Israel; the *Daily Mail* created 'Newssight'.

Bob Edwards wanted the *Sunday Mirror* to be in on the fashion and he had originally appointed James Pettigrew as his 'investigative reporter'.

Pettigrew had produced a remarkably good Shock Issue for the *Daily Mirror* on housing that had been highly praised in Parliament, so Bob thought he was the man for the job.

Actually James had gone to the north-east, knocked on the door of a run-down council house, introduced himself to the housewife and told her he had 'come to write about squalor'. She was a *Mirror* reader, so invited him in, and he asked whether she had that morning's edition. She moved the cat off it and showed it to James, possibly thinking she had won some sort of prize. But he opened it at the centre pages, spread it on the sofa, and sat on it.

Bob sent him to Switzerland to investigate and 'expose' a professor offering a 'rejuvenation treatment' involving monkey glands. James decided that the way to expose it was to sign up for the full course regardless of expense and it ran in the paper as a three-week sensation.

Pictorial evidence seemed to show that he did in fact look considerably younger and James, between marriages at the time, reported that his 'love-life' was better than ever.

But weeks away from the office... and a big bill... even if it was recovered by a massive increase in sales...

So his next assignment was much closer to home, and less expensive. When an eagle called Goldie escaped from London Zoo James was sent to find it.

Goldie was reported to be still in the vicinity so he was instructed to hire an eagle outfit from Berman's, the theatrical costumiers, then take lessons in how big birds strutted on the ground and the rate and fashion in which they flapped their wings, and told to stalk Regent's Park. Nothing came of it and Bob's first sortie into 'investigations' was abandoned.

Jimmy Pettigrew would have his unique moment of glory when Lord Lucan, who lived next door to him in Lower Belgrave Street, mistakenly staggered, literally drunk as a lord, into the Pettigrew home before going to his own house and bludgeoning his children's nanny to death, under the drunken impression that he was killing his wife.

After Poulson *et al* Bob decided to try again and tempted me to defect from the *Daily Mirror* to work with George Martin and Victor Sims, two old reporters (I use the adjective kindly, but they could probably have given me more than twenty years each), and men of immense experience. He created his *Sunday Mirror* Investigations Bureau afresh.

What Bob had forgotten was that 'investigations' required both time and money. The biggest obstacle once again was time. Sunday newspapers usually had a week to work on a story, and that was generally considered sufficient. A thorough investigation, handled properly, could take weeks or months.

I was given a story to chase about a racketeering landlord and shot off to Manchester to 'investigate' it, but it didn't stand up. Another, about suspected mis-spending by a charity, also failed; whoever had told the paper about it had simply got it wrong.

Six weeks on the staff and I hadn't had a word in print. My father phoned to ask whether I was ill.

With nothing to do, no story to write, I called Donald Herrod, Poulson's former defence counsel – who was by now a judge – for a chat. When I whined to him about my lack of productivity he told me to phone Poulson's trustee in bankruptcy, a Leeds solicitor.

'It's all happening, here,' the trustee told me.

People who had been the recipients of the corrupt architect's largesse had started to pay back their ill-gotten gains. Four and a half years earlier he had gone bankrupt with debts of £247,000. When I called him the trustee had recovered more than £300,000, with promises of more to come.

Even Andy Cunningham, the grasping 'Lord High Everything' in County Durham, had met all the trustee's claims. Some of the other repayments were from people who had gone to jail; some were from people who had narrowly escaped it.

It was lunchtime on Saturday. I told Joe Grizzard, the deputy editor, what I had learnt and I could immediately see the cogs in his brain start to turn, thinking in headlines.

'These repayments are mostly bribes?'

'Yes.'

'Then you have the splash tonight.'

The paper led with POULSON BRIBES BONANZA.

It certainly looked like the result of an 'investigation', but had taken about half an hour to compile.

And I was back in business.

The next one took Victor Sims and me a couple of weeks to uncover but we eventually revealed that eighteen heart patients had died after being prescribed a 'life-saving drug'. Newspapers love medical stories, they are even happier when they lead to a Parliamentary Inquiry. This one scored on both counts.

'WONDER DRUG' SHOCK was the splash headline.

I got a charity-style agency, set up to provide work for jobless youngsters, closed after revealing that it was creaming a fiver each off their weekly government grants. That came from a friend in Newcastle – as did the story that energy secretary Tony Benn had ordered a stop to Britain's fuel expansion programme after learning that the nation currently had too much of it.

One of my old prison contacts told me that pop-singer Janie Jones, serving seven years for controlling prostitutes, had had her mink coat burned by other inmates in Holloway Jail. (Women prisoners were allowed to wear their own clothing, and Jones had been the first woman prisoner to have a bubble bath in jail.)

My prison pals stayed in touch. From one of them I learnt of a Home Office decision that Moors murderer Myra Hindley would never be freed. This made a full page – MYRA 'IS TOO EVIL TO FREE'. And was followed the next week with a list of male killers about whom the same decision had been made: THE NO-HOPE LIFERS.

Both stories brought complaints to the editor from the self-styled 'prison reformer' Lord Longford, who said that whoever was feeding me with this information was clearly in breach of the Official Secrets Act.

Bob Edwards told him: 'Frank, I didn't take any notice of the Act when I was in the RAF. Why do you think I would concern myself with it now?'

News editor Graham Gadd had heard of a racket to provide British wives for illegal immigrants so that they could stay in the country – and even that one woman had 'married' seventy-five foreigners for £300 a time.

'Seventy-five?' I said. 'It must be possible to find at least one of them.' And I did. Photographer John Cleeve and I had to chase him through the restaurant and kitchen of a burger joint in Wembley but when we caught up with him he agreed to talk and even to be photographed. I had the front again:

HOW I BOUGHT A BRIDE – SUNDAY MIRROR EXCLUSIVE.

So that was the trick: instant 'investigations'.

My next Page One splash was – I am happy to report – inspired in the Stab over a couple of pints with my chum Alasdair Buchan who pointed out that there was to be a massive anti-race march in London on the following Sunday, so wouldn't it be a great idea for the paper to run an exposé of the racist National Front that would coincide with it.

I agreed, provided that we would work on it together, for Al (whose parents were both MPs) was interested in politics while my interest was restricted to the politicians. I'd met Kingsley Read (a graduate of Leeds University) who'd been chairman of the NF before resigning to form the National Party which had won two seats on Blackburn Council; Read won one of them but the other councillor was disqualified over 'election irregularities'. I thought he might have something interesting to say about his old comrades.

He had quite a lot, especially about his successor and former deputy John Tyndall. But he also mentioned in passing that the NF had banned three little girls from marching in a pipe band during the London Cenotaph ceremony on Remembrance Day – on the basis of 'race'.

We struck gold there, for Alasdair had been at the wreath-laying, and had noted the name of the band hired by the Front, possibly with a view to enquiring, some time in the future on a quiet day, about the connection, if any, between the NF and a children's band.

The band was traced and the story stood up; National Front party officials had spotted three twelve-year-old girls and told the band organiser: 'Take them out. We are not having coloureds.'

And the girls volunteered to stay on the coach rather than spoil the day for their friends.

So the following Sunday's front page would be:

VICTIMS OF HATE.

And for reasons best known to himself Front chairman John Tyndall agreed to be interviewed by Alasdair and me, so the spread across pages six and seven was:

THE MAN WHO WANTS TO BE FÜHRER,

Another instant production.

I had never been on a march or a 'demo', but Alasdair asked: 'How can you produce a paper like that and not go along to support the cause – or at least to watch it in action?'

So I went. Police lined the route from Marble Arch to Trafalgar Square. So did the *Sunday Mirror* news vendors, who had to call for extra copies. Most of the marchers found the front page irresistible. It was a rare example of seeing what sells newspapers.

John Tyndall was livid, not least because the 'wants to be führer' line and some of the other content came from our interview with Read, rather than from him. He threatened to sue us. Bob Edwards, who had never been on the receiving end of a writ, said he was looking forward to it, but Tyndall eventually thought better of it.

Only a few days later two men buzzed on the answerphone at the door of the block of flats where I was living.

'Mr Barker… We are home security specialists. Can we come up and talk to you about better security for your home?'

'Why would I need extra security?'

'Well, mainly because of the job you do.'

'What job is that?'

No answer.

'I don't need extra security, which is why you can't get in.'

When I mentioned the visit, totally informally, to a friend in the Special Branch I pointed out that my name was not in the London telephone directory and nor was it on the front door.

'That will have been the National Front,' he said. 'They'll have got your home address from their members among your printers. They're supposedly all ardent trade unionists and left-wingers, but a lot of them support the Front. It's odd really – the *Daily Telegraph* has more Commies on its editorial staff than the *Morning Star*; most of the *Daily Express* are Labour supporters, and the majority of *Mirror* staff are Tories.'

*

It all goes to show that you can't judge by appearances.

Talking to some people who had been at Trinity, Cambridge, with Prince Charles I heard the seemingly unlikely story that the heir to the throne had toyed with the idea of joining the university's Labour Club.

It sounded unreal, but they told me he had been influenced by a student friend with rooms on the same staircase.

Some said that he had been persuaded after actually attending a meeting of the Club – which sounded even more unlikely.

Trinity, which could claim to have produced more Nobel Prize winners than the whole of France, had also educated traitors like Kim Philby, Donald Maclean, Guy Burgess and Anthony Blunt. Perhaps there was a left-wing bug in the college air.

It could certainly make a piece, if true. So I asked Lord 'Rab' Butler, who had been Master of Trinity when Charles was there.

'Well, yes…' he told me. 'The Prince used to come to see me to ask for advice and on this occasion he asked whether I thought it would be all right for him to join the University Labour Club.

The Master's immediate response: 'Hell, no!'

So it stood up. The boy most likely to succeed could have been set to become the first King – perhaps of any country – to have been a member of the Labour Party.

A day's work… another 'instant' investigation.

Having escaped conscription I quite enjoyed being with the army – exercising with the Yorkshire Hussars, a territorial unit, on Catterick Moor, flying out to British Honduras with the Green Howards, training in Germany for 'IS' (internal security) operations in Northern Ireland, then reporting 'The Troubles' there.

Part of the attraction, without doubt, was that national newspapermen were given the 'equivalent rank' of major. In BH that entitled me to the services of a 'batman' and a driver.

The army also enjoyed entertaining 'friendlies' from the press and endeavoured to involve them fully.

At Catterick I was blown off my feet by a 'Thunderflash', a type of dummy grenade that landed between them and is officially 'noisy but harmless'. But my slit trench was dug for me by a sergeant-major.

Reporters were shown how to fire machine guns and drive tanks. I went on a sniper's course where, just as you got a gunman in your sights, there was a strong likelihood of a woman pushing a pram crossing your line of fire.

On a moonless night I ventured along 'Booby-Trap Alley' which involved spotting trip-wires and other obstacles on a forest path. (If disturbed they triggered thunderflashes.)

I trekked through dense jungle with the Gurkhas and even drove army helicopters in BH, Berlin, Denmark and north Italy.

Later we would hear of journalists being 'embedded' with the forces when covering wars. An interesting terminology. Was it a good idea for us to get so close to the armed forces?

Well, it could have saved one editor's job.

When the *Daily Mirror* bought faked pictures of 'British soldiers torturing prisoners in Iraq' it announced its supposed scoop by putting the photos on TV the night before. Retired photographer Eddie Rawlinson did a screen grab at home and – before the paper even hit the streets – sent me an email saying that there was rabbit off, somewhere.

Eddie knew what soldiers were supposed to look like. The lacing on a soldier's boots was wrong, he wrote. The rifle held by one of them was the wrong type. The vehicle in the picture was the wrong vehicle for Iraq. The fastening on a soldier's webbing was wrong. The trousers, at the ankle, were wrong.

If Eddie had still been running a picture desk those photos would never have got across it. The editor, Piers Morgan, would not have been fired. And the paper – once the most highly rated and respected by soldiery of all ranks – would not have been brought into shocking disrepute.

It would not have run the page one headline VILE, nor had to apologise on the whole of the front page: SORRY... WE WERE HOAXED.

*

The *Mirror* introduced a system of 'sabbaticals' by which reporters could take paid leave in order to learn something useful for their work. Hearing about this, a couple of friendly officers suggested that I apply for a short service commission in the army; I had the basic educational qualifications, was still young enough at the time, and they said they would provide me with the requisite references. It would give me a better insight into military life, they said. Better still, I thought, I would get to meet future commanders, and probably even the odd foreign potentate, that would be useful contacts in the future.

Importantly, I would be able to opt out after twenty two weeks. The maximum allowance for a sabbatical was six months.

I'd put the idea to Bill Freeman along with the offer of a big feature, or even a series of features, at the end of it, but he said the *Mirror* would not countenance subterfuge: I would need formal army approval to do it. Otherwise he thought it was a great idea.

As did the MoD top brass, who said I could go to Sandhurst.

The only stipulation, I said, was that nobody should know what I was doing. Impossible, they told me – they couldn't allow a *Daily Mirror* reporter into the Royal Military Academy without the commandant being aware.

Fair enough, I said. But only the commandant.

The commandant also thought it was a good idea. But he

couldn't allow it unless the regimental sergeant major was also in on the secret.

I had to draw the line there. The RSM would not handle a *Mirror* reporter like any other cadet; I would either get an especially tough ride, or a soft one. And if I were to be treated any differently from the other officers the plan simply wouldn't work.

'Think about it,' urged the MoD. You can have a place at the Academy if you want one. It would be silly to give it up. We have never offered such a facility to any other reporter.'

But I turned it down. Nevertheless, for years afterwards I would tell people over dinner in officers' messes in various parts of the world that I had been offered a place at Sandhurst, but that I had refused it.

Now, on the *Sunday Mirror* at the height of the Cold War, I was having lunch with the director of press and public relations (a brigadier) at the Ministry of Defence and he asked: 'Who are we supposed to contact on your newspaper if the balloon goes up? It would be helpful if there was somebody who knew the difference between a brigadier and a bombardier.'

I passed the question to Bob Edwards who told me: 'You are obviously interested. Would you like to do it? Become our defence correspondent; use the title, it might even help get more stories.'

That's what happened. The *Mirror* papers were totally pro-soldier (not always necessarily pro-army, but always on the side of the squaddies) and the stories started to trickle in.

We could even combine 'investigations' with defence – for example when I learnt about a firm in Bournemouth that supplied aircraft parts to the manufacturers of Concorde and fast fighter jet planes for the RAF. The problem was that the parts they sold – mostly nuts and bolts, known as 'fasteners' – were recognised in the trade as 'bicycle quality', which was a long way short of aircraft quality.

The story ran for three weeks – first the exposure, including a $56 source invoice for low-quality goods that that had been altered to $16,600 for top-quality fittings. Then the frantic search for the inadequately weak parts that had been supplied and fitted in aircraft and finally the arrival and searches by the fraud squad and the MoD police. Each story took less than a day to report and write up, but made the best part of a full page in successive weeks.

More instant investigations.

*

During and after the War the *Daily Mirror* had employed Barbara Betts as a sort of agony aunt for servicemen and their families, an interesting occupation for a young woman with an Oxford degree in philosophy, politics, and economics. She maintained her concern after marrying picture editor Ted Castle and becoming an MP.

Mirror reporters went everywhere the armed forces went and they – all ranks, about 300,000 of them, and their wives when their men were posted abroad – bought the paper (although officers also bought the *Daily Telegraph* to find out what they were supposed to be doing.)

Ellis Plaice, former *Daily Mail* reporter, became the *Mirror* services correspondent with a brief to write about members of the armed forces – any forces, anywhere in the world.

After one particularly exhausting trip to Viet Nam he arrived home, poured himself a large whisky, sank into an armchair and switched on the TV to find a programme about a day in the life of Fleet Street.

It showed the mid-day news conference in his own editor's office and to his amazement Dan Ferrari was presenting a story that Ellis had written.

'Wonderful, wonderful stuff,' Dan was saying. 'He was trapped and surrounded with a platoon of US Marines and they were told they had no chance of survival. They should all write their last letters home and prepare to die.'

The system, Dan explained, was to tape your last letter into your armpit. When their base was overrun the Viet Cong would usually mutilate the bodies with machetes, but they didn't hack the armpits because they were too tough. When the Marines recaptured the spot, they would check the armpits for letters, photographs and valuables before putting the corpses into body bags.

Ellis was by this time sitting upright and pouring another drink.

154

Everybody in the conference agreed it was a great story – especially when Dan told them that they had been miraculously rescued at the eleventh hour and Ellis had collected several of the last letters including some written to relatives in the UK, and of course including his own last letter.

'Excellent, excellent,' said the editor, Tony Miles. 'That's the splash and the centre spread, tonight.'

Ellis hadn't seen the paper while he'd been away. He would enjoy going through the files in the office and seeing his story in print. He poured another Scotch and watched on.

The cameras moved to the noon conference at *The Times*, followed some reporters and photographers around on stories in the afternoon, and then returned to the *Mirror* six o'clock conference.

Everybody was still raving about Ellis' brilliant copy.

But there were other pages to fill.

'Anything from Parly?' asked Miles.

'Nothing yet,' said political correspondent Victor Knight. 'But Mrs Thatcher [secretary of state for education, the voice-over explained] is likely to abolish free school milk.'

Somebody murmured 'Thatcher, the milk-snatcher.'

'That's it!' exclaimed Miles. 'That's the splash. With reactions on the centre spread. Terrific story!'

'But...' protested Ferrari, 'what about Ellis' great stuff. Where is that going to go?'

'On the spike,' said Miles. 'Nobody's interested in Viet Nam. It's thousands of miles away.'

Ellis, now with sad eyes still glued to the TV set, poured himself another drink...

*

When he was covering the Black September uprising in Jordan, in 1970, Ellis had been trapped at the height of the fighting in the lobby of the InterContinental hotel, Amman, Jordan, with John Edwards from the *Mail*. The hotel was under intense rocket attack because of its strategic position on a hilltop.

The two reporters decided to find a more secure place to shelter but as they ran through the lobby towards the basement stairs another rocket exploded, knocking them both down onto the marble floor. The place filled with choking smoke and dust. But Ellis crawled off through the debris towards the main door. Edwards thought he was bravely going to check who was doing the shooting and yelled at him to come back but he disappeared from sight. Some time later he reappeared squirming through the rubble as if swimming side stroke. He had the hotel's American Express machine and a whole box of blank receipt slips under one arm.

Showing it to Edwards, he said: 'We're set for life.'

What he hadn't realised was that the machine had the words 'InterContinental hotel, Amman' sealed into it. They were 'set for life' in terms of Amex receipts for their expenses, only if they could claim to eat all of their meals, for ever, in Jordan.

*

The rules of reporting wars were that correspondents did not carry or use weapons, so that if captured they could not be classed with enemy forces nor subjected to the same treatment. Donald Wise, who worked in the Far East and covered more wars than anybody I know, usually wore a Waikiki beach shirt so that not even a sniper at long-range could mistake him for a soldier.

Following the rules wasn't always easy.

On the front line reporters were frequently under fire. If the squaddies were forced to retreat – and in Viet Nam that often involved slithering backwards on your belly – the system was to provide cover for the men in front and behind you. Your life was at stake. You were expected to take your turn.

When – if – that happened, it was never recorded or reported.

John Pilger, allocated a hut for the night in a de-militarized zone, was handed a rifle by a US Marine sergeant. 'If anybody shorter than six-feet tall comes through that door you fire this at him.'

He then offered him two grenades.

'If that don't stop 'em, pull the pins out of these and throw them at them... Roll away with your helmet over your head...'

Pilger's response was to refuse the arms. 'I am a reporter,' he said. 'I don't support your war. I am here to write it, not to fight it.'

'Listen, suh,' the sergeant told him, patiently. 'If some gook comes in this hut there's no way he's gonna pause at the door and ask: "Excuse me, bub, is you a news guy?"...'

During the Falklands conflict Alastair McQueen was always at the front with the Paras – sometimes too far forward to get his stories to the rear for daily transmission by the Navy.

In the black of night his platoon forced back an attacking Argentine unit that had shelled and shot up a forward observation post. The gunner was in agony:

'I've lost my leg,' he cried.

'No you haven't,' the first-aider told him. '...It's over there.'

*

During the seventies Middle East terrorism was spreading to the UK, often with Arabs and Israelis fighting openly on the streets of London, so I took in security as part of my brief.

This provided an entrée to the security services (I had already made contacts in the Special Branch of the Met Police) and I discovered that – even without the benefit of RMA Sandhurst – officers that I had met along the way had aged with me and been promoted and transferred.

An infantry officer I'd befriended in Germany was now on the Russian desk of MI6; another from Catterick was liaising with the Irish desk in MI5. Yet another was handling Nato planning...

It all paid dividends. When Turkey staged a military coup, the RAF flew me in there while all other foreign pressmen were being evicted.

The day the Berlin Wall came down I somehow happened to be in Germany already as a suddenly invited guest of the army... with a helicopter waiting to fly me into the city.

*

The 'home news' pages of the popular papers were becoming increasingly occupied by stories about television, especially the soaps, like *Coronation Street* and *Eastenders*, and their plots and their 'stars'. They were effectively competing with *TV Times* and *Hello* magazine rather than with the hard news stories in the 'heavies' – the serious or 'unpopular' press. And Bob Edwards liked the idea of 'security' to provide some sort of balance and also a degree of credibility for what he considered to be a proper newspaper.

There was no shortage of real news, but stories about 'celebrities', that by now included even news readers and weather presenters, seemed to be what the readers wanted. Meanwhile Bob, who had never seen a TV soap opera, wanted more serious stuff.

When the Royal Wedding (Charles and Diana) was imminent, and fearing that I might somehow be roped in to the inevitable mass coverage, I decided to get myself as far away from it as possible and told the office I needed to go back to Belize (formerly British Honduras) to visit Our Boys – we kept four Harriers, a couple of infantry platoons and a Navy destroyer there 'to protect British interests in the Caribbean'.

I few out on the eve of Wedding Day and, changing flights at Dulles Airport in Washington, found TV screens everywhere broadcasting the preliminaries for the ceremony. Thank God I was escaping all that jamboree. But when my RAF Hercules landed in Belize I was met by an army corporal who handed me an envelope. It contained an invitation from the British governor-general to join him on the lawn of Government House that evening... to celebrate the wedding of the Prince of Wales.

Then came a message from the features editor. They were desperate for something different. Could I get a picture of some 'natives' – loyal subjects of the Queen – watching the wedding on TV in the jungle? If the local women were topless, it would probably be best to photograph them from behind, watching the screen. Presumably the army engineers could rig up a TV set. They were sending Eddie Sanderson, a freelance based in Los Angeles, to do the pictures.

Eddie, an old friend – he hailed from Berwick on Tweed – read the menu in the Fort George Hotel and spotted the 'wild jungle pork'. Had I tried it? I said that I had, only once, but this time I was opting for the fresh swordfish.

I didn't tell him that the reason I'd had it only once was that the day after I'd eaten it, I'd seen a waiter carrying a massive rat, the size of a dog, and asked him where he'd found it.

'Dis ain't no rat,' he told me. 'Dis is a jungle pig.'

Eddie, however, found it delicious.

We went up country to visit the Gurkhas who, football mad, had cleared a pitch in the middle of the jungle and were kicking a ball around on it. When I told them that Eddie had once had a trial for Berwick Rangers they invited him to join in. He tucked his trousers into his socks and ran down to play.

'It's a great privilege for your colleague to be invited to join them,' said the commanding officer as we sat watching.

'How so? It's only a kick-about.'

'It might look like a kick-about to you, but to them it's the quarter-final of the King George the Sixth Cup.'

Fortunately there had been no score when I beckoned Eddie off the pitch, and a hitherto disconsolate Gurkha was finally able to take his rightful place with his team.

*

I went to Berlin more frequently than I went anywhere, occasionally crossing into the East via the iconic Checkpoint Charlie. There were defecting agents, and escapers who found intriguing and innovative methods of crossing the Wall. And there was Spandau, a military prison with (until his death in 1987) only one inmate, Hitler's deputy, Rudolf Hess.

I told Bob Edwards I thought I ought to go to Berlin. I can't even remember the reason, now, but it doesn't matter because Bob's instant reply was: 'Okay... Go to Berlin.'

Didn't he want to know why?

'No... if you think you ought to go to Berlin, go to Berlin. I agree that you should go.'

This seemed to me – even in the indulgent tradition of the newspaper – to be adopting an overly lax attitude to foreign travel and expenses so I asked why he didn't want to know.

He rummaged through the pile of paperwork on his in-tray and produced an internal memo.

It was from the editorial manager (a non-journalist) and referred to my previous week's expenses:

'Are you aware that it cost more to keep Mr Barker in London last week than it normally costs to keep him for a week in Berlin?'

That was all it said.

Bob told me: 'I am not having arseholes in management write memos like that to me about my reporters – so if you want to go to Berlin, go to Berlin!'

*

Chris Hutchins, our gossip columnist, told me that he'd met a young man at a party who said he'd had a homosexual relationship with 'a leading member of the government in East Berlin'. It wasn't a story for Chris, but he thought it might be of interest to me. He had arranged to meet the chap for lunch at Langan's so, if I also happened to be lunching there...

I was introduced as the *Sunday Mirror* defence correspondent.

'Oh, then you'll know Sir James Dunnet... I had sex with him.'

Sir James was permanent under-secretary of state at the MoD and chairman of the D-Notice Committee, which occasionally gave advice to newspapers and broadcasters on matters affecting national security. I looked at this chubby-faced youth with long black hair in sweater and jeans and thought it a bit unlikely.

'I picked him up while he was looking in the window of an antique shop, just behind the Hilton, near Shepherd Market. He had no idea that I was male. Darling, you should see me in the gear! With my hair all shining and the lipstick and eyelashes, the long fur coat and the boots. I look stunning!'

Maybe... But, Sir James Dunnett...?

'He took me to his home and we had sex. Just oral, so he never knew. At least, he didn't know at the time; he found out later when I went to see him at the ministry...'

Chris had warned me that the gossip writers considered the guy, who called himself Vikki de Lambray, to be an unreliable source, and he could probably recognise an expression of incredulity on my face. He opened the briefcase that was at his feet.

'He paid me with a personal cheque...' And with a flourish he produced a photocopy of it.

'Afterwards, while he was washing, I lifted the credit cards from his wallet and took them home.'

He produced photocopies of those, too.

'So I knew who he was and the following day I rang him at work and told him that I had inadvertently – Lord knows how – left his home with his credit cards in my pocket and that if he would meet me on the steps of the ministry at noon I would return them to him. After all, I may be a prostitute, but I'm not a thief.'

Dunnet's relief at retrieving his cards – including his MoD pass – must have been overwhelmed by the horror of now seeing 'Vikki de Lambray' dressed in his street clothes, as a man. He wasn't aware that he was also being photographed as the cards were handed back to him.

'So you're a prostitute but not a thief. What else are you…? A blackmailer?'

'Not at all. This documentation is for my own protection. I have upset a lot of people and I am famous. But I'll be dead before I'm thirty if I don't take precautions – I'll probably be found dead in a ditch somewhere with a heroin overdose.'

He said he had 'a 900-page memoir, naming names' in his briefcase.

'Even people in Germany,' prompted Chris, recalling the original point of our meeting.

The East Berliner sounded even less likely than Sir James Dunnett, and yet, as the story unfolded…

De Lambray said he didn't know the man's name, only his nickname, but he could describe him, and tell me where he worked – in Normannenstrasse in Lichtenberg, in East Berlin. But I knew who he was, not only from the description, but also because what was referred to as his nickname was also actually his 'trade' name, as a spy. And he was the head of the East German security service.

Fantasist though he might be – if fantasy this was – the young transvestite hooker had certainly done his homework. He knew a tremendous amount about the man. He said he had visited him in Berlin twice.

But if a guy in a position like that was looking for a bit of rough, or even a tarted-up bit of trannie rough, he surely wouldn't need to go to London's Shepherd Market to find it.

I needed proof, or something resembling it.

'I don't suppose he also paid you by cheque…?'

'No – cash, in American dollars.'

I pocketed the Dunnett paperwork and went that night to confront the MoD's top civil servant at his home. Sir James, I knew, was recently widowed, so I wasn't about to embarrass anybody other than him.

He astonished me by inviting me in and saying: 'Yes, I am afraid that's true. Would you like a drink? Bit depleted at the moment… I have only…' he looked about the apartment '… Cointreau.'

He poured two glasses of the orange liqueur and continued: 'All I can say in my defence is that, well, my wife was terminally ill. She told me she was sorry she was unable to satisfy my natural male urges and said that if I felt the need for it, she would have no objection, so long as she didn't know about it.'

But… a prostitute…? Did he have no respectable female friends?

'They would have been my wife's friends, so that would have been an impossibility. But one night – admittedly perhaps a little the worse for drink – I found myself near the Hilton and got into conversation with what I thought was a young woman and one thing led to another and I invited her back here.'

'And you paid by cheque.'

'Why not? I didn't see anything wrong with what I had done.'

'The Permanent Under-Secretary and a prostitute? A man in your position?'

'Prostitution isn't illegal. The following morning when I realised that my cards were missing I reported everything to security, and they also told the police. When she… he… came to the ministry to return them, I reported that, too.'

So he probably wasn't a security risk, nor a candidate for blackmail. On the other hand, there was a gossipy newspaper tipster running around the capital telling the story and providing the evidence to anybody who, like me, would listen.

'Are you going to write the story?'

'I'll discuss it with my editor but, probably, yes. I will be just as sensitive as I can, but the top man at the MoD picking up a transvestite tart in Shepherd Market is a story, I'm afraid. There's no two ways about it, sorry.'

'If you must, you must, I suppose. Have another drink. But you must understand that I was... lonely.'

The Special Branch knew all about the incident. They confirmed that Sir James was no security risk and were still considering the implications of charging the man with theft. There appeared to have been no 'intention to deprive' him of the cards, but the fact that he had photocopied them complicated the issue.

They also knew quite a lot about 'de Lambray'. His real name was David Christian Lloyd-Gibbon (or maybe only David Gibbon) and at one time he'd changed his name by deed poll to Louis de Rothschild and been paid ten thousand pounds by the Rothschild family to change it back.

The Special Branch, and MI6, were more interested in the East Berlin encounter. They didn't believe it, either.

That story could keep for now. Meanwhile I had the Dunnett copy to write.

Bob Edwards wasn't sure about it: 'You say yourself that he was no security risk. So who benefits, if we run this story?'

'We do. The readers love spy stories. They are all lapping up George Smiley on TV. And here we have the top man in the MoD who picks up a tart, takes her home, has a blow job and next morning discovers he's had sex with a bloke. If that's not a Sunday newspaper story, tell me what is.'

'But he was a lonely old man,' said Bob. 'We are not in the game of exposing every senior civil servant or prominent figure who has sex with a prostitute, are we? I suggest what we do is keep this one in the safe and if anybody else looks like breaking it, we'll use it because it's coming out anyway. And we'll do it better because we will have the cheque, the cards, and the photographs.'

And that's what happened. Six weeks later the Special Branch phoned to tell me that the *News of the World* had the story and was running it that night. We waited until it appeared in their first edition, then ran our version, which was considerably better.

A short time afterwards 'Vicky de Lambray' was found dead,

163

apparently from a heroin overdose (although the autopsy found no puncture marks) – not in a ditch as he had forecast but sitting in an armchair in his flat in Stockwell, South London. He was thirty-six.

We never got to the bottom of the East Berlin accusation.

*

Terrorism – on which I was meanwhile increasingly concentrating – became international. Both the Arabs and the Americans were supplying arms to the IRA. The Libyans started training the Provisionals. And the IRA in turn trained the Basque ETA separatists at a farm outside Dublin.

Baader-Meinhof, the Red Brigades, the PLO and factions as distant as Argentina and Japan offered each other advice, arms, tactics and training, and ultimately sanctuary. Public Enemy Number One was the assassin known as Carlos the Jackal. They even held a 'summit meeting' in Rome to exchange information. Bob sent me there to cover it.

*

When Russia invaded Afghanistan Bob Edwards called me in to his office. I found him standing at his desk with his deputy, Vic Birkin, at the other side of it. Between them was the oversized *Times Atlas of the World*, open at a map of the whole world.

'You'll know this,' Bob said to me. 'Which… is Afghanistan?'

I jabbed a finger, roughly where China and Iran met India and Pakistan.

'There you are,' said Bob to Vic, peering and finding it on the map. 'I told you he would know.'

My work done, I returned to my office. The phone rang. 'I didn't ask you to leave. Come back, will you?'

Bob was opening a bottle of white wine from his built-in fridge.

'I was thinking… it would be very useful to this newspaper if you were to become foreign editor.'

Evelyn Waugh, in *Scoop*, couldn't have made it up.

The first point of contact on returning from a foreign trip, even before regaining one's desk, was always the office pub and the usual suspects were there when I entered The Stab In The Back with my bag still over my shoulder.

Alastair McQueen, who in all but title was the *Daily Mirror* War Correspondent, ordered up the drink and asked: 'Are you okay? We nearly got you, last week.'

'How did you nearly get me? Where were you?'

'On the other side. I was watching you through the bins, running about like a mad thing through a deserted village. You silly bugger! Why did you zig-zag when you were being shelled? You zig-zag when you're being shot at. But under mortar fire you are just as likely to zig into it, as to zag out of it.'

Alastair and photographer Bill Kennedy had been with the PLO in South Lebanon; I had been moving fairly freely between the Israeli Defence Force and a bunch of totally useless idiots called UNIFIL – the United Nations Interim Force in Lebanon.

Alone in a small settlement I found a garden wall to hide behind. It had thirteen shell holes in it through which I would be able watch a battle that was obviously imminent.

Suddenly I was joined by an Israeli reporter who asked: 'You Barker, from the *Mirror*? There's a telex for you at the cable office.'

The message might have been telling me to come home, so I ran for it, in the centre of Metullah, the northernmost town in Israel. 'Cable office' was something of an exaggeration: it was just a general store serving maybe three hundred inhabitants. But it had a telex machine.

First, I needed to venture from behind the wall and cross a wide dust road. That was when the mortar fire started. As I reached safety behind a building, a sandy hole opened in the stretch I had just crossed. I got my breath, then ran – zig-zagged, it was a natural reaction to being shot at or shelled – across the next road. A loud CRUMP and another hole. And so my journey went.

'I told the gunner: Don't shoot at him. He's a white man. And a friend of mine,' said Alastair. 'But you know what the Arabs are like. They take no fucking notice.'

George Thaw, who edited the Old Codgers' letters page, took a swig of white wine and said: 'Crikey! I hope the cable was worth it, when you got it.'

I produced a folded square of rough yellow paper from the breast pocket of my jacket and handed it to him: 'Judge for yourself.'

It was from my secretary.

> PRO MIRRORMAN BARKER METULLAH ISRAEL. DEAR REVEL IS IT OKAY WITH YOU IF I TAKE TUESDAY AFTERNOON OFF TO GO TO THE DENTIST?

'That's the best cable I've seen sent to a war zone,' said Paul Callan. You should frame it.'

'Not the best one ever, though,' said McQueen. 'That has to have been in the Hungarian uprising when Noel Barber on the *Mail* was shot and Sefton Delmer from the *Express* got a cable in Buda, or maybe in Pest:

> BARBER SHOT WHY YOU UNSHOT?'

Alastair must have been at school when that had happened. And George remembered – although he wasn't born at the time – that, while covering the Italian invasion of Abyssinia for the *Daily Mail* in 1935, Evelyn Waugh – before writing *Scoop,* the best-known novel about newspapers – received an order from his editor:

> 200 WORDS UPBLOWN NURSE

After an exhaustive investigation Waugh determined that rumours of an English nurse having been killed in an Italian air raid – or, indeed, of any nurse being blown up anywhere – were in fact bogus. He cabled back:

> NURSE UNUPBLOWN.

This reminded me of a story, I think originally told to me by George Gordon of the *Mail,* of an exchange between the *Telegraph* foreign desk and its man in the Congo:

> WHY UNNEWS QUERY
>
> - UNNEWS HERE STOP
>
> UNNEWS THERE COMMA UNJOB HERE STOP

- UPSTICK JOB ARSEWARDS STOP RUDE LETTER FOLLOWS STOP

Michael Christiansen, while editing the *Sunday Mirror*, loved sending them and had his own clever cable signature, XSEN, Callan recalled.

When John Knight was on a job in Johannesburg he received a cable – PRO MIRRORMAN KNIGHT JOBURG HYATT – from the boss saying:

SALISWARDS SOONEST REGDS XSEN STOP

And he replied:

MY DEAR CHRIS COMMA IMAGINE MY ASTONISHMENT WHEN ON ANSWERING THE DOOR OF MY SUITE AT THE HYATT I ENCOUNTERED A DUSKY HOUSEBOY BEARING A SILVER PLATTER AND ON IT YOUR TOTALLY INDECIPHERABLE MESSAGE STOP

THE WEATHER HERE BY THE WAY IS DELIGHTFUL AND THE HOTEL IS DECIDEDLY GRAND STOP

THIS IS REALLY THE SORT OF PLACE WE SHOULD THINK ABOUT BRINGING THE GIRLS FOR A HOLIDAY COMMA ESPECIALLY DURING OUR WINTER COMMA WHEN THE CLIMATE HERE COMMA I HAVE IT ON THE BEST AUTHORITY COMMA IS SUITABLY TEMPERATE AND THE SCENERY AT ALL TIMES OF YEAR IS PERFECTLY STUNNING STOP

THE STORY ON WHICH YOU SENT ME HAS FAILED TO STAND UP COMMA SO I INTEND TO SPEND A FEW DAYS GETTING MY BEARINGS AND IF NOTHING PRESENTS ITSELF I MAY TAKE A TRIP TO SALISBURY LATER AND HAVE A LOOK ROUND THERE STOP

HOPING THAT THIS FINDS YOU AS IT LEAVES ME STOP BEST REGARDS STOP JOHN STOP

PEE ESS COLON INCIDENTALLY COMMA IF YOUR MESSAGE WAS IN ANY WAY IMPORTANT COMMA PLEASE DO NOT HESITATE TO TELEPHONE ME STOP

OPEN BRACKET COLLECT CLOSE BRACKET ENDIT

It was of course the '(Collect)' that did it. Telex messages were charged by the key-stroke, including spaces, and with the single word '*Collect*' at the end John Knight had made his cable reverse-charge.

Thereafter XSEN stuck to using the telephone.

In the days before internet keyboards and mobile phones with 'international roaming', getting a story when working overseas was often the easy part; the difficult bit was transmitting the story home.

As I have mentioned, public telephone systems in the UK were still being developed. You could often drive for miles across deserted English countryside in search of a telephone that worked, or a kiosk that hadn't been used as a lavatory. Pubs were usually the best bet which – the thought has only just crossed my mind – may be why reporters had such affection for them.

Abroad, the best option would be a four-star hotel (reporters liked them, too); it would probably have an international line and maybe a telex machine. Otherwise a call to file copy could often take days.

Even then you could find yourself with a crackling and near incoherent connection. Worse, you got a copy typist whose native language wasn't English.

Robin Stafford, the *Daily Express* man in Greece, was thrown out of the country at the start of a military coup but managed to sneak back in. He found a friendly face at the central telephone exchange who secretly got him a line but he was connected to a new copy taker who had never heard of him.

'Stafford...'

'How do you spell it?'

'For fuck's sake get on with it! I'm crouched in a cupboard in Greece.'

'Don't talk to me like that!' yelled the copy-taker as he disconnected him. It was several days before he could get through to the office again.

Military coup...

Just as the lift doors were closing from the rooftop bar of the Hassler Hotel at the top of the Spanish Steps, our man in Rome, John Penrose, was joined in it by a well-dressed man who smiled at him in apparent recognition.

'Don't tell me,' said Penrose. 'We have met, haven't we?'

The man nodded.

'You had a big job and you gave it up... Don't tell me. It will come to me...'

When the lift reached the ground floor, Penrose confessed that his memory had failed him.

'King of Greece...?' said the man, as he walked away.

It was time to report to the office.

15. Foreign affairs

Foreign editors' names went on a list that was circulated to the London embassies by the Foreign Office. Holders of this highly esteemed title were supposedly people of influence, classed as 'opinion-formers'.

Different embassies made different types of approach. I had already established contacts with the Israelis; now, recently elevated, I'd be invited for dinner at the ambassador's home, and for a private lunch at the Travellers' Club with their Belfast-born president Chaim Herzog.

The PLO invited me for a drink in a pub, the Americans to a barbecue at the ambassadorial residence in Regents Park. The Libyans wouldn't speak to me after I described Gaddafi as 'Colonel Mad'. The Russians took me to lunch.

*

The big story was Anthony Blunt, regurgitating the Burgess-Maclean-Philby saga that had been running spasmodically for nearly 30 years. I interviewed author Andrew Boyle, who had exposed Blunt in his book *Climate of Treason*, and Malcolm Muggeridge who knew them all and had worked with Philby (and Graham Greene) in the secret service during and after the war.

The big prize, still alive, would of course be an interview with Kim Philby. Assistant editor John Knight got close during a visit to Moscow, ostensibly to cover the 1980 Olympics, by finding a phone number and calling him.

'What do you want?'

'I'd very much like to meet you, and to interview you…'

'Of course you would.' Click.

The nearest I got was meeting and getting to know Philby's son John, who lived in Tufnell Park and occasionally visited Moscow and fed me with tit-bits of information. I had feelers out everywhere, and eventually got a call from somebody who said he represented something called the Soviet Copyright Agency but was in fact based in the Russian Embassy.

We met in a bar and he told me that an interview would be 'not impossible' to arrange, subject to a few rules. First, the interview, once written, would need to be approved by the authorities, but solely on the grounds of security; second, there would have to be a nominal payment to his agency because everything that 'Colonel Philby' said for publication was their copyright, and they would want a share of the money if the interview was syndicated – as it surely would be, world-wide.

It all sounded very positive. I said I thought I could live with that.

Fine, said my new contact. It would take some time to set up, but in the meantime would I be interested in writing some freelance articles? His agency would very much like somebody in a position like mine to write for it, chiefly about the political attitudes of the British press, and probably also about the relationships between politicians and Fleet Street.

To avoid any potential embarrassment with depositing Russian cheques in my bank account he could pay in cash at whatever was the Fleet Street rate, which he would expect me to advise him on.

I said I thought I could live with that, too.

But, back in the office, when I told Victor Knight (by now political editor on the *Sunday Mirror*) about this interesting invitation to enlighten a hungry and uninformed Russian readership and explain the British press and politics to them, his reaction was swift.

'Don't do it,' he said. 'Of course they will pay you in cash, but you'll obviously have to sign a receipt. Once they have your signature on a document accepting payment for information they can wave it at you for the rest of your life. They can ask for more sensitive information that you might not want to give. For God's sake, the next Soviet defector could name you to the British authorities as a source!'

Even if I appeared only on a Soviet agent's expenses, he said – and my man had paid for lunch, and for alternate rounds of drink in the pub – my name would be on a list, somewhere, accepting hospitality as 'an informant', for how could he claim reimbursement, otherwise? (The reciprocal side of this was that the man would not be named on my *Mirror* expense docket, appearing merely as a 'diplomatic contact', for, frankly, the editor didn't want to know who any of these shadowy sources actually were).

So I prevaricated over writing articles for the 'Copyright Agency' and possibly as a result of that the proposed interview with Philby never took place.

Perhaps it never would have happened, anyway.

The *Sunday Times* eventually tracked Philby down and talked him into an interview. Reporter Murray Sayle, aware of the defector's devotion to test cricket, simply hung around the main post office in Moscow until Philby turned up to collect his copy of *The Times*, and intercepted him. The interview took place with Philby's loaded revolver on the table between them.

*

As Victor Knight had predicted, defecting Soviet agents did indeed reveal names on the KGB contact lists – even people like Jack Jones, the acceptable face of militant trade unionism; apparently he provided them with 'information about the Labour Party and the TUC'. Scores of his contemporaries would also be later 'outed' by British Intelligence on similar grounds. Who wouldn't have done the same, in those days, for anybody who would share a drink at a bar, and listen to stories? But my name didn't appear.

For my part, I have no idea after this length of time what information I may have disclosed to my would-be benefactor – although I know that it would not have been anything that I wouldn't have written, or couldn't have written, for publication in my own paper. In other words, it's highly unlikely that I told him anything he didn't already know and, assuming that he was a KGB man (as, of course, was every Russian who was permitted to talk to foreigners in London), I probably told him far less than he already knew.

*

The hairs on the back of a foreign correspondent's neck have a life of their own.

You probably wouldn't be aware of them normally, but they stood to attention whenever you went through a checkpoint, whether it was in Northern Ireland, the Middle East, or approaching the iron curtain.

What, after all, were you doing there? Gathering information. Isn't that what spies do? And aren't all western journalists spies?

There's a fine line to be drawn, somewhere.

Suppose you are going to – pick a place at random – Lebanon; it may not be a bad idea to take a chap from the appropriate desk at the Foreign Office for lunch and find out the latest intelligence on what's happening there, before you go. And if he reciprocates the hospitality on your return and asks about your experience on his patch, and you tell him what you saw and heard, does that amount to…?

Yes; it's a very fine line.

I once, as a change from flying in or taking the military train, took my car along the corridor to West Berlin. Because I was officially a defence correspondent and the MoD knew I was making the trip, the Military Police at the inner German frontier post at Helmstedt invited me to stop for lunch, gave me a card with a union jack on one side and words on the other saying that I was British and Britain did not recognise East Germany, so if stopped I would speak only to a Russian officer, and then I passed through the Soviet – rather than the GDR – checkpoint.

The Military Police major who gave me lunch warned that I should not exceed the 100kph speed limit because I would be timed at either end. But if I didn't turn up when expected at Checkpoint Alpha, near Marienborn, they'd send a helicopter along the corridor to search for me. And, incidentally, he'd consider it a kindness if, once in Berlin, I mentioned 'any unusual or interesting troop movements' that I saw along the route.

I asked what he meant by 'unusual' and he said that, well, *any* troop movement would be of interest.

That's another example of the fine line. If I am going about my normal job and I see anything that anybody else along the autobahn could see and I talk about it later in a bar in Berlin, that's one thing. If I make a point of giving the information to a British officer, that's another.

But if I just write about it in the paper, where anybody can read it, it's only journalism.

Passing on information is what journalists do to earn a crust. And businessmen and politicians of course do it all the time, too. There's a constant to-and-fro. When George Brown was deputy Labour leader and wanted information about the 'loony left', he asked Chapman Pincher of the *Express*. Like you would. Who knows what goodies George offered the doyen of spy-writers by way of exchange?

*

Long before I arrived in London the *Mirror* actually had a real-life spy (some say there were at least two) on the payroll.

There was one guy who wasn't required to write anything. There was not much unusual about that – one feature writer, name of Eric Wainwright, boasted that he hadn't had a word in print for five years, going on for six. Eric appeared in the office regular as clockwork or at least regular as calendar-work, once a month, only to compose his expenses. For his retirement party they had to bring somebody out of retirement just to introduce him to the features editor.

The other chap – I have just checked and he is still alive so it would probably be impolite to name him – appeared in the office even less frequently than Eric.

When the editor made enquires about what this employee was supposed to be doing for a living, he was directed straight to the chairman, Cecil King, who told him: 'Don't ask!' But, when pressed, King said that 'duty to country comes above all else'… and that was why he had put the man on the editorial payroll.

Discreet checks revealed that the 'journalist' in question was – at least when last heard of – also on the books of the Secret Intelligence Service. Come to think of it, he never had a farewell party… perhaps he's still on the staff.

Small wonder, then, that old reporters on the *Mirror* titles developed a habit of looking about them before exchanging confidences.

Were there others?

I don't know. They wouldn't be very good at being agents if I did know. But I once walked unannounced into the office of a *Sunday Mirror* executive and found him cleaning a pistol at his desk, and then I discovered that he and another senior colleague regularly visited a private gun club 'to practise' (although to practise what, I never found out). And a feature writer of my acquaintance kept a revolver in his desk drawer but as far as I know he never took it anywhere to practise using it.

What to make of it all?

The likely answer is, never tell anybody anything. We had a fair number of journalists who managed to live by that rule.

16. El Vino veritas

In between writing stories – which meant most days and most evenings when in London – there was the pub. In our case this was The Stab In The Back, the name chosen by the staff but rejected by the brewers who insisted on hanging a sign over the door suggesting it was called the White Hart.

It was an integral part of the building, and was owned by the Mirror group. I could never understand why we didn't keep it and simply install a manager, but the best explanation I got was that we were 'not in the business of running pubs'. So the brewery got the inevitable vast profit.

The pub would start to fill up with journalists at opening time and (apart from a two-hour closure, mid-afternoon) would remain fairly full until closing twelve hours later.

The news, picture and features desks always knew where their people were, if they couldn't be seen in the office – if they went anywhere other than the Stab they'd leave a contact number – but at least in theory they were still in the building and could easily be called back.

Some of the feature writers left a (spare) jacket round the back of their chair, so they had presumably just nipped out to the bank, or maybe to move their car. Another left a pair of shoes under his desk, clearly suggesting that he couldn't have gone far, padding along the carpeted corridor in stockinged feet. But in truth they could have been anywhere.

There were lot of alternative pubs around the office. Keith Waterhouse once ventured into the Printers' Devil and asked the manager to turn down the volume on the juke box. He was told that was impossible – because 'the staff like it'. Waterhouse asked him for some change, then fed ten coins into the machine, pressed *Amazing Grace* ten times… and left the pub.

So the Stab – no juke box, no background music – remained the favourite.

Nevertheless, occasionally people strayed.

Tony Smith, sports editor of the *Sunday Mirror*, a short, balding and immensely humorous figure who had sometimes been mistaken for music hall comedian Max Wall, came into my room and leaned against the wall.

'Just coming back from lunch,' he said. 'Is this a record?'

I looked at the clock. Five forty-five. 'No,' I told him. 'It's impressive, but by no means a record.'

Tony looked at me and grinned; I hadn't got it.

'I mean from lunch... yesterday.'

It still wasn't a record.

John Knight once went for lunch and failed to reappear for the next three days.

When he returned, Bob Edwards asked where he had been.

'On the piss,' John told him.

'Oh, thank goodness,' said Bob. 'We were worried in case you were ill.'

Outrageous, reckless, irresponsible behaviour – at least to today's young minds.

But the difference between their type of journalism and today's is that both Tony and John returned from their alcohol-fuelled absences with stories that would feature prominently in the following weekend's paper. They didn't find news – or inspiration – on diets of mineral water and cress sandwiches while sitting at their 'work stations'.

Nevertheless, neither of them came remotely near a record.

Sun reporters Dougie Thompson and John Hiscock went for lunch together in the upstairs bar of the Tipperary. Hiscock flashed his brand new air travel credit card – issued to allow on-the-road reporters to get a flight anywhere, to cover a breaking international news story at a moment's notice. Thompson opened his wallet and produced his own card, also issued that day.

'Where could we go with these?'

'Anywhere.'

'Let's try them out, and see how they work.'

They took a taxi to Heathrow, and booked club class flights to Los Angeles.

They haven't come back to the office... yet.

Those two may, in fact, be the current record holders.

Drink and journalism went together like… well, like gin and tonic.

In spite of living a life often involving greatly excessive food and alcohol, I have been the worse for drink only once that I can remember. (There may have been other times that I can't remember.) But there were many stories, revolving around reporters and drink that I can still recall.

Surprisingly nobody, not even the people who would be in the Stab all day, seemed to get drunk. Or maybe they did get drunk but when the occasion demanded and they were recalled to the office to work on a suddenly breaking story the adrenalin kicked in and sobered them instantly. Drunkenness seemed to be something that usually happened only when they moved on after closing time to the Press Club. And there were never any fights – something else that seemed to figure more often after the Press Club.

Sports writer Hugh McIlvanney was once involved in a fracas outside the Club. He knocked his opponent to the ground but the man somehow moved his feet around McIlvanney's ankles and brought him crashing to the pavement.

Impressed, McIlvanney conceded: 'Well, you've got to admire his choreography.'

Generally, however, camaraderie was the name of the game, as Hughie Saker, popular one-eyed reporter on the *Mirror*, discovered.

In the early hours one morning he was slumped across the bar in the Press Club replete with cognac which he insisted was necessary to relieve the pain in his eye-socket – evacuated, he claimed, during his time as an RAF rear-gunner (although Keith McDowall of the *Mail,* who'd been at school with him, said it happened when they were in the playground playing soccer with a one-inch marble and Hugh had tried to head the 'ball').

His colleagues, being kindly gents concerned for his welfare, wondered what to do with the body. And somebody thought of ringing his good lady wife and telling her to come and collect him.

Mrs S, a reporter on the *Evening Standard* called Vivienne Batchelor, had, after all, been prevailed upon to collect him at other times in similar circumstances. And as far as Hugh's drinking chums were aware she had always complied without complaint.

And so she did this time; her husband's supper had been on the table since 8 o'clock, and she'd heard no word of him since morning, but she was a wise woman who knew that he could just as easily be in Rio or Berlin (although, if she'd been invited to put a bet on, the Press Club would have been favourite).

So she pulled a raincoat over her nightie and drove her own car into town. She had worked out a strategy – there'd be plenty of room for parking off Fleet Street at that time in the morning. She'd leave her car near the office in Shoe Lane and bring her hapless husband home in his car, then go to work by train next day and bring her car home that night.

It all worked well. She found her husband unconscious in the passenger seat and the keys under the mat on the driver's side, exactly as arranged by his drinking companions. She got behind the wheel and set off home. Simple, how these things work out.

Cruising down an empty open road she was overtaken only by the need to spend a penny. No problem, she pulled into a lay-by and nipped behind a handy clump of bushes.

…At which point our hero awoke from his slumber to find himself mysteriously parked on the roadside and in the passenger seat of his office car. Funnier things had probably occurred after a night on the cognac in the Press Club, so he hitched himself across the gearstick and drove home.

Hurriedly readjusting her clothing the poor wife ran after him, gesticulating wildly, as one might. But Hughie, on a traffic-free run, had seen no need to check his rear view mirror.

So there, on the main road, stood Mrs Saker, wondering about the possibilities of thumbing a safe lift home clad in only a raincoat and a full-length night-gown and the first vehicle to pull up alongside was a police car.

This was pre-breathalyser but nevertheless the girl from the *Standard* knew that driving south of the river under the influence of drink was considered a sin. She span out the story – possibly nearly as long as this one – for fear that the cops would chase and apprehend her man. In the end she told them the truth of the matter and the knights of the road laughed, and offered her a lift home.

There was no sign of the car when they pulled into Saker Magna, but a constable opened the garage doors and found the car perfectly parked. They bade her goodnight, watched her safely into the house, and went off to catch criminals – as, in those days, the boys in blue mainly occupied themselves.

In the kitchen, the steak dinner that had been pointedly left to go cold on the table had been picked clean. In the bedroom was a dormant husband, snoring.

Viv looked at her watch and decided it was hardly worthwhile getting in to join him. She had an early shift, so showered and started to get dressed.

Hughie woke to find his ever-loving standing half-dressed beside the bed.

'What are you doing?'

'I'm getting ready for work.'

'Oh...' But she could see the tumbrels of his mind revolving slowly.

'Just a minute! – Where the fuck were you when I came home last night?'

*

Mirror reporter Bill Marshall once committed the unforgivable sin of getting drunk after doing a story, but before writing it, and collapsed unconscious in a pub.

Sean Bryson, on the *Mail*, generously thinking that it was something that could happen to anybody (it couldn't – discipline, though lax, was tougher than that) altered his own copy and filed a freshly rewritten version to the *Mirror* copy-takers in Bill's name.

The following day the two men met on a different job. Bill, completely unaware of the previous night's events, produced a copy of the paper from his pocket and said: 'See this, arsehole? Don't ever tell me that I can't write a story when I'm pissed!'

*

At the end of an all-night (and early morning) drinking session in Liverpool Press Club Bill remembered that his musical hero Hoagy

Carmichael was in town and suggested to his drinking partner Ian Skidmore that the two of them should visit his suite at the Adelphi Hotel and pay homage.

Inevitably they asked him to play the piano. Hoagy agreed: but he wouldn't play his signature tune *Stardust*. He said he couldn't stand the damn thing, and he'd written it.

So for an hour or so he plied the two reporters with Scotch and entertained them with tunes for which, he said, he had not been able to find a publisher.

A yelp from Bill brought the performance to an abrupt end. He had remembered that he should have been across the city covering a trial at the Assizes.

'Anything I can do?' asked Hoagy.

Bill said yes, there was. He knew Hoagy didn't like *Stardust* but could he ring his news editor and, when he came to the phone, hold the instrument over the piano keyboard while Hoagy played a few bars of it and then say, 'Hello, this is Hoagy Carmichael. I am afraid I have detained your reporter Bill Marshall.'

Good as gold, Hoagy did as Bill asked him. He played the opening bars down the phone and said his piece. There was a pause and then a suddenly angry Hoagy said, 'No, this is not Bill Marshall, I am not pissed at half past eleven in the morning and I have no idea what is on at the Assizes.'

*

A *Mirror* sub turned up late for his shift and told night editor Vic Mayhew: 'Sorry I'm late, Vic. I'm a bit pissed.'

Mayhew's response was: 'Oh, I'm sorry to hear that, mate. Are you OK? Why don't you go down the pub and if you feel better come back later.'

*

Drinking was one thing; organising drinking was quite different.

Joyce Hopkirk was without doubt an exceptional journalist, one of the greats. She'd been women's editor of the *Sun*, launch editor of *Cosmopolitan*, and would become women's editor of the *Sunday Times* then editor in chief of *She*.

But as assistant editor (features) of the *Daily Mirror* she messed up the dates for a lunch with Spike Milligan, and editor Mike Molloy, in a rare fit of unoriginality, told her: 'Hopkirk – You couldn't organise a piss-up in a brewery.'

A day or so later she handed out invitations to:

A PISS-UP IN A BREWERY

Joyce Hopkirk is delighted to invite you to a gala piss-up at the Whitbread Brewery, Whitechapel Road, London, E1, on Wednesday July 16th at 7pm.

Guest of Honour: Mike Molloy.

Art editor Paddy O'Gara asked her whether she had put many invitations out.

'Yes, why?'

'Because the Whitbread Brewery is in Chiswell Street in Smithfield; the brewery in Whitechapel Road is Watney's.'

To be fair, Hopkirk wasn't a beer drinker, and both breweries began with W.

She let out the sort of scream only bats can hear and began racing round the office snatching up envelopes from in-trays, while instructing her secretary to do the same.

It was fairly late on Tuesday that somebody noticed that it – not the following day – was the 16th. Joyce's secretary had once again to run round all the editorial notice boards altering the date, and then ring everybody when they came back from lunch to tell them that the organised piss-up was occurring that very evening.

Nobody seemed to mind much – especially when they learnt that it was perfectly acceptable to visit Watney's brewery and drink gin and tonic, and a good time was had by all who managed to attend. Molloy however, was seen to be wearing a fairly smug expression, throughout.

John Knight, assistant editor, columnist and chief feature writer of the *Sunday Mirror* slipped the carver a few coins in return for our hefty slices of roast beef from the trolley and turned to face me across his table at the Savoy Grill with a worried expression.

For his regular *Face To Face* feature he had, he reminded me, interviewed the past three prime ministers, and a couple of leaders of the opposition parties, two American and several European presidents, Prince Philip, Prince Charles, a few other assorted kings, queens and princes, a couple of gallant generals...

He had, he felt, a reputation to maintain. So who should he do next?

In those days we were still a few rungs above rating anybody with a bit-part in *Coronation Street* as 'a celebrity'. We were interested only in people who were world famous or at least nationally important. And, more to the point, actually interesting.

Over the second round of vintage port he had solved the problem for himself.

'It'll have to be the Pope,' he decided.

'Of course,' I agreed. 'He's the only one left. However...'

The well-established knowledge that popes didn't grant interviews to newspapers was no deterrent for John who had been with him on his visit to Ireland. He had even been photographed sitting on the Pope's bed. Back in the office he rang Paul House, Our Man in Rome.

'Fix me an audience with the Pope,' he said.

No sooner said than done. Organised. Booked.

It was, in fact, remarkably easy. The Pope held a public audience once a week. Normally, given about six weeks' notice (applications made only by fax), members of the public could get in to the Vatican and spend a few hours in the papal presence. The Pope would pick out a few of this congregation for a very brief exchange of words; the rest would simply be in his company for a communal blessing.

For a personal audience you normally needed to be a head of

state. Otherwise, the best chance for a quick chat was to be on the front row of the public shows. Paul House could fix that. What he couldn't guarantee was that His Holiness would pause for even a few short words with John.

The best he could do was to get him on the end of the row and organise the official Vatican photographers to take non-stop motorised snaps of him all the time he and the Pope were in the same camera frame.

Came the day and John Paul II started working the front line of the faithful. As he approached the end John Knight let out an audible sigh and appeared (some said) as if he might be about to stumble. Quite the opposite – he was preparing some fancy journalistic footwork. But the Pope automatically grabbed John's shoulders, to prevent his falling at the papal feet. John grabbed the Pope's shoulders – and clung on.

'Are you all right, my child?'

'Yes, thank you, your holiness. But...'

'Yes, my son?'

John was still holding on to the Pope.

'You will come to England, Holy Father, won't you?'

John Knight wasn't letting go until he got an answer.

The Pope beamed his beatific smile and said: 'Yes, my son. I will come to England.'

And he moved on.

The Hollywood actor James Stewart, a couple of seats away, got nothing except the smile.

That was it.

Within the hour the pictures dropped in London and Bob Edwards was on the phone to John's hotel in Vatican City.

'Christ! This is a great scoop. Where's the copy?'

'Put me over,' said John. And he began to dictate:

> The Pope in an exclusive interview told me in the Vatican...

For the front: World Exclusive –I WILL VISIT ENGLAND POPE TELLS THE SUNDAY MIRROR. *From John Knight in Rome.*

For the double page spread on the centre pages: MY AUDIENCE WITH THE POPE.

184

In order to get to the more remote parts of the nation in time for breakfast, Sunday newspapers started rolling off the presses at about seven on a Saturday night. By 7.30 the first editions had found their way on to the news desks of the rival papers.

By eight, editors and news editors and foreign editors were staring at the front of the *Sunday Mirror* and asking why they didn't have the story about the Pope.

They read, and re-read, the front and the spread.

There was nothing in the story to confirm it, they decided. Only one quote in the entire thing. Which was true. The thousand words in the centre spread were about the people visiting the Vatican for the audience, and the entrance into the chamber of the Pope himself. And the description of his appearance, right down to his white Gucci slippers.

There were photographs. The Pope greeting priests and nuns… and then the Pope with John Knight, first, holding him by the shoulders and looking serious and concerned… then, smiling at him, with their hands on each other's shoulders. There was no doubt that the meeting, some sort of meeting, had taken place. If the Pope was planning to visit the UK, this would be a truly historic event. And they had missed it. If the Pope wasn't – and with not a lot to substantiate it – the story was 'a John Knight flyer'.

And that was how the frustrated news executives explained it away to their editors. At least, temporarily.

Meanwhile Our Man in the Eternal City had been busy. At six-thirty he had telephoned the Vatican press office and asked the duty staff about the Pope's plan to visit the UK. They knew nothing about it.

'You'd better check,' House told them. 'Because His Holiness has promised a British journalist that he will be visiting England. The story is running in tomorrow's newspapers.' Enquiries were made. The story was confirmed. A press statement was issued immediately.

Fleet Street was astonished, not to say appalled.

'If the Pope decides to visit England…' they were asking, 'why does he choose to announce it exclusively to the *Sunday Mirror*?

185

And why did he choose John Knight? Is he even a Catholic?' They never learnt the answers. They had missed the big story.

There were repercussions. Some days later Cardinal Bruno Heim, *Papal Nuncio* (the Pope's ambassador to the UK) unexpectedly invited me, as *Sunday Mirror* foreign editor, to his home for lunch. I was shown into the dining room by his chaplain and when Heim appeared, a bottle in each hand, he greeted me with 'Well, what do you want?'

I was puzzled. 'You invited me,' I reminded him.

'Precisely. So… what do you want?'

'Excuse me…?'

'What do you want – sweet, or dry?'

We sat together sipping dry white cocktails at a large refectory table.

'…So… Now that the *Sunday Mirror* has invited him, and now that he has agreed to come… what are we going to do with him?'

And we started planning the first Papal visit to the United Kingdom. The organisation took more than forty meetings, during which plans were made and frequently revised, improved and altered. As a head of state and the head of the Church of Rome he would obviously meet the Queen, head of the Church of England. But as international events unfolded he couldn't meet the prime minister, Margaret Thatcher, because Britain was going to be at war with Catholic Argentina. The itinerary would eventually take in nine British cities and feature sixteen public addresses.

My reward for this was the presentation by the Cardinal of two – two – papal medals for 'good works', a rare honour for a non-Catholic.

'I can't wear even one of these,' I told Heim.

'The Holy Father is aware of that,' the Cardinal said. 'But he has learnt that your children are Catholic. He has blessed the medals so that you can pass them to your son and daughter in recognition of his holiness's appreciation of their father's helpful work in organising his historic visit.'

John Knight, naturally, got nothing.

Not even Scoop of the Year – which of course his story was.

*

The Pope was a big story, but eventually only a three-day wonder, and not as big as the Falklands – Britain At War – was going to be.

The Argentine invasion started on Thursday April 1, which could have been a significantly foolish date to pick because the British forces – Royal Marines and Royal Navy – were changing over, so were twice their usual strength.

News reached London on the Friday and Bob Edwards asked me: 'So... what's our line on this?'

My view was that the Falklands, being inhabited by Brits who couldn't bear to live in their own country and opted to settle as far away from it as they could get, even if that meant on a freezing windswept rock (I had met members of their council and considered them a miserable bunch of buggers) were 'not worth the life of a single Marine.'

Bob thought about it. 'We can't say that. Suppose one Marine is killed. How could I tell his parents that he died for nothing? We have to support our troops.'

'That's the same thing,' I said. 'But the truth is that if they die, they die defending a useless rock. Anyway, I've told the MoD to get me on the first ship out. They say they're putting all the correspondents' names in a hat.'

'I don't want you to go,' Bob told me. 'It'll be three weeks cruising down the Atlantic, and the Argies will surrender when we get there, then three weeks sailing back. I don't want you swanning about on a ship for six weeks when you could be doing something useful here.'

My name wasn't drawn from the hat, but Alastair McQueen's was; fair enough, he could cover for both the *Daily* and the *Sunday Mirror*.

18. War games

The nation seemed excited about the prospect of being at war again. Perhaps, nearly forty years on, the last unpleasantness was too distant to remember what war meant, or what it was like. We had to capture and report the mood.

The first thing was the usual Whitehall cock-up. The GCHQ listening post at Cheltenham, expecting an invasion, had monitored a call from the islands' Cable & Wireless station:

'I'd better sign off now. We have some unwelcome visitors.'

The GCHQ man phoned the Foreign Office: 'Did you hear that? British territory has been invaded. You'd better tell Downing Street.'

'He didn't say that. He didn't mention Argentina specifically.'

'Who else could he have meant? And we could hear gunfire in the background. You must have heard it too...'

'It may have been our Marines, discharging their weapons...'

They didn't tell the prime minister until nearly four hours later.

Meanwhile Our Boys – the Task Force and our correspondents – were sailing south. I learnt that the method of delivering mail and supplies would be for the RAF to fly close to the ships and drop packages alongside, so they could be picked out of the water by the Navy. So I suggested that we should send copies of the *Sunday Mirror*, to keep them in touch with news from home. The MoD liked the idea, but wondered whether they should make the option available to all newspapers. They decided that, since nobody else had asked, the initiative should stay with the *Sunday Mirror* alone.

Newcastle Breweries agreed to brew a special strong winter beer, based on their famous Brown Ale, and called it *Sunday Mirror Task Force Ale*. They'd provide it free, if we could arrange delivery to the troops – and of course we could; it went with the newspapers to twenty-nine separate ships.

Families at home sent us news and photographs to print in our 'Task Force Edition' then they asked whether they could send letters and photos via us. We could also do that. By the end of hostilities my desk was handling 30,000 pieces of mail every week, including news of newly born children and proposals of marriage (and acceptances), all courtesy of the *Sunday Mirror*.

The rest of the time I was based inside the MoD, picking up and trying to decipher the news that eventually started to dribble back.

With virtually no news for the first three weeks (Bob Edwards had been right about that) we busied ourselves by interviewing experts, mainly retired commanders, about what was likely to happen. The MoD didn't like that. We were telling the enemy more than they needed to know – and one of the predictions was likely to be the right one.

So the Task Force Command HQ reached an agreement with the defence correspondents: they would be told what the actual plans were – on condition that when reporting speculations they didn't include the genuine tactics that would be used.

It was a fair and sensible compromise.

I learnt from Intelligence that, when the Task Force was nearing the battle zone, the Argentine government intended to announce the sinking by its navy of HMS *Exeter*, a type 42 destroyer (built at Swan Hunter on Tyneside).

Exeter meant something in Argentina where its namesake was famous for having helped sink the German cruiser *Admiral Graf Spee* in the Battle of the River Plate in 1939 after which it had been taken to the Falklands for repair.

In reality the ship would not have been sunk by the Argentine navy but the intention was to create alarm among the British population. This was merely *psy-ops* – psychological operations – (I was learning the technology) and the Argies wrongly assumed that, as the Caribbean guard ship, it would be one of the first to arrive at the scene.

However Royal Navy plans did not include *Exeter* for the Falklands, so the message was passed to the ship. It put in to port in Florida and the crew told to phone home and tell their families that if they heard news about the sinking of their ship they could ignore it, because they were not involved. So far, so good. (It would, in fact, be deployed later, following the sinking of its sister ship, HMS *Sheffield*, and would shoot down four enemy aircraft.)

So, I knew, and the crew's relatives knew, what was going to happen but true to form the Navy didn't tell the BBC – nor even its own press desk. When the 'news' came over the wires from Buenos Aires the Navy was unable to deny it and reports of the sinking were broadcast worldwide by the world's most dependable news service. The families were not alarmed but the rest of the nation was shocked. It was several hours before the mis-information was corrected. *Psy-ops* had worked.

*

The war, when it started, would last ten weeks, during which time the Pope would come to the UK, as invited by the *Sunday Mirror*, and pray for peace in the Falklands (and in Northern Ireland) at Canterbury Cathedral – with John Knight being photographed in the front pew.

When the conflict ended more stories started to drift back. A friend in the Foreign Office told me he had heard a story – but didn't know the details – that revolved around an heroic Green Howards officer and a beret, and a Ministry of Defence balls-up. If I could dig out the facts, he suggested, it might be a good story.

I knew that the Green Howards, a North Yorkshire regiment, had not been deployed to the Falklands, so my first task was to find out which officer from the Princess of Wales' Own had been there, and why.

It transpired that a captain from the regiment had been on the islands, serving with the SAS. Then that he had been killed in action, while protecting the retreat of his radio operator after being surrounded by enemy troops. In an effort to draw fire, Capt Gavin Hamilton had stood up – and been shot down – five times.

After the Argentine forces surrendered, the commander of the unit that had shot him said he wanted to record the action of 'the bravest soldier I have ever seen' and recommended him for 'the highest possible award for gallantry' – which, to the British forces, meant the Victoria Cross. So there was my story. The beret figured because the Argie officer said he wished to send the captain's widow his own beret and cap badge as a mark of profound respect. And the MoD had lost it in transit.

The follow-up was when the medals were awarded. A recommendation for a VC required the testimony of an officer, but the Army apparently wasn't prepared to accept the eye-witness evidence of the enemy, so the gallant Captain Hamilton was awarded the Military Cross instead – becoming the first soldier to receive that medal posthumously.

For my own efforts, having avoided the mud and bullets of the actual fighting, I received a Cudlipp Award – for covering the Falklands conflict without leaving London.

19. Endgame

The printing industry had started to evolve in the service of the church; early woodcuts show monks producing bibles with a backdrop of stained glass windows, to make the point. That presumably explains the use of a number of ecclesiastical expressions within printing (and, later, in journalism).

A group of print workers – what other industries might call 'the shop floor' – is called a chapel, and the shop steward is the Father of the Chapel or FoC; the source of any style of type is a fount (pronounced font). When type was spilled it was said to have been devilled and the chapel apprentice – perhaps the person most likely to spill a tray of type – was known as the printer's devil.

A year after joining the *Sunday Mirror* I was elected FoC of the sixty-strong journalists' chapel on the paper, and very shortly afterwards as convenor (chairman of the FoCs) of all the group's journalistic chapels – nearly 900 souls in all.

The FoCs normally met once a month, then held individual chapel meetings to report back to their own members on the *Daily* and *Sunday Mirror*, the *People, Sporting Life, Reveille,* the joint *Daily-Sunday Mirror* Manchester chapel, and when necessary the Scottish *Daily Record* and *Sunday Mail.*

Once a year we would put in a claim for increased pay and expense allowances. We would usually hear about pay rises on the printing floors and would often be influenced by those.

The other Fleet Street chapels would wait until the Mirror Group got its increases and then enter their own claims. (They did the same when David Thompson, Mike Gallemore and I successfully fought the Inland Revenue with our claim that what we spent buying our own newspapers should be reimbursable by the company and be free of tax.) What was good for the Holborn Circus goose was good for all the Fleet Street ganders.

Unlike the print unions who could and would threaten a stoppage on a demand for 'hot weather money' in summer or for an increase in the number of pages being produced on one night, and did tax-free casual shifts under names like M Mouse and A Hitler, relations between the management and the editorial staff were basically cordial.

Even by Fleet Street standards overmanning on the print floors was ridiculous. If everybody rostered for a nightly shift had turned up for work there wouldn't have been room for them to stand. So lots of them didn't bother and their mates signed in for them. While being paid to print newspapers some of them were operating as self-employed black-cab drivers. Others signed in for their own shifts and then went off to work for other newspapers.

When the Queen paid a rare visit to the Mirror building she was taken to see the vast printing hall.

'My word,' she said. 'How many people work here?'

'About a third of them,' the editor, Mike Molloy, told her.

We, the journalists, didn't do badly. In the seven years that I was leading negotiations the average journalist's pay increased 300 per cent. And there were more reporters and writers than there were stories for them to handle.

There was more to it than that.

The journalists also jealously guarded what they referred to as 'the editorial integrity' of the titles. The newspaper was owned by Reed, a vast paper, paint, wallpaper and magazine company that kept its distance. Unlike the other nationals, the Mirror Group therefore didn't have a proprietor, as such, and it didn't want one.

*

The spectre of Robert Maxwell had been hanging over the *Mirror* titles for more than a year before his eventual purchase.

In July 1983 *Daily Mirror* FoC David Thompson and I had gone to see Joe Grizzard who as director of editorial administration was the executive we dealt with on a daily basis, and asked him about rumours that Maxwell was planning to make an offer. It was, Joe said, news to him. Later that day he called us to a meeting in his office where we found chief executive Douglas Long waiting. We could forget the rumours, said Long. There had been no bid from Maxwell who, in any case, did not have the money.

According to Long, Maxwell had been about to conclude a deal with the *Telegraph* to print their daily and Sunday papers in

London's Dockland. His plan was to establish himself as a contract printer for Fleet Street, thus separating the functions of publishing from printing and hopefully, in the process, easing some of the traditional trade union problems with which the industry was beset. Everything had been settled, the contracts drawn up. But Maxwell had failed to show with his share of the money – proving, to Long at least, that despite the size of the Pergamon/British Printing and Communications Corporation empire, there was a serious cash flow problem at Maxwell House.

Joe and Douglas reminded us that the Mirror was owned by one of the biggest companies in Britain. Reed International had made a £61million profit in its trading year to April 1983. They didn't need the money a sale would bring. They had no intention of selling our titles, which had contributed £8 million to their profits. They depended on their *Mirror* ownership for 'ready' cash.

There was a long-standing belief that, because in theory a roll of wallpaper could take a year or more from design to point-of-sale, newspapers provided a terrific advantage; conception to actual sale took less than 24 hours: at newsvendors' stalls and sub-post-offices throughout Britain and the world the papers produced at midnight collected ready money at breakfast time.

It does not, of course, work quite like that. The man with a kiosk at King's Cross did not desert it at lunchtime to deposit his collection of 12p's (the *Mirror* share of the 1984 cover price of 18p) at Holborn headquarters; he paid the wholesaler and the wholesaler returned the money, less three pence each for himself and the seller, by cheque at the end of the month. Nevertheless, it was obviously a faster return for Reeds than producing Crown Paint, designing Sanderson wallpaper, manufacturing Twyford bathroom fittings, or marketing Polycell.

David and I had no reason to doubt Long, exactly, although we wondered whether Reed would have told him if Maxwell was hovering on the sidelines. Still, the story about lack of cash seemed fairly conclusive: sufficient, anyway, to bear repetition in chapel meetings and at the bar of the Stab each time the rumour was resurrected.

194

What we did not doubt at all was that Reed International would sell if the price was right.

Reed had bought the International Publishing Corporation, which included the *Mirror* group and a bunch of profitable magazines ranging from *Woman* and *Woman's Own* to *New Scientist*, in a share exchange deal worth £115million in 1970. Their main interests were packaging, paper, and paint and it was patently clear that they would dump their troublesome, overmanned and costly national newspaper interests without shedding a tear.

The previous Christmas they had definitely entertained an approach from *Observer* owner Roland 'Tiny' Rowland, the boss of Lonrho, for MGN's English titles, the *Daily* and *Sunday Mirror*, *Sunday People,* and *Sporting Life*. By all accounts he had offered first £70million, and then £80million, but Reed had held out for £100million. Maxwell, as always with his ear to the ground, had offered to help by taking the *Observer* off Rowland's hands for £7million. Rowland, who had bought the world's oldest Sunday newspaper for a pound, suggested that he might part with it for perhaps £10million.

Robert Holmes à Court, an Australian millionaire businessman unheard of outside the City pages, was another rumoured would-be purchaser. He was busy piling up shares in Fleet Holdings, which owned the *Daily Express, Sunday Express* and *Daily Star*. Yet another was Sir James Goldsmith, whose full-colour weekly news magazine *Now!* had recently folded.

But, according to Douglas Long, these were rumours we could discount, along with a practicable recurrence of a Tiny Rowland bid.

Journalists returned from City lunches almost every day with the names of other would-be press barons, most of them now faded into obscurity, who were reportedly eager to buy the Mirror.

But the Mirror Group did not look like a particularly good deal at Reed's valuation of £100million. The book value of its assets stood at only £34million. Nearly half its £8million profit came from the two relatively-small Scottish titles; two years earlier these had accounted for only one-fifth. On their share of £262million sales the

195

London and Manchester print operations showed a return of only 2.1 per cent, while the *Sun* contributed £22million to News International's pre-tax profit of £36million.

The *Daily Mirror*, flagship of the Group and once proudly claiming the World's Largest Daily Sale, was entrenched in a fierce circulation battle with Rupert Murdoch's *Sun*, the recently-launched *Star*, and other popular tabloid dailies. The Sunday papers were fighting a losing battle against rivals each with (admittedly, loss-making) colour magazines, Murdoch's *News of the World* at the lower end of the market, and Associated's *Mail on Sunday* at the higher.

Production of all titles in London faced a nightly crisis caused by so-called 'new technology', the switch from traditional hot metal to computer typesetting techniques. Print unions had responded aggressively to this national newspaper innovation, and management exacerbated the situation by introducing inappropriate and untried technology. From a catastrophic start in 1978 which allowed the *Sun* to overtake the *Mirror* as top of the pop dailies, the system had been a disaster. New methods intended to reduce costs, manning, and time spent in production, had had precisely the opposite effect.

Industrial relations were diabolical. Constant demands for higher payments to production workers making spurious claims for their 'extra' duties were – because of the instant perishability of newspapers – inevitably and speedily met by management with cash payments.

Sales (due largely to a costly sale-or-return deal with newsagents and to an even costlier 'bingo' game promotion with big cash prizes) were in the meantime improving. From the first to the third quarter of the year circulation of the *Daily Mirror* increased by 245,000 to 3,451,000 a day. The *Sunday Mirror* went up by 265,000 to 3,674,000, and the *Sunday People* by 200,000 to 3,530,000. The Queen Mother's favourite paper, *The Sporting Life*, benefiting from the demise of the *Sporting Chronicle*, increased sales by 20,000 to 78,000 but nevertheless lost £3million a year.

North of the border and making £3.5million a year with realistic manning levels, computer-setting and colour printing, the *Sunday Mail* was selling more than 800,000 a week, and the *Daily Record* about 745,000 a day.

But in spite of selling more than 33 million newspapers which were read by more than half the population of the United Kingdom, Reed's subsidiary MGN board found difficulty in making more than a pittance of the millions passing through their hands stick to their fingers as profit.

So, was Maxwell really interested? 'I never comment on rumours,' he told the *Mail on Sunday*, adding: 'Privately, it's balls.'

Nevertheless, the same newspaper reported at the end of August that he had 'offered, or at least mooted', a price of £98.7million for MGN.

That is a curiously contrived figure, either to offer or to 'moot': appearing sufficiently accurate to suggest a top-level leak at either Reed or Pergamon – as was clearly the intention. It is even more curious, with hindsight, in that Robert Maxwell's first – public – offer was a round-sum £80million and his second, a much rounder £100million. All it really showed was that Associated Newspapers' City office thought that the Reed estimate of MGN's value was not far out.

But then the parent company had good reason to know the worth of its newspaper division; it had had it valued separately and been monitoring it all year.

The board had been examining two possibilities – either to sell off part of MGN (Robert Maxwell was interested in this option), or to float the group as a separate company.

Ironically, while the group wrestled with computer techniques, it was another company's electronic technology that made the difference between book and real value.

Reuters, the international news agency that had started with carrier pigeons, had developed a computer service supplying information to banks and brokers about world currencies. Money rates could be called up within seconds on a small screen, the 'Reuters Monitor', from anywhere in the world onto the desks of businessmen for whom time literally was money. When the service started in 1973 it had five subscribers; ten years later it had 13,000 in 78 countries, and nearly 35,000 viewing terminals.

The idea of possibly putting the *Mirror* on the stock market followed the suggestion of a flotation of Reuters which had made an operating profit of £36.5million and just distributed its first dividend since 1941. Keen to exploit this newly-discovered asset Britain's national and provincial newspapers (who between them owned 82 per cent of the agency's shares) pressed for it to go public. Reed's holding was 8.5 per cent, of which 7.8 per cent was owned by the Mirror.

And the most commonly quoted figure as the value of Reuters was £1,000million. An even more optimistic estimate was £1,500million, so the Mirror group's holding could be worth £80million, perhaps £120million...

On the back of this information, shares in Associated Newspapers which published the *Daily Mail* and the *Mail on Sunday* had almost trebled during the year; shares in United Newspapers, publishers of a string of provincial papers, more than doubled; Reed International was not far behind; while Fleet, undervalued on its flotation at 16p, watched its shares soar to 184p in the same period.

And the Mirror Group's Reuters shareholding was shown in the Reed accounts at a nominal £5,000.

But was the Group for sale? 'Arrant nonsense,' said Douglas Long.

All was to become clear on October 13 (a Thursday), in a week during which speculation about a sale had reached new and dizzy heights, when Reed chairman Sir Alex Jarratt interrupted his holiday 'because of leaks' and announced his intention to sell the Mirror Group.

But... not to any one person or company, because this would be against 'maintaining the traditions, character and independence of the newspapers'. Jarratt said that shares would be sold to 'small investors' during the first half of 1984. Reed shareholders and the 7,434 Mirror employees would be given priority to buy shares and, with thousands of investors, 'we will be able to ensure that no-one will have a major controlling shareholding in the company.' The Mirror Group was 'a good company with a strong board and a good bunch of assets to see off any predators.'

He said that the appointment of an 'independent' chairman to head the new, public, company, would be announced in the near future. He was likely to be a prominent figure, intended to reassure staff that editorial independence would be protected under the changed arrangements. He declined to name possible candidates, saying only: 'We know who we want.'

The decision to sell, said Jarratt, did not reflect disenchantment with national newspapers, but rather a desire by Reed to consolidate its interests in other areas of publishing. Any big company, he said, was 'obliged from time to time to look at its portfolio and decide what it can live with'. The intended flotation was not a demerger, but the creation of a 'free-standing, publicly-quoted company with a new set of shareholders.'

He added, for good measure, that 'no approaches to take over the Mirror Group have been made by Robert Maxwell, Robert Holmes à Court, or anybody else.'

David Thompson, wearing his journalistic hat as the *Daily Mirror* chief parliamentary correspondent, and Joe Haines, the paper's chief leader writer, were both in Blackpool covering the Conservative party conference. They hurried back, David to deal with questions being raised by anxious journalists in his chapel, and Joe to settle the fears of anxious readers and writers in a leader column headlined WHERE WE STAND:

> The sale of the *Daily Mirror* will not weaken our voice nor our independence. We are changing owners but not our policy.
>
> The modern *Mirror* has never had a proprietor. That has given us a freedom unknown to other mass-circulation newspapers.
>
> We want to keep it that way.
>
> And a widespread sale of shares to the general public will, we hope, ensure that independence is strengthened.
>
> The editorial freedom of the *Daily Mirror* is the most precious asset we have. It is not for sale to anyone.

The *Mirror* is not a party newspaper, it is not an establishment newspaper, it is not a newspaper for protecting privilege.

It stands, unmistakably and alone among the popular national dailies, on the sane Left of politics.

That is our tradition and the editor of the *Mirror* is its custodian. The *Mirror's* views are not, and never have been, subject to commercial or political pressures.

Nor should they be. Nor will they be.

If ever our freedom to declare what we believe to be right is damaged or destroyed, then the heart of the *Daily Mirror* would be destroyed, too.

We hope that our readers will want to buy a part of the *Daily Mirror*. It has always been their paper more than ours.

The *Mirror* means something special to those who work for it and to the readers who buy it.

That will not change.

It was, largely, what the *Mirror's* journalists wanted to hear. And if it was what Reed and MGN were saying, that was all to the good.

There were, however, questions.

If MGN was, after all, such a marvellous prospect, why was Reed selling us? And how on earth could Reed prevent anyone, Maxwell and Holmes à Court to name but two, from acquiring large blocks of shares – even if they couldn't buy them in the first issue?

There were several answers to the first question. Despite their statement, Reed was less than enchanted with its Fleet Street interests; nobody could remember reading about a strike of wallpaper printers, there was no gold-plated overmanning among paint mixers, a day's lost production by hand-basin moulders was not an irretrievable loss of both income and goodwill. The Mirror Group's profit on turnover was pathetic, almost as if the directors were not concerned about making a profit, so long as they didn't make an actual loss.

But more important was the aspect of the Reuters shares that could turn out to be worth £120million, if the agency had been correctly valued at £1,500million, but in reality might realise only £40million, depending on unknown factors such as the state of the market, and the rules that the Reuters board might impose prior to floating the company. The time to sell, clearly, was while there was a prospect of getting the higher figure.

The second question, already occupying the minds of *Mirror* directors, journalists, and would-be purchasers (among them, Mr Robert Maxwell) was never answered.

We felt that we ought to be doing something, so David Thompson, Mike Gallemore from Manchester and I went to speak to City lawyers. We enquired about 'golden shares' and other options that could prevent anybody acquiring sole ownership of a company. We investigated the possibility of a Parliamentary Bill that might do the same thing.

Finally we went into the City and raised, first, £35million (the book value), then £100million (the asking price) to finance a staff-management buyout so that we could buy it ourselves.

But the response we got from Reed was still that the Group was 'not for sale to any individual or to any group of individuals'.

They appointed Clive Thornton, maverick chief executive of the Abbey National building society, as chairman to oversee the flotation on the recommendation of *Daily Mirror* city editor Robert Head. So far, it seemed, so good.

Thornton was a self-confident – in fact he was an over-confident – Geordie, a former Newcastle solicitor who had lost a leg in an accident as a teenager.

When he made his first appearance on the editorial floor art editor Paddy O'Gara commented: 'In the land of the legless, the one-legged man is king.'

At my first meeting with Thornton he mentioned that the *Daily Mirror* had more journalists in London than the Sun had, worldwide. I said nothing; we had more journalists in Manchester than the Sun had worldwide. When a sub-editor went for his break he'd come back and find that somebody had nicked his chair.

But he wanted the journalists' support and confidence, so could we agree to a deal for non-automatic replacement of non-essential staff? I said we didn't envisage that as a problem; there were no plans to increase our numbers – there would be nowhere for any new people to sit.

But even then the Maxwell rumours didn't go away.

20. Black Friday

At two minutes into Friday the thirteenth of July, 1984, the telephone rang beside my bed. I had only just arrived home after a frustrating day in which eighteen months' rumours and denials that Robert Maxwell was buying the Mirror group of newspapers had peaked. The caller, a financial journalist on another newspaper, said: 'He's bought it!'

I somehow knew, not only because of the timing, that this was right. There was also the excitement and conviction in the reporter's voice, and probably more importantly the fact that with his own contacts inside the Reed organisation (which was selling), Pergamon (which was buying) and with access to new *Mirror* chairman Clive Thornton (who frequently told outside journalists what he was doing before his own staff, and even members of his own board, knew) this reporter's information about what was happening to us had to date never been wrong.

In return for the financial details of the deal I gave him some hopefully non-committal quote for his paper on behalf of the 860 journalists in the Mirror Group. Then I rang Clive Thornton at his London flat.

'He's in. He's got it. A hundred and thirteen million.'

A newspaperman, which Clive wasn't although he tried desperately to be, would have cursed: he didn't. In any case, it wasn't that much of a surprise. Paul Quade, in the *Mirror* City Office, had told me at noon that 'Maxwell will own us by five o'clock'. Three hours after that deadline my own financial 'mole' had joined me for a drink in The Stab. 'The Reed board is meeting now,' he said. 'And Maxwell's in it.'

From the lobby phone of Orbit House, the *People* building built over the pub, I had rung Clive Thornton and repeated the information.

'It's not true,' he said. 'It can't be. Look, I have this arrangement with Leslie Carpenter [chief executive of Reed International]; he rings me every time the board is meeting to tell me what they're going to discuss about the *Mirror*, and he rings me after every meeting to tell me what they've decided. He hasn't phoned me, so they can't be meeting.'

'I'm telling you! They are meeting. And he is in there.' Clive said he would try to contact Carpenter, and would ring me back. Ten minutes later the phone rang beside the bar of The Stab.

'It looks as if you're right,' said Clive. 'Carpenter's secretary said he was in a meeting and not available. I asked if it was a board meeting; she said she didn't know. I asked if Maxwell was there, she didn't know that either. But she said he couldn't be interrupted. He's supposed to be ringing me back, but I don't know whether he will... You know, I've never been in that pub of yours – what's it like?'

I told him that we prided ourselves, with some justification, in frequenting probably the worst pub in London, and possibly the worst anywhere outside Carlisle, where pubs were designed in the better interests of the temperance movement. At one time it had had a carpet, but so much beer was spilled that it you didn't keep your feet moving they stuck to it as if glued, so it was removed and replaced by linoleum.

'However bad it is, I'll buy you a drink there tomorrow.'

'Are you serious? You don't drink.'

'I will tomorrow, either to drown our sorrows and say goodbye... or to celebrate having got over this thing for once and for all.'

Now at home, sitting on the edge of my bed at five minutes after midnight I could picture him shrugging his shoulders as he said there was nothing we could do at that time of the night: we'd talk about it in the morning.

There was still plenty for me to do. I had to contact all the leaders of the National Union of Journalists chapels to relay the news, and to decide on our official reaction when reporters would be phoning other reporters for quotes in the morning. Typically, most of the people I called told me they had already heard the news, which must have meant that many were aware of it before Clive Thornton.

Also fully informed about the sale before the chairman were

several senior *Mirror* directors who were sitting as though in the last days of the Raj finishing off the contents of editorial director Tony Miles' fridge and office drinks cabinet. Chief executive Douglas Long phoned there from Reed House and announced the news of the purchase to Miles who relayed it to the assembled company.

'That's it, then,' said Miles. 'I'm going home.' *Mirror* editor Mike Molloy was next to the phone. He rang his back bench and told night editor John Parker: 'You'd better do another Page One – Maxwell's bought the company.'

The information must have come as some form of relief to Parker who, at that stage, had been unable to find a story to lead the paper. Thursday had been a slow news day and the *Mirror* had three stories on the front.

Column one was a story about Nigeria's High Commissioner and two other diplomats being banned from Britain because of their involvement in the attempted kidnap of their country's former Transport Minister who, drugged and locked inside a crate labelled 'diplomatic baggage', had been rescued by police at Stansted Airport. The bottom four inches referred to the possibility of a dock strike being called off after three days; employers and union leaders were meeting to discuss a new peace initiative. At the top, beneath a blurb for '£25,000 bingo', and occupying almost twice as much space as the docks story, was 'the official engagement picture' of Koo Stark, a former soft-porn actress – 'once courted by Prince Andrew' – with her fiancé, the 23-year-old heir to the Green Shield stamp fortune.

The only change the night desk was planning for this page was the late news that Nigeria had expelled two British diplomats in retaliation for the expulsion from Britain of three of theirs.

Parker hurriedly redesigned Page One with MAXWELL BUYS THE MIRROR replacing the docks story and took the page scheme to show Molloy on the ninth floor. That was fine, said Molloy.

But should it be bigger? No, said the editor; his readers were not interested in Robert Maxwell.

The phone rang again. It was the night news desk announcing

that Robert Maxwell was in the building, on the editorial floor, and about to leave it for the chairman's office in search of the editor of his paper.

'That's it,' said Miles. 'I'm definitely leaving. If he wants me, tell him I've gone.' He went to the back lifts for the staff entrance where his driver would be waiting.

As John Parker entered the front lifts, chinagraphed page scheme in hand, he passed Maxwell, who asked where he could find 'Mike'. Having found him, he asked for 'Tony' and on being told that Miles was at home said 'Get him back, I'm calling a board meeting.'

When he returned to his desk, Parker cropped an inch off the Koo Stark picture and added the space to the story about his new boss.

My phone started ringing while early morning television, still in its infancy, boosted shaky viewing figures by showing a jubilant Robert Maxwell and some of the Mirror Group board members he'd been able to contact and summon arriving at the Holborn headquarters at two in the morning. That morning's *Mirror*, and the front page of virtually every other national newspaper, was now splashing the story.

When Clive Thornton arrived in his ninth floor office he found it occupied by a team of strangers from Pergamon Press. He had miscalculated, badly. For some reason he had reckoned that Robert Maxwell would wander in to Holborn mid-morning, perhaps around eleven, to assume control of his new acquisition. Clive, normally an early starter, had no special reason to rush to work that morning, so he turned up, planning to await Maxwell, at about ten o'clock. On the chairman's desk, beaming, sat the new owner of the *Daily Mirror*, *Sunday Mirror*, *Sunday People*, *Sporting Life*, and the two Scottish titles, the *Daily Record* and *Sunday Mail*.

The conversation between the new and the ex-chairman didn't last long. Thornton complained that he'd been let down by the endless leaks of confidential business information from the boardroom; Maxwell said that he wanted to keep the directors who would be useful to him – which didn't include Thornton.

In the foyer of the Holborn building Clive Thornton was interviewed by excited journalists as he left.

Did you actually meet Mr Maxwell? – 'I could hardly miss him, he was sitting on my desk!'

On the pavement in Holborn Circus he posed for photographers, happily complying with the suggestion that he be pictured ripping up that morning's edition of the *Mirror*. It might have been a true reflection of his feelings, but it was another thing that no real newspaperman would have done. To the journalists, who had pledged their support to Clive Thornton throughout his six-and-a-half-month tenure of office, that act was somehow deeply offensive. However wronged he felt, someone remarked later in the day, he had gone over the top; 'ripping up the *Mirror* was like tearing off a baby's arm.'

Thus Friday the thirteenth, traditionally 'Black Friday', began.

It was 'black' for most of the 7,500 staff on the Mirror titles because they had opposed the Maxwell take-over or, indeed, a take-over by any Press 'predator'; and because of the infamy of the Reed board which had persistently promised that the Mirror Group was not for sale to anyone, not to any individual, nor to any group, nor to any group of individuals.

Clive Thornton was entitled to feel bitter. He had actually been employed by Reed to prepare a flotation of the company for them with the sole intention of putting the newspapers into the hands of as many small shareholders as possible. While Thornton was working on this plan, and writing a prospectus to be published in the *Mirror* papers as a pull-out supplement, while he was trying to concoct codicils to prevent large share ownership, trying to interest pension funds and insurance companies in taking up options, and while he was checking with the Stock Exchange about writing-in guarantees against predation, Reed had been negotiating secretly with Robert Maxwell.

Clive and I never had the drink, nor even the promised talk, not on that Friday morning nor at any time afterwards.

*

It was a rare experience for me, a reporter, to be interviewed by fellow journalists. But that day I had sixty calls from the press in my capacity as convenor of the nine National Union of Journalists chapels. I spoke to most of them. There wasn't much left to say, except to complain feebly that we felt betrayed by Reed International.

In one interview, with the London *Evening Standard* on the front steps of the Mirror building I suggested that, since the presumed value of the Group was a hundred million, in accepting one hundred and thirteen million Reed boss Sir Alex Jarratt had taken 'thirteen pieces of silver' adding, 'admittedly, very large pieces.' Reading this aloud on the sub's table of the *News Of The World*, Malcolm Munro Hall, our former chief sub editor, said 'Good old Rev - talking in headlines', but was told by Dixie Dean, another sub: 'Well, Revel's obviously not very well up on his Bible; the actual quotation is *thirty* pieces.'

Jarratt, I said, having shown that his word and the word of his board was meaningless, should now resign, and take his fellow directors with him. Although they had a duty to their shareholders, they had another duty, a public duty, touching on a matter of great national interest and importance, namely the stewardship and independence of the Mirror newspapers.

It remained to be seen whether the new owner would be able to keep his word about continuing editorial independence, I said. 'Meanwhile all we can say is that, whatever his failings, he has certainly shown more guts and determination than our last one.'

In mid-afternoon my secretary brought me an update of phone callers. At the bottom she had written: 'And Ian Hall says, if you have a minute!!! (his exclamation marks) would you please give him a ring.'

A chat with Ian – neighbour, bridge partner, ski companion, the man who introduced me to sailing, and managing director of a London advertising agency – would be a welcome and refreshing change from being interviewed by the world's print and broadcast media. I called him immediately.

'Been sacked yet?' he asked. Not yet, I said, but I was seeing the new owner at four o'clock and anything could happen.

'I expect he'll sack you,' said Ian. 'And I just wanted to say, well... I don't know how much you earn, but when he does sack you, I thought you might like to come and work here and look after media for us.'

Greater love hath no man.

*

All the FoCs of the Mirror Group's sixty-odd chapels were summoned to a four o'clock meeting with the new proprietor in the Rotunda, the circular dining room at Holborn Circus. They represented the National Graphical Association's powerful and militant skilled printers and compositors; SOGAT '82's clerical and machine-room workers, secretaries and advertising and circulation representatives; the NUJ's journalists in London, Manchester, and Glasgow; the electricians, engineers, catering staff, security, heating engineers, builders, plumbers, carpenters, messengers, nurses, painters, drivers, cleaners, and all the other ancillary staff required to produce newspapers 361 days of the year.

By four-twenty they were debating among themselves what sort of insult a twenty-minute delay represented. Consensus favoured waiting until half-past four before returning to the more important job of producing newspapers: at four-twenty-two a mountain of a man ambled in and picked up a microphone that he plainly did not need.

'Good afternoon, ladies and gentlemen,' he boomed. 'My name's Robert Maxwell, and I own this company...'

Although he was about to protest, as he did frequently that day, that 'this is not an ego trip', Maxwell, clearly, was on a supreme high. His self-introduction, especially with hand-mike in one hand and large Havana cigar in the other, was fairly reminiscent of 'Good evening, ladies and gentlemen, my name's Frank Sinatra and it's great to be back in London.' If he expected applause he was disappointed: nobody clapped. In any case, he was not telling us anything we did not know.

What we didn't know, and what certainly most of those present did not grasp, was how much this meeting warned of the shape of things to come.

Both journalists' and printers' chapels had held post-midnight meetings at which suggestions that the paper be stopped had been considered, but they had decided to continue and produce the last edition. Maxwell said he was pleased that we had 'shown good sense' by producing a paper that morning. If we hadn't printed, he said, we would have closed – 'and never again reopened'. He wanted the newspaper to work, he said; it was his intention to produce newspapers, but if the staff stopped him, then so be it: it was not as if he needed the money.

It was a strange-sounding threat from someone who had just bought the newspaper he'd been hoping for half his life to buy.

We didn't know what, if anything, to make of it. It sounded like a brash, bullying and probably empty posture. But it was nothing of the kind; we were to hear the same threat, and suffer from it, several times over the coming eighteen months.

The main board, he said, would be very much as before, with one exception. He had met all the directors and asked all, except one, to stay. He didn't mention Clive Thornton by name, but he was the only one not sitting behind the new owner. Maxwell reeled off all the names: Douglas Long, chief executive; Tony Miles, chairman and editorial director; Lawrence Guest, finance; Roger Eastoe, advertising; Roy Woolliscroft, manpower; Jack Ferguson, production; Tony Boram, editorial administration; the three editors – Mike Molloy (*Daily Mirror*), Bob Edwards (*Sunday Mirror*) and Richard Stott (*Sunday People*). He momentarily forgot the name of Roger Bowes, the deputy chief executive, referring to him with feigned familiarity as 'Roger... er... the dodger'.

Events were to show that he could have forgotten more names. By the end of the month Miles and Long had left 'by mutual agreement'; Boram, whose early retirement had already been planned, also left; Wooliscroft retired and remained for a short time as a 'consultant'; Bowes went back to his old trade in an advertising agency and the following year joined the *Express* Group, briefly, as its chief executive.

Maxwell spoke, without notes, for perhaps half an hour. It was a great honour, he knew, to own the *Mirror* titles, the achievement of one of his biggest ambitions. He was going to restore the *Daily Mirror* to its rightful place at the top of the popular newspaper market and was starting immediately by reducing the cover price by a penny to restore price parity with the paper's main rival, the *Sun*. Before long, we'd be printing the *Mirror* titles in colour. He was going to launch a new and much-needed evening newspaper for London in September (at a Press conference later that day he gave the launch date as September 15, but when a reporter pointed out that Saturday was an odd start-day for an evening paper, he changed it quickly to September 17 – the first inkling we had that the plans were not fully thought-out).

Everybody knew that the biggest problem in national newspapers was overmanning, said Maxwell, and the *Mirror*'s staffing was ridiculous even by Fleet Street standards. But there would be no compulsory redundancy; staff numbers could be reduced painlessly by natural wastage – retirement, and people leaving voluntarily for other jobs. Most unions had promised Thornton that they would consider non-automatic replacement in other than key jobs, and Maxwell would expect similar agreements. Other than that, despite everything that had happened in the past, there were no 'hit lists'; everybody in a job with MGN would remain in employment.

Maxwell was, he assured us, a total supporter of the principle of the closed shop, and this would continue throughout the company. All union agreements would be upheld by him, provided they were adhered to by the chapels. This was to mean no disruption of production and no industrial action other than through established procedures. It meant the end to 'wildcat' strikes, but sounded otherwise unoppressive.

'I believe in negotiation,' he said. 'I like negotiating. I consider myself a tough negotiator and I think that most things can be resolved in that way. If the procedures don't work, if we get to the end of the line and you have to strike, that's all right with me. Eventually the strike will end and we will see who was right, but we will resume work with no hard feelings on either side – because we will have followed procedures.'

There would be union consultation and involvement in everything, at all levels, including representation on the working party for the new evening paper. But confidentiality was to be the watchword; if there were any leaks, 'and this building leaks like a fucking sieve', the union representatives would be sacked.

There were two problems here. First was the expletive before the word sieve and several FoCs, possibly grateful to get a chance of self-expression, complained noisily, as if to suggest that bad language was rare in the newspaper business. Maxwell apologised and said that, anyway, the building leaked like a *bloody* sieve.

The second issue came when questions from the floor were invited. Introducing myself as convenor of all the Mirror Group journalists, I said that if I had heard him correctly, and that if he had meant what he said, he would get no union representatives on his working parties, nor on anything else; it wasn't the unions that leaked, I said, but the management and the board. Another apology: he hadn't meant it quite like that; nobody would be sacked, but the working party would be disbanded, so everybody would suffer if there were leaks.

David Thompson, FoC of the *Daily Mirror* NUJ in London, asked what would happen to the independence of editors, since Maxwell had said that he was in total control of reshaping the papers and, by inference, of the editorial content.

Maxwell's reaction was that this question was an insult; what did we think his editors, Mike Molloy, Bob Edwards and Richard Stott, would say if he asked them to print anything they didn't want to print?

Having identified me as a journalist, he gesticulated in my direction as he asked this question. Almost certainly, he was not looking for an answer, but I said they'd probably say yes; otherwise they'd have to stop being editor: in either case the result would be the same.

Maxwell grinned. 'Perhaps you're right,' he said. 'So I'll guarantee now that I'll never ask them to do anything they wouldn't want to.'

Maxwell was an enormous man, a giant, a great bear, with a

voice like Bovril. At my first meeting with Clive Thornton I had found myself obsessed by the fact that he had only one leg; with Maxwell my chief awareness was, strangely, of his Czech origins. I was listening to his voice, his sentence structure, trying to identify the alien nuances, but there was none. Rather, his vocabulary was amazing in its range, his accent impeccable. Perhaps the whole package was so perfect that he could only be a foreigner. In fact one of the few outward signs of Maxwell's background, I'd discover later, was his tendency to wear his shirt buttoned up to the neck, without a tie, when off-duty – a strangely un-English but very *mitteleuropaisch* fashion (another, perhaps harking back to his childhood poverty, was to eat quickly – and not necessarily only from his own plate – without using cutlery.)

What did strike me was his resemblance to Orson Welles: the voice, the size, the appearance, the impressive personality. What didn't strike home immediately was that the meeting was not actually with Welles, but with that actor-director's most famous creation – Citizen Kane.

He even laughed like C F Kane, especially at a print FoC's comment about the number of times he'd handed Maxwell his matches to relight his frequently-extinguished cigar: 'I don't know, Mr Maxwell, you've told us your plans, and how rich you are... but sitting here all we see is a bloke bumming a light all the time.'

The similarities between Maxwell and Kane – modelled on America's most famous and eccentric newspaper magnate, William Randolph Hearst – were many, although some took longer than others to emerge.

Kane styled himself 'Publisher'; so did Maxwell, after toying with 'Chairman', 'Chief Executive', and even 'Editor-in-Chief' – or possibly all three titles. (Actually, for me, this was the clue to Kane-ism; every newspaper except the *Mirror* had had a proprietor – but who had ever heard of a newspaper 'publisher'? Hell's bells, it *was* Charles Foster Kane!)

Kane was a 'Democrat', Maxwell was former Labour MP for Buckingham, although they both were variously described as 'Communist' or 'Fascist' by their enemies.

Kane printed his 'declaration of principles' on Page One of his *'New York Inquirer'*: 'I'll provide the people of this city with a daily paper that will tell all the news honestly. I will also provide them with a fighting and tireless champion of their rights as citizens and as human beings.' Maxwell published his – FORWARD WITH BRITAIN – on Page One of his first *Daily Mirror*.

Kane was 'always trying to prove that he was an honest man'... In response to a question from one FoC – that Maxwell had been quoted as saying that he was an admirer of Margaret Thatcher, and had once voted for her, 'so how can you expect us to believe you when you say you're a Socialist?' – Maxwell said that he had never voted anything but Labour since the War. He had said that Margaret Thatcher was the best prime minister we had, no more than that, but thought that some of her policies were in the best interests of Britain.

'But I do not tell lies,' he said. 'I never tell lies. I might change my mind sometimes, but I have never told a lie. If anybody can provide proof that I have lied about anything, I'll promise here and now to give that man a million pounds.' There were no takers.

Like Kane, Maxwell considered himself 'more newsworthy than the names in his own headlines'. And in some respects this belief was substantiated by the fact that rival newspapers often rated him or his business dealings as Page One material.

They both saw themselves, too, as ambassadors of their country. 'Kane' returned from a European visit in the 30s having 'talked with the responsible leaders' and declared to a Press conference that 'There'll be no war' (although this sounded like a lift from the life of Beaverbrook, rather than of Hearst). Months later, when talking to Ethiopia's leaders about the delay in world reaction to that country's famine, Maxwell would tell them: 'I speak only for the people of Britain.'

It was all there, even to the monogrammed shirts in which they each prowled the editorial floors in the early hours of the morning.

Like Kane, he was to start writing for his own publications (although political editors Terry Lancaster and then Joe Haines did the actual writing). Maxwell resurrected an old, defunct, house-

214

name for his articles. Charles Wilberforce was a pen-name Hugh Cudlipp had used for 'anonymous' articles written while editorial director for the *Daily Mirror* and the six-million circulation *Sunday Mirror* – in the days when it was called the *Sunday Pictorial*.

Both men even stuck their fingers in their mouths and whistled to attract the attention of their employees...

And both wanted to be loved.

At the end of the FoCs' meeting, Maxwell walked over to me as I was leaving. He put a big arm around my shoulder and, although perhaps three inches shorter than I am, he appeared to dwarf me.

'How do you think I went down?'

'Considering how much hostility there was towards you when you came in, I think you went very well.'

'It's going to work, you know.'

'It had better. I've got eight hundred journalists' mortgages to worry about...'

Maxwell, I knew, had served for a time with British Intelligence during the War. His business intelligence service, I suggested, had done well with the timing and background information for his purchase of MGN.

'Intelligence service? I didn't need one. Not the way this company leaks information. But it appalled Clive Thornton.'

'Appalled him?' I said. 'It totally screwed him.'

'Yes. That's what Clive told me this morning.'

'Oh, it's Bob and Clive now is it?'

'Well, I called him Clive. I don't think he called me anything. But everybody calls me Bob.'

'Be that as it may, Mr Maxwell, everybody liked Clive.' That was a slight exaggeration.

'You'll get to like me, too. You'll see.'

'What I actually see, Mr Maxwell, is that it is Friday the 13th. I am trying to decide whether or not I am superstitious.'

'Aren't you? I am. Thirteen is my lucky number. That's why I waited until just after midnight, last night, before concluding the deal with Reeds.'

Tom Harrison, convenor of the NGA, stopped with his team on

the way out of the Rotunda. Maxwell still had his hand on my shoulder. 'You okay, Revel? Do you want me to keep a couple of the lads here, for protection?'

I remember reporting back on the FoCs' first meeting with the new owner, and describing Robert Maxwell as 'probably the most impressive man I've ever met'.

Someone asked: 'But do you like him?'

I said I didn't know, but he was the best proprietor we had.

*

With the arrival of Robert Maxwell the writing was clearly on the wall for the print unions, and the NGA and SOGAT head offices wanted a three-pronged (with the NUJ) attack on the Maxwell empire. Tom Harrison and I each rejected the idea without reference to our members, but the officials got together and decided to pursue the idea.

I was called, with the rest of the Mirror Group NUJ FoCs, to union headquarters in Acorn House, a short walk away from Holborn in Grays Inn Road. I argued against the proposition on the grounds that, apart from the fact that the NUJ and NGA were ridiculous bedfellows, now that he owned the Mirror, to 'wreck Maxwell' (that was how the proposal was worded) would be to wreck the Mirror because the two entities were now inseparable. I was astonished to be outvoted by my colleagues – and felt that I obviously had no option but to resign as their chairman and spokesman. In the event, the threesome never got off the ground.

*

A week after I resigned as convenor, I was summoned upstairs. The phone rang and a lady's voice asked: 'Can you see the Publisher?'

'Not from here, I can't.'

'Are you free to come up here and see him?'

Apart from Thornton's brief tenure, I'd never had such a politely put request from the ninth floor. Never had one afterwards, come to that.

I was shown straight in, another experience bordering on the unique. I didn't know what to expect. A convenor can at least hope that his colleagues would support him in the face of trouble,

216

especially if the trouble arises directly out of the convenor's role. An ex-convenor has no such protection. There were two likely options: a handshake, let bygones be bygones, from an overweight Czech... or the handshake and a small cheque.

The big man was in his shirt sleeves. 'Have a drink.'

'Thank you, a cold lager.' He had to send to the kitchen, there was none in his office fridge.

'I bet Clive Thornton never offered you a drink.'

'I always got the impression that he didn't want people to hang about in his office. Anyway, he didn't drink, himself.'

'I drink. I smoke, too. All my vices are above the belt.' He beamed at his own humour. I smiled. 'And I want you to hang about. Help yourself to a cigar.'

I took a Havana from the humidor on his desk and used my own cutter on it. The tobacco leaf was as dry as dust. The cigar crumbled in my hand so I produced my own from my jacket pocket.

'Why have you resigned?'

I told him, briefly, about the preposterous plan for a three-pronged attack – about which he had obviously been aware. Was my resignation irrevocable? It was. Who would succeed me? If the FoCs had any sense, they'd elect Mike Gallemore. Would that be my choice? Without a shadow of doubt. Would they elect him? After an argument, they would.

David Thompson would have appeared the more logical choice, but against him was the workload involved in running his own multi-faction chapel, and the urge to call a mandatory meeting of his 270 members every time a thought crossed his mind. In Gallemore's favour was his level-headedness, his constant pulling of David and me 'off the ceiling', and the fact that I thought he was the best negotiator going.

Maxwell asked what I planned to do 'next'. I told him I thought I'd 'play foreign editors again', and get back to some real reporting, and earn my pay. Maxwell said he approved of that. Did I want any help from him, in anything?

I said I didn't, and that if I did I wouldn't ask him for, nor expect, any favours. After all, I'd tried my hardest to keep him out of the building. He knew all that. But that was the past. He'd asked people about me. They'd said I'd done a good job for my colleagues, he said. And if Bob Edwards had appointed me his foreign editor I was 'obviously no slouch'.

He said, as if the thought had just entered his mind (and maybe it had): 'Incidentally, what do you think of *The Sporting Life*?'

It was a reasonable question; I'd represented its journalists in negotiation, it was in financial difficulty and I was concerned about its future. So I started talking about the loyalty of the editorial staff and the high price we paid for printing it.

'...Because I'm looking for an editor for it. Could you edit *The Sporting Life* for me?'

Could I? 'Of course I could!'

'Write me a paper. Tell me what you would do as editor. I suppose I'll have to draw up a shortlist, but your advantage at the moment is that yours is the only name on it, and I've put it there. It's a shortlist of one.'

As suddenly as he had raised it, he dropped the subject. How had I got along with Thornton? What did I think of him? Maxwell thought Thornton was too self-satisfied, too smug, and he was right about that. If Thornton had floated the company it would have been bankrupt in twelve months, he said. In any case, nobody would have bought the shares; if Reed hadn't sold to him he would have announced that he would never buy any Mirror shares in the future – and what would the shares be worth if nobody could sell them?

How had Clive Thornton achieved the non-automatic replacement agreement? To help him keep Maxwell out. Which non-NUJ FoCs did I know? Which would give him the same agreement? Where would the trouble come from? Not difficult, that: the NGA, and SOGAT machine men. The NUJ had already lost interest in causing trouble.

'How did you get on with Glasgow Harry?'

Harry Conroy, a *Daily Record* staffman, was general secretary of the NUJ. He didn't wait for an answer.

'You know... the first call I got on this phone was from him. He said: "Clive, I think we've found a way to keep the bastard out!" I said, "Is that you, Harry, you Scots bugger? This is Bob Maxwell. What's the matter – don't you read your papers?" I'd recognised his voice.'

He talked, sometimes asking questions, about the editors, all the titles, the Manchester operation, the new evening paper (he didn't suggest the editorship of that, but he'd like me on the planning committee for it).

'You've got a lot of experience,' he said. 'Both in newspapers and trade unions. That's what we need. Can I knock on your door, if I want to?'

'It's your door now: you can do what the fuck you like with it.'

'Of course, but can I expect to find your advice at the other side?'

'If the advice you want is in the best interests of the journalists, and the papers.'

He laughed. 'I know... once a hack, always a hack. That's fine. Similarly, my door is always open to you. But, now you're no longer convenor, I'll expect you to knock on it first, not kick it open.'

We both laughed.

As I left, he reminded me to put my thoughts about *The Sporting Life* on paper without delay because 'I want to do something about it very soon.'

It had been a totally friendly meeting, I hadn't been sacked and I'd been half-offered an editorship, but I still didn't know whether I liked the man.

*

Tony Boram was a director of the *Sporting Life* and most of the editorial executives were at his farewell party in the White Swan. The attendance, even for a director as popular as Boram, was increased by the sudden resignation of Tony Miles and Douglas Long who had respectively been chairman and chief executive and who obviously decided to save money by sharing Tony's planned drinks party. Despite his pay-off Miles, who had been 30 years on the *Mirror*, was totally depressed by the thought of his departure; his wife Annie, a former *Mirror* secretary, was in tears.

Maxwell, eighteen days in charge, was much in evidence. He

took me to one side. 'Don't worry about the *Life* job. There's no competition.'

A day or so later Bob Edwards put his head round my door: 'Revel! I never knew you were good at sport!'

I had no idea what he was talking about.

'*The Sporting Life*. The chairman's just told me you're on the short list.'

Meanwhile the shortlist lengthened. *Life* features editor George White applied; Ted Graham, sports editor of the *Daily Mirror*, and the man I'd have put my money on, was a contender, as was Monty Court, racing editor of the *Sunday Mirror*. Henry Kelly, television presenter and racing fanatic, told me he wouldn't mind if I'd put in a word on his behalf with Maxwell. Several racing commentators also threw their brown trilbies into the ring.

Bob Edwards had been editor of the *Sunday Mirror* for 13 years and he told me privately that Maxwell, rivalled only by Michael Foot, was his 'oldest friend since the war'. In recognition of one or both of these facts Maxwell appointed him 'senior group editor'. He would have preferred to be called editor-in-chief but Maxwell quite clearly still hadn't ruled out that role for himself.

I was summoned to the ninth for another cold lager and dry cigar. Bob Edwards stood beside him.

'The chairman wants you to become his editorial adviser.'

I turned to Maxwell. 'Er ... what about the *Life*?'

'If you'll take my advice, you'll forget about the *Life*. I'd rather you didn't pursue it, for your own sake. I'm afraid the *Life* has no life left in it. I told you before that I would ask for your advice. Now I want you to advise me about what the staff and the readers are saying and thinking about what we are doing, and advise me about news stories. But the important thing is that I'd rather have you inside the tent pissing out, than outside it, pissing in.'

'Well,' I said, 'if your advice is that you want to take my advice, I'd better take it. A nod's as good as a wink to a blind horse, as they say on the *Life*. I'll try it and see how it goes for a couple of weeks.'

In the end that job outlasted him. And so did *The Sporting Life*.

*

There was however no doubt that the gravy train was about to hit the buffers. We were still using the Stab In The Back but we were drinking in the Last Chance Saloon. Pick your own cliché.

When he couldn't sleep, which was most nights, Maxwell started reading the journalists' expenses claims. Understandably surprised, if not appalled, by what he read, he put me in charge of – for which read 'made me responsible for' – them.

He loved the very idea of journalism, kicking against the establishment, and puncturing the powerful; he found vicarious pleasure in the constant air of mischief, the camaraderie, intrigue, excitement and even sometimes the living dangerously. He just didn't understand it.

'I don't object to reporters spending money to get stories but I will not have them lifting pound notes out of my back pocket to slide into theirs. And I am not willing to be the uninvited host at all these staff lunches.'

He appeared unimpressed when I explained that 'working lunches' were often where ideas and inspiration sprang from. To me it was part of the system, so when I saw a show-business writer and a photographer lunching together I asked: 'Just so I'll know, when the expenses drop, which one of you is Liz Taylor?'

When sports editor Tony Smith introduced me to former Grand Slam tennis star Sue Barker, I told him: 'I thought she'd be fatter. According to the exes dockets she had seventeen lunches with our staff last week.'

'Why,' Maxwell asked, 'do sub-editors get expenses when they never leave the office?'

'So they can get home when public transport has stopped at night.'

'But one of them apparently lives in fucking Winchester – and that's seventy-five miles away!'

(I didn't tell him that the sub in question rented a room across the road in Smithfield Market, where he stayed during the week, for a fiver a night.)

He next hit on foreign travel: no more trips abroad without the personal approval of 'the Publisher'.

So no more sudden jaunts to the southern hemisphere in winter months to follow up spurious 'sightings' of Martin Bormann in Rio, Dr Mengele in Argentina, or Lord Lucan in Johannesburg.

(When a reader rang to say he had spotted Lord Lucan in North Wales, he was told: 'Nah. He wouldn't be seen dead in Wales. Now, if you'd found him in Bali, or Hawaii...')

In the year that Maxwell bought the company it had been on course to make a profit of £156,000. At the end of his first year in charge the profit was £80million. He had achieved that without shedding a single job – by the simple expedient of spending less money.

Nevertheless the single red line on his spreadsheet was foreign travel. And that was his own fault.

He wouldn't approve even necessary travel for overseas sporting fixtures until the last minute. It would be obvious that we would be sending a sports writer and a photographer (and sometimes a news reporter) to major events. But by the time we got Maxwell's okay the opportunity to take advantage of group bookings for flights and hotels had been missed. Our people had to get there and check in however and wherever they could – long after all the teams and the fans had booked – which meant increased costs, and often accommodation in hotels that were miles away from the stadiums.

'We've spent a whole year's foreign budget in six months,' he complained. 'How do you explain that, mister?'

'I suppose you'll want to sack the bugger who's responsible?'

He thought about it. '...Is it me?'

'Well, it isn't fucking me!'

'Then it had better be fucking you from here on in, mister. You can now assume responsibility for all foreign trips. I'll tell the editors.'

So I did business travel deals with Thomas Cook, British Airways, British Caledonian and Air France. I was starting with a fresh budget and in the first year was £250,000 in pocket.

And everybody went where the editors wanted to send them, and often could afford to stay on for a couple of days when their assignment was finished. They could use the time to look for other stories, I suggested; and sometimes they found them.

He next put me in charge of the journalists' pay claims and my system was to negotiate a deal with him, first, then wait to see what the chapels wanted. Frustratingly, most years – and I did it for six – the claims were lower than I had already negotiated for them.

There was the inevitable 'poacher-turned-gamekeeper' jibe, but then you can't keep a sub-editor away from a cliché.

*

Maxwell brought in people from industry and commerce to handle the marketing. They may have known lots about selling baked beans and tonic water but they knew nothing about newspapers – which they referred to as 'the product'.

They knew even less than Maxwell himself, which was saying a lot.

When the editors bridled about the publisher's face appearing on their front pages virtually every day (sometimes it was fair enough because a lot of the things he did were actually news, and were also being featured in other, rival, newspapers) they turned to me. He failed to understand my point when I told him about the Catholic paper that had only two pictures on the front of its Easter edition. They were 'Our Lord'… and 'Our Editor'.

So I offered him a deal. If he would give up his insistence on appearing on the front page – where inevitably the space for photographs would often be limited by competing 'news' – I would get the editors to allot him the whole of Page Two, which I described to him as 'the next best thing', to use as he liked.

'The whole of it? Impossible! They'll never agree to that.'

I said I would persuade them, provided only that he would agree to it before I approached them.

'I'll bet you can't talk them into it.'

'You'll bet?'

'A bottle of champagne.'

Daily Mirror editor Mike Molloy couldn't believe it either when I told him about the deal I'd just made.

Then he thought about it.

'Yes… I can see him going for it. That's the thing about Bob – he's newspaper-blind. He has no idea how they work.'

What Mike and I knew, but Maxwell didn't, was that in terms of news the first inside page was the newspaper graveyard. It was the page that nobody read.

The phone rang on Mike's desk. 'You got Mr Barker with you?'

'We've just opened a bottle of Champagne, Bob. I believe you're going to come down and join us, with another one,' Mike told him.

*

Sales were erratic, going up and down with various stunts, like 'Millionaire Bingo' and Maxwell, accompanied by a team of security men, appearing on TV with a million pounds in notes on a trolley, to show viewers what a million quid actually looked like.

But we were still selling fewer copies than the Murdoch *Sun*.

*

Bob Edwards retired the year after Maxwell had arrived. Mike Molloy succeeded him, insisting on the editor in chief title.

I was summoned into the presence and told I was booked to fly to Sydney that night. Great, I said; my favourite city.

'I know it is – that's why you're going. Give your passport to the secretary and she'll get you a visa.'

'Why am I really going?'

'It's a secret mission. You don't need to know.'

'I think it might be helpful if he does know, Bob,' said Mike. 'So he knows what to do when we get off the plane.'

'Okay… I want to buy the Fairfax group of newspapers.'

'And what do you want me to do?'

'Buy it. But I don't want anybody to know, especially that bastard Ned Kelly.' (That was the way he usually referred to his rival media mogul, Rupert Murdoch.)

While we were in the air Maxwell was interviewed about the New York *Daily News* by a reporter on the *Financial Times*.

All part of his plans for global expansion of the Mirror group of newspapers, he said. For example, as he spoke, his son Kevin was en route to Australia with the editor in chief and his editorial adviser to negotiate for the *Sydney Morning Herald*.

And this from the guy who had complained on day one about leaks from the building.

The news reached Sydney before we did. My pal Bill McKeown, who had worked with me on the *Yorkshire Evening Post* and now worked for the Australian government, phoned the bank that we were to use as a base.

'Is Mr Revel Barker there, please?'

'Not at the moment.'

'Has he come here to buy a newspaper?'

'Yes,' the receptionist told him. 'In fact he's just popped out to buy one.'

Negotiations successfully (we thought) concluded, I asked: 'Now that it looks as if we are buying this group, who are we going to get to run it?'

'Oh, hasn't my father discussed that with you?' asked Kevin. 'He is rather expecting that you will be doing that.'

*

Richard Stott, who had been editing the *People*, was Mike Molloy's natural successor for the daily editorship.

Stott had been a tenacious reporter – one of Dan Ferrari's favourites on the *Daily Mirror* – with a string of scalps to his credit, including former transport minister Ernie Marples, Leeds United manager Don Revie, John Stonehouse MP and Martin Edwards, the Manchester United chairman. He even provoked Reggie Maudling into issuing a writ (which was quietly withdrawn after I produced the notes of my interview with the former deputy prime minister).

He had continued his fervour for investigation and exposure of people in high places and restored the traditional role of the *People* as a campaigning Sunday newspaper. Readers were mostly at the poorer end of the market and liked to see self-important figures being brought down a peg or two, so circulation was beginning to rise under Stott's editorship.

Maxwell had already identified him as a 'cheeky chappy' and appeared to enjoy his company and, sometimes, even to listen to him on the subject of newspapers, especially the *Daily Mirror*.

Arguments between them were frequent but often ended with a

resigned concession from the publisher. 'OK,' he would say. 'You are the editor.' But sometimes it would be: 'OK, so you're the editor – but I am right.'

It was perhaps fortunate for both of them that much of Stott's ready wit and acerbic humour passed over the Maxwell head. But by the end of 1989 Maxwell was becoming visibly irritated by him and tired of his arguing that a newspaper could have only one editor.

The crunch came on Christmas Day when Stott was planning to splash on pictures of Romanian President Nicolae Ceausescu and his wife Elena lying dead after being sentenced and executed by a 'military' court. Maxwell, fairly typically, wanted to lead the paper with an appeal to *Mirror* readers to donate cash for 'poor Romanians'.

They fought angrily. Stott won the day. But on Boxing Day Maxwell offered Stott's job to Roy Greenslade (managing editor of the *Sunday Times*), who had previously turned down the editorship of the *People*.

To save face all round, Maxwell told Stott he was accepting his suggestion of a management buy-out of the financially ailing *People*, and Stott returned to edit it, in anticipation of becoming his own 'publisher'.

He would become chairman of the new company and they both somehow decided that I should be managing director; I was in Austria when that decision was made and Maxwell phoned and asked me to meet him in Munich. I drove there; he flew in to offer me the job at a meeting that lasted about half an hour and after which he flew back whence he had come.

But there were complications with separating the paper from the Mirror stable because the group as a whole was about to be floated, so Stott as chairman and editor and I as managing director and managing editor would be given a year to prove that we were capable of both financing and running a newspaper successfully and independently.

Maxwell was planning to retain a minor shareholding, and said he wanted to keep the printing contract. I told him he could have it for the first two years, but thereafter we would be looking for the best deal.

'Excellent!' he said. 'You're already thinking like a managing director.'

No other proprietor had ever given journalists the opportunity to own and run their own newspaper, he said. But was it the slaves taking over the cotton fields, or the lunatics running the asylum?

By far the biggest obstacle was that Maxwell prevaricated about putting a price on the title. Its real value was about £15million but it was shown in the prospective flotation documents at £50million – despite the fact that nobody could remember when it had last made any net contribution to group profits.

Planning reached the stage where we had negotiated rents for new premises and established new deals for staff and services. Stott went down well presenting the relaunched title to the major advertisers and agencies:

'We've done our research into how the average British male spends his Sundays... sleep in late, have a shag, read the paper, then go down to the pub to talk about it, come home to eat, fall asleep watching *The Great Escape* on TV, and wake up to find the telly's still on and Harry Secombe is singing in a graveyard.'

But we made the mistake of holding and slightly increasing circulation against the trend and bringing the paper notionally into profit in that first year of independent editorial and budgetary control.

At that point, to nobody's genuine surprise, Maxwell reneged on the deal and kept it within the group flotation plan.

Thus Stott's ambition to become his own publisher – our fifty *People* journalists hadn't thought twice about it when I told them they could either remain in the employ of a big fat nasty bastard, or 'cross the road and work for a little fat nasty bastard and a tall thin nasty one' – came to nought.

His initial consolation prize was to be offered the editorship of the newly acquired New York *Daily News*, which he turned down because he didn't think a New York paper should have an English editor.

Asked by Maxwell what he wanted, Stott replied: 'I think it's pay-off time, now, Bob... unless you want me to return to the *Daily Mirror* as editor.'

And Maxwell offered him his old job back.

I was *de facto* the managing editor of the *People*, so I stayed at my desk as Bill Hagerty took over the editor's chair.

I'd had a lot of desks (one of them, Clive Thornton's old one). I was still director of Mirror Colour Print (having been sent to Hamburg to learn how the Springer Group managed it); I'd been managing director designate of the *Sydney Morning Herald* (which the Australian government wouldn't let him buy); pre-launch managing editor of the *European* (until he switched it from a daily to a weekly, which I told him wouldn't work); consulting editor of the *Moscow News*... I was also editorial relations manager, group managing editor, and assistant managing director of Mirror Group – titles he'd bestowed on me but never relieved me from.

I could have kept Mirror Colour Print in profit (it was always in profit) simply by printing my own business cards. But I used only the one that said REPORTER.

I sent him a note saying I wanted to leave, and was invited to 'pop up' to see him.

'How many times have you told me you want to leave?'

'I haven't kept count, but it's five, I think.'

'Look... if you are really serious about leaving, I won't stand in your way. But either go back to your office and find something useful to do, or go back and write up your terms for departure and bring them to me.'

I pulled a dog-eared sheet of paper from the inside pocket of my jacket and passed it across the desk. He raised his polished black eyebrows.

'How long have you had this in your pocket?'

'Since Friday, July 13, 1984. But I have retyped it from time to time to adjust the figures.'

'I had no idea that you were so unhappy.'

'That's because you never listen to anybody.'

'Okay. I'm listening now. I am agreeing to all of this.'

He went down my list, scrawling his initials against each point.

'You look depressed, Bob. Tell me it's because of the thought of my leaving.'

'No; I've got flu. The doctors always said that one day the flu would kill me.' (He had only one lung.) 'So I am going to the boat to get some fresh air. Come back to me on Tuesday' – this was Thursday, the last day of October – 'and we'll revise these figures.'

He walked me to the lift, something he hadn't done for Margaret Thatcher, nor even for Mother Teresa, with his arm round my shoulders, just as he'd had it there on his first day. Only this time he didn't appear so massive.

'You've always been a good friend to me... You have never given me anything but good advice.'

'Perhaps you should have listened to more of it.'

'Perhaps I should... So... Tuesday.'

We shook hands. And that was it.

I was the last person in his office in his lifetime. He went to the helicopter, then to his private jet, and to his yacht, *Lady Ghislaine*.

Five days later, when he was reported lost at sea, the Stock Exchange sealed his office and my piece of paper was the only document on his desk.

*

When Maxwell dropped off the back of his yacht in the Atlantic on Monday, November 5 1991, it fell to Stott, as editor, both to manage the coverage and to man the bridge in Holborn; after hearing the news one Mirror director flew off to the Caribbean with his wife on a holiday they had won in a *Mail on Sunday* competition.

Deputy chairman Ernie Burrington went home to play bridge.

Stott led the paper with a big picture of his late boss and the headline THE MAN WHO SAVED THE *DAILY MIRROR* – BY THE EDITOR. Fifteen inside pages were devoted to the one story. Then he walked outside the building to face hordes of newsmen.

Asked how Maxwell had sounded, last time the two of them had spoken, Stott replied: 'He seemed very buoyant.'

He told me later that he regretted having said that. But he didn't regret the *Mirror* headline, because he honestly believed that by sorting out the print unions, buying the best colour presses in Fleet Street and introducing a 'new technology' system that actually worked, Maxwell had secured the papers from an otherwise inevitable slow death.

He didn't change that opinion even when, a few days later, he had to lead the paper with MILLIONS MISSING FROM THE *MIRROR*, detailing how the publisher had stolen around £500 million from the company pension fund. And now Stott revealed how, when Maxwell's wife and daughter had flown out to Spain, ostensibly to make arrangements about the body, they had immediately started shredding documents from Maxwell's files on his luxury yacht.

It was a unique predicament for any editor – investigating his own newspaper and exposing his own board of directors. When it was discovered that Maxwell's head of security, a former chief superintendent with Scotland Yard's serious crimes squad, had bugged some of the executive offices, Stott led the paper with a snatched picture of him and the headline: THIS IS THE BUGGER!

While much of it appeared good knockabout (and it is true to say that Stott was personally having great fun wreaking discomfort among the ineffectual executives who had clung to the publisher's shirt-tails for the past seven years) it was serious stuff. Stott was running investigations again.

His reporters followed the money, revealing the names and the detailed dealings of high-profile city firms that had handled finance for Maxwell, often with little or no regard for the sourcing of cash nor even for the whereabouts of tangible assets.

He ignored pleas – and eventually direct instructions – from the board who told him that to run these stories was damaging to the company. Stott replied defiantly that it might be damaging to the directors, but that it was vital to the integrity of the newspaper, and pressed on.

He had originally gained the editor's chair by being called from the *People* to Maxwell's office to be told that the publisher was 'minded' to offer him the *Daily Mirror* job and would put him on a short list. In what was to be a typical reaction to Maxwell's pomposity, Stott told him:

'Bollocks. You are either offering me the job or you are not.' Taken aback, Maxwell said that, in that case, he was offering him the job.

Instead of taking over immediately, Stott confidently spent a full month writing the terms for his employment, which in part laid out a revised editorial policy for the paper but essentially said that he would brook no interference from anybody. To his astonishment, Maxwell accepted the document and signed it without demur.

This did not of course mean that Maxwell didn't attempt to inject his own ideas, but it meant that Stott could remind him of the deal, and rebuff him, even to the point of describing the publisher's suggestions as stupid. Nobody else ever did that.

The basic problem for Maxwell was that he had no sense of humour and was never sure whether his editor was being funny, cheekily rude, or downright insulting. The fact was that when he spoke with him Stott was being earthily honest. He believed that he worked for the *Daily Mirror*, not for Maxwell, and would frequently tell him so.

After one blazing row about the most trivial of matters – how the rival papers were delivered to Maxwell's front door by a messenger around midnight every night – Stott told him, from home: 'You make this job a fucking misery, Bob. You can stick it.' He slammed down the receiver and when Maxwell called him back, Stott hung up the phone.

Next morning he was summoned to 'pop up' into the presence and asked 'What are we going to do about this situation? You know... I always accept resignations.'

'You are going to apologise for your behaviour,' Stott told him. 'And I, of course, will accept your apology. Then I expect you will open a bottle of Champagne.'

Maxwell thought for no more than a matter of seconds. He walked to his fridge and took out a bottle of Krug and opened it. 'I'm sorry,' he said. 'I was wrong.'

Stott's humour could be dry, or it could be cutting. Introduced to his prospective father in law, a high-ranking RAF officer, he had immediately asked him for his views on the Spitfire. Although he had flown Lancaster bombers, the Air Vice Marshal spoke in high praise of the fighter aircraft before being interrupted by Stott saying 'Because I came here in one...' and took him to the window to show him the little red Triumph sports car parked outside. '...It's so much smarter than the Herald, wouldn't you agree?'

When meeting Peter Jay, former ambassador in Washington who had been recruited as Maxwell's chief of staff and was experiencing marital difficulties, Stott asked him: 'If it's true that you are one of the brightest minds of our generation, why didn't you wear a condom when you shagged the nanny?'

After Maxwell's death the company was sold and Stott found himself working for another unworthy chairman, this time a man he had originally known as an exceptionally irritating sub editor.

David Montgomery, who had failed as editor of the *News of the World* and of *Today*, told Stott that his job was safe – and sacked him two days later.

But the song had ended before he did. Only the malady lingered on.

After thirty years of real journalism it was time to take a rest from it.

I felt that most of Fleet Street had already made that break.

#

Books published by Revel Barker

These titles are available – with free delivery worldwide – from
The Book Depository: *www.bookdepository.com*

Slip-Up by Anthony Delano
> *How Fleet Street found fugitive Great Train Robber Ronnie Biggs –*
> *and how Scotland Yard lost him.* The sub-title tells it all, really.
>   No journalist can afford to miss this cautionary tale... it has one
> rolling in the aisles. Mr Delano's eye is astute, his ear a credit to
> his profession at any level; and his wit is accompanied by the
> ability to write clear English. – *The Times.*

Joyce McKinney And The Case Of The Manacled Mormon by Anthony
Delano
> The story of a former Miss Wyoming who was accused by a young
> Mormon missionary of abducting him, chaining him to a bed in a
> Dartmoor cottage and raping him. I kid you not. – **Roy
> Greenslade** *(Guardian).*
>   Anthony Delano brings 60 years of high-voltage journalistic
> experience to his books on stories that fired the imagination of
> newspaper readers, worldwide. He has again struck gold. His
> research, and attention to detail, is faultless. Any journalists who
> were involved in the story will nod their heads in approval
> of Delano's meticulous investigation into what really happened
> when McKinney manacled a Mormon to her bed. And any
> journalists who were not involved will for ever wish they had
> been. A superb read. – **Barnes & Noble**, New York.

Crying All The Way To The Bank by Revel Barker
Liberace v Cassandra and the *Daily Mirror* in the High Court of Justice
(Famous Trials)
> Bizarre and hilarious... Nothing shorter than a paperback could
> achieve a balanced report of the advocacy and summing-up.
> – **Hugh Cudlipp.**

Man Bites Talking Dog by Colin Dunne

Colin Dunne entertained (and is still entertaining) millions of readers with his canny ability to spot, and to report, the strange, the odd, the unlikely and the just plain daft, producing interviews with celebrities including film star Brigitte Bardot and Corky The Talking Dog. Meanwhile back in the office were the immoral, the completely unreliable, reckless, feckless but richly talented and endlessly amusing colleagues wondering whether they would ever be given an assignment, or whether they should simply go for a long lunch and moan to each other about their lack of employment.

From Grub Street To Fleet Street by Bob Clarke

From the broadsides of the sixteenth century to the broadsheets of the 19th century, taking in the Civil War newsbooks, the gutter press of the 18th century, the rise of Sunday papers full of sex, sport and sensationalism, and the birth of the popular press, Bob Clarke describes the journey of the English newspaper from Grub Street to Fleet Street. It vividly portrays the way the news was reported, to provide a colourful, if often gruesome, picture of the social history of the past.

Publish And Be Damned! By Hugh Cudlipp

The book that should be on every journalist's shelf. Subtitled *The astonishing story of the Daily Mirror*, it records the first 50 years of that newspaper – which Cudlipp controlled as editorial director and chairman but never formally edited – culminating in its position as the best-selling daily newspaper in the world.

'Sparkles and flashes like a welder's arc' – **Cassandra**.

The Street Of Disillusion by Harry Procter

When people heard of an unusual story they would say: 'Tell Harry Procter about it'. There hasn't been a reporter with that sort of fame (or notoriety) since. *The Street of Disillusion* is a classic tale following a young man's ambition to reach The Street and make his name there covering all the big stories – murders, fraudsters, runaways, wayward priests and nuns... and then to lose all faith and hope in what some hacks referred to as The Boulevard of Broken Dreams.

The Best Of Vincent Mulchrone

A lifetime of wit and observation of the folly and splendour of his fellow humans by the *Daily Mail*'s finest reporter.

Waterhouse On Newspaper Style by Keith Waterhouse

The first living author to have a book (*Billy Liar*) on the GCSE syllabus, Waterhouse succeeded Cassandra as chief columnist on the *Daily Mirror* (for 26 years) before moving to the *Daily Mail* (23 years).His stylebook is still revered and read avidly and with joy by students and practitioners of the trade.

A Crooked Sixpence by Murray Sayle

Described by Phillip Knightly (*Sunday Times*) as 'the best novel about journalism – ever', it's a thinly disguised account of a young investigative reporter's life on a sensational Sunday newspaper... too thinly disguised for some – its original publication was withdrawn and pulped after characters in the book thought their identities were too easily recognised.

Forgive Us Our Press Passes by Ian Skidmore

'Skiddy' was one of those happy newsmen who stumbled across unlikely stories and even less likely characters. His book charts his life as a reporter, news editor and hack-about-town... Chosen by the BBC as Book Of The Year, it had the highest listening figures on Radio Four and was read twice on the BBC World Service.

Cassandra At His Finest and Funniest

William Connor (Cassandra) was possibly the most famous columnist in post-war journalism. For more than thirty years he set new styles for writing, commentary and straight-forward reporting – copied often, but never matched or beaten.

Ladies Of The Street by Liz Hodgkinson

It's now more than 100 years since the first woman became editor of a national daily newspaper. She lasted in the job only a few weeks... before being replaced by a man. Liz Hodgkinson pays tribute to some foot-soldiers and commanders of the regiment of women – many of them household names – who by their courage and determination helped shape and humanise national newspaper journalism.

CPSIA information can be obtained at www.ICGtesting.com
Printed in the USA
LVOW07s1947081015

457493LV00023B/721/P